Sport in Britain 1945–2000

Making Contemporary Britain

General Editor: Anthony Seldon
Consultant Editor: Peter Hennessy

Published

Northern Ireland since 1968
Paul Arthur and Keith Jeffery
The Prime Minister since 1945*
James Barber
British General Elections since 1945*
David Butler
The British Economy since 1945
Alec Cairncross
Britain and the Suez Crisis*
David Carlton
Town Planning in Britain since 1900
Gordon Cherry
The End of the British Empire*
John Darwin
Religion in Britain since 1945
Grace Davie
British Defence since 1945*
Michael Dockrill
British Politics since 1945
Peter Dorey
Britain and the Falklands War*
Lawrence Freedman
Britain and European Integration since 1945*
Stephen George
British Social Policy since 1945
Howard Glennerster
Judicial Politics since 1920: A Chronicle*
John Griffith
Sport in Britain 1945–2000
Richard Holt and Tony Mason
Consensus Politics from Attlee to Major
Dennis Kavanagh and Peter Morris
The Politics of Immigration*
Zig Layton-Henry
Women in Britain since 1945*
Jane Lewis
Britain and the Korean War*
Callum Macdonald
Culture in Britain since 1945*
Arthur Marwick
Crime and Criminal Justice since 1945*
Terence Morris

Electoral Change since 1945
Pippa Norris
Youth in Britain since 1945
Bill Osgerby
The British Press and Broadcasting since 1945
Colin Seymour-Ure
The Labour Party since 1945
Eric Shaw
Third Party Politics since 1945*
John Stevenson
The Trade Union Question in British Politics*
Robert Taylor
The Civil Service since 1945
Kevin Theakston
British Science and Politics since 1945*
Thomas Wilkie
British Public Opinion*
Robert M. Worcester
Local Government since 1945
Ken Young and Nirmala Rao

Forthcoming

British Industry since 1945
Margaret Ackrill
British Foreign Policy since 1945
Anthony Adamthwaite
The Conservative Party since 1945
John Barnes
Education in Britain since 1945
David Crook
British Social Policy since 1945 (Second Edition)
Howard Glennerster
Britain since 1945
Ed. *Jonathan Hollowell*Parliament since 1945
Philip Norton

* Indicates title now out of print

The series *Making Contemporary Britain* is essential reading for students, as well as providing masterly overviews for the general reader. Each book in the series puts the central themes and problems of the specific topic into clear focus. The studies are written by leading authorities in their field, who integrate the latest research into the text but at the same time present the material in a clear, ordered fashion which can be read with value by those with no prior knowledge of the subject.

THE INSTITUTE OF CONTEMPORARY BRITISH HISTORY
Senate House, Malet Street, London, WC1H 7HU

Sport in Britain 1945–2000

Richard Holt and Tony Mason

The right of Richard Holt and Tony Mason to be identified as authors of this work has been asserted in accordance with the Copyright, Designs and Patents Act 1988.

First published 2000

2 4 6 8 10 9 7 5 3 1

Blackwell Publishers Ltd
108 Cowley Road
Oxford OX4 1JF
UK

Blackwell Publishers Inc.
350 Main Street
Malden, Massachusetts 02148
USA

British Library Cataloguing in Publication Data
A CIP catalogue record for this book is available from the British Library

Library of Congress Cataloging-in-Publication Data
Holt, Richard, 1948–
    Sport in Britain, 1945–2000 / Richard Holt and Tony Mason.
        p. cm.—(Making contemporary Britain)
    Includes bibliographical references and index.
    ISBN 0–631–17153–3—ISBN 0–631–17154–1 (pbk.)
    1. Sports—Great Britain—History—20th century. 2. Sports—Social
    aspects—Great Britain. I. Mason, Tony. II. Title. III. Series.
GV605.H66 2000
796′.0941′09045—dc21
00-009033

Typeset in 10½ on 12pt Sabon
by SetSystems Ltd, Saffron Walden, Essex
Printed in Great Britain by MPG Books Ltd, Bodmin, Cornwall.

This book is printed on acid-free paper.

Contents

General Editor's Preface

The Institute of Contemporary British History series, *Making Contemporary Britain*, is aimed at school students, undergraduates and others interested in learning more about topics in post-war British history. In the series, authors are less concerned with breaking new ground than with presenting clear and balanced overviews of the state of knowledge on each of the topics.

The ICBH, which produces the series, was founded in October 1986 with the objective of promoting the study at every level of British history since 1945. To that end it publishes books and a quarterly journal, *Contemporary Record*, it organizes seminars and conferences for sixth-formers, undergraduates, researchers and teachers of post-war history, and it runs a number of research programmes and other activities.

A central belief of the ICBH's work is that post-war history is too often neglected in British schools, institutes of higher education and beyond. The ICBH acknowledges the validity of the arguments against the study of recent history, notably the problems of bias and of overly subjective teaching and writing, and the difficulties of perspective. But it believes that the values of studying post-war history outweigh the drawbacks, and that the health and future of a liberal democracy require that its citizens know more about the most recent past of their country than the limited knowledge possessed by British citizens, young and old, today. Indeed, the ICBH believes that the dangers of political indoctrination are higher when the young are *not* informed of the recent past of their country.

I am delighted to have *Sport in Britain 1945–2000* in the series. For too long the contemporary history of sport in Britain has been ignored, sensationalized or trivialized. Yet no understanding of how Britain has developed since the Second World War can be complete without comprehending the importance of sport and its complex interaction with the media, social history and government policy.

A key reason why there has been a gap in the literature is because the subject is so vast and amorphous that no-one has been able to bring it clearly into focus, least of all within the confines of a book of just 200 pages. It has required the considerable combined talents of Richard Holt and Tony Mason to execute this task. They are both deeply versed in the history of sport and in British social history and their combined knowledge and enthusiasm has produced a book which is erudite, penetrating and highly readable.

Anthony Seldon

Preface and Acknowledgements

For much of the second half of the twentieth century, British sport was poised between an amateur past and a free-market future. This complex transition is the main theme of our book, in which the media play a key role as a driving force for change. Surprisingly, there are very few works of social and cultural history on post-war British sport, although there are numerous factual accounts of individual sports and chronological lists. Our book aims to give equal attention to the post-war years and to the more immediate present. Its organizing ideas are drawn directly from sport itself but also linked closely to wider social issues. A key difference between a sociology of contemporary British sport and a social history is that history takes an interest in the past in its own right rather than using it as a source to explain the present. With the exception of chapter 1, which is a survey of participation by class, gender and ethnicity, the historical approach we have chosen weaves these themes into the story itself. We have tried to piece together what mattered *then* rather than what matters now. Women, ethnic minorities and the disabled are more important in the 1990s than they were in the 1950s and we try to explain this. But the 1950s cannot be understood simply in terms of the absence of disadvantaged groups. Post-war sport had its own agenda which has to be understood in its own terms.

This book aims to be a work of original historical synthesis, not a conventional textbook summarizing an established secondary literature. No such body of material exists, although there are a few outstanding books and articles. There is, however, a vast amount of material drawn from newspapers, government reports, census data, player memoirs, social studies and histories of individual sports or clubs. These are mentioned in the notes, though we have tried hard to keep them to a minimum. Not all sports get equal treatment. Neither of us ride or sail, and equestrian and aquatic sports deserve more space than they get. So do motor racing, speedway and dog racing, which were all popular forms of spectator sport in the last fifty years. Too many sports would have spread the jam too thinly. Our aim was to give more extensive coverage to the most popular organized and competitive activities which had both an active and a spectator dimension: football, cricket and rugby as team sports; athletics, tennis and golf as individual events, which also have an important female component. Other sports like rowing, boxing and swimming are discussed more briefly.

The structure of the book requires a few words of explanation. Chapter 1 gives a brief account of the general pattern of change, looking first at spectators but then in more detail at the ordinary sportsman or woman. As the main focus of the book is on excellence, it seemed important to have a general idea of grass-roots change at the outset to allow the reader to fill in the general picture. This chapter is more factual than the rest of the book and those who prefer to skip the description of sport by category can go straight to chapter 2. The rest of the book falls naturally into three sections of two chapters each. Chapters 2 and 3 look at the amateur world, from post-war revival and through the slow, uneven decline of the amateur ideal. Next come sporting heroes as artisans and celebrities, tracing the history of the professional in chapter 4 and the growing media obsession with sport in chapter 5. Finally, sport as a form of national representation is examined in chapter 6 and sport as an element in government policy is the subject of chapter 7. With the exception of chapter 2 on the immediate post-war period, all the other thematic chapters have a loosely chronological approach, starting from the post-war era and working forward, sometimes combined with case studies of specific sports. We have tried to balance an appreciation of personalities and performances with a wider explanation of change to capture a little of the dramas and characters which so many people found so compelling.

This book has been a long time in the making. Writing contemporary history is like trying to hit a moving target; sport, in particular, changed fundamentally in the 1990s around issues of media control and professionalism. However, the shape of British sport is a lot clearer now than when we began to write. The 1990s have proved to be a decade of enormous importance because of satellite television. Amateurism, which for so long was the ruling ideology of British sport, no longer has any influence at the top level. We can start to see the long century of 'sportsmanship', which ended in the 1980s and 1990s, in better perspective. The year 2000, therefore, is not just a convenient finishing date. It brings a distinctive period to a logical close.

Anthony Seldon of the Institute of Contemporary British History first suggested we should write this book. We are grateful to him for both the initial idea and his patience. Our editor at Blackwell Publishers, Tessa Harvey, has prodded us when we needed it and commented thoughtfully on the work as it came in. Louise Spencely was very helpful in the final stages and so was Tony Grahame. We are grateful to Paul Wells for casting a critical eye over the first draft of chapter 5.

Our colleagues at the International Centre for Sports History and Culture – Tony Collins, Mike Cronin, Pierre Lanfranchi, Matt Taylor and Wray Vamplew – have been good fun, encouraging and generous with their time and ideas. We are grateful to the research students doing the MA in Sports History at De Montfort in recent years and our current doctoral students. The many colleagues whose work has shaped our thinking are acknowledged in the notes. They all deserve our thanks but a special word of appreciation must go to Gareth Williams, Jeff Hill and Chuck Korr for their encouragement. Finally, a vote of thanks must go to Ros Lucas, who did some of the typing quickly and carefully. Instead of us thanking them, our wives – neither of whom like sport – will surely just want to thank us for finishing.

Richard Holt and Tony Mason
International Centre for Sports History and Culture, De Montfort
University

Abbreviations

AAA   Amateur Athletic Association
ARA   Amateur Rowing Association
BOA   British Olympic Association
CCPR   Central Council for Physical Recreation
FA   Football Association
FIFA   Fédération Internationale de Football Association
GAA   Gaelic Athletic Association
IABA   Irish Amateur Boxing Association
IOC   International Olympic Committee
IMG   International Management Group
LTA   Lawn Tennis Association
MCC   Marylebone Cricket Club
NARA   National Amateur Rowing Association
PGA   Professional Golfers' Association
R&A   Royal and Ancient Golf Club of St Andrews
RFU   Rugby Football Union
TMS   Test Match Special

1 Playing and Watching

On the eve of the 1966 World Cup, Walter Winterbottom, the former England football manager, gave a lecture on 'the pattern of sport in the United Kingdom'.[1] He made no reference to the prospects of the national team under his successor, Alf Ramsay, except to say the event would be watched in 29 countries by an estimated audience of 400 million. Perhaps Winterbottom was disappointed to be out of the football world at such a moment. Since leaving the England job, which he had held since 1946, he had run the Central Council for Physical Recreation – the co-ordinating body for sports associations – and went on to be Director of the newly formed Sports Council. Here was someone truly at the heart of things, a powerbroker behind the scenes of British sport. Why then did he ignore the England team on the eve of its greatest triumph? Was it awareness of celtic sensitivity? Sport was a powerful vehicle of national identity within that unique constitutional federation called the United Kingdom of Great Britain and Northern Ireland. He knew only too well the deep England–Scotland rivalry. 'Anyone but England' was – and remains – the watchword of Scottish football.

Or did he simply think the World Cup had little to do with the active sporting lives of ordinary men and women? Winterbottom knew there were two worlds: the best and the rest, professional sport and everyday recreational sport. Most of this book – but not all – is about elite sport and its changing role in British society. But before scaling the heights, there are the depths of all those born to blush unseen: the Comptons of the village green; the Cottons of suburban golf, the Bests of so many street games before the car – or was it 'the coach'? – snuffed out the 'tanner ball player'. What happened to ordinary players is both important in itself and for a proper understanding of spectator sport and its meanings. Sport was unusual in the performing arts in that spectators often knew what was involved in the performance – or, at least, thought they did. Not many theatregoers had tried to play Hamlet. Most cinemagoers knew nothing about making a film. But most of the spectators at the Open had played golf. Football crowds were full of men who had played football. The same was true of cricket and tennis.

These foot soldiers of sport followed their heroes from afar, admiring their talent, will power and sense of fair play. As Winterbottom stressed, 'sport was part of our behaviour – the way we lived'. The British had invented modern sports and the cult of sport was part of what made us distinctive. It was not so much what we played as the way we played. The code of sportsmanship was built into the brickwork of Victorian amateurism and still influenced the post-war middle classes and the respectable artisan. There was – and is – a large constituency for sporting nostalgia. The rhetoric of 'warm beer' and 'long shadows over county grounds', made famous by John Major's tribute to cricket, was the stuff of countless pastoral elegies from Edmund Blunden's wartime *Cricket Country* to John Arlott's Hampshire and Hambledon.

But this was not Winterbottom's style. Here was an insider who took a matter-of-fact approach, not a dewy-eyed gent clinging to the amateur ideal. He was from Oldham and had trained as a physical education teacher at Carnegie College in Leeds, where he became a lecturer. He also played professional football for Manchester United. During the war he rose to be a wing-commander in charge of physical training at the Air Ministry. Here was a new kind of public figure, a man who had seen sport from several sides: as a player, a teacher, a manager and an administrator. He resented being told what to do by committees of amateurs. The 'old pros', who thought football was a natural gift, resented his modern coaching methods and fitness training. 'Articulate, good humoured, a devoted enthusiast, practical but also visionary', he was one of the new 'meritocracy', which was to have so profound an effect on Britain in the second half of the century.[2]

Watching

Like so much else in the sixties, British sport was in flux. Some bastions of traditionalism like the MCC and Wimbledon reluctantly abandoned amateurism; others like the Rugby Football Union or the Amateur Athletic Association (AAA) refused to budge. For them sport was set in aspic, preserved from the corrosive forces of commerce by former Olympians like Lord Burghley, who was President of the AAA until 1976. Winterbottom took a quietly different view. 'In an age of change where the benefits of technological progress, particularly affluence, mobility and mass communication, were radically transforming our lives', he wrote, 'it was inevitable that our attitudes and habits in sport and physical recreation would change also.'[3]

He was right. The media turned out to be the prime mover of high performance sport in the later twentieth century. In 1950 less than one adult in twenty watched television. By 1970 less than one in twenty did not. When combined with steadily rising real incomes, television coverage meant that sports-based advertising reached a vast number of consumers. This was a global phenomenon with Formula One leading the way. Hitherto unimagined sums of money were injected into sport by the end of the century, especially into football, via the sale of broadcasting rights, and recouped by satellite television from advertising and monthly subscriptions.

All this was in the future as Winterbottom surveyed the post-war decades. The professional sportsman was still relatively untouched by the media, though the fascination with George Best was a sign of things to come. Yet even 'El Beatle' and his co-stars in the Manchester United forward line, Denis Law and Bobby Charlton, had to bargain for their own wages. There were almost no agents to negotiate special contracts and transfer deals. Players had to go and deal directly with 'the boss', no easy task at Manchester United under Matt Busby; it would be another thirty years before players effectively had freedom of movement under the Bosman ruling of the European Court of Justice. The ethos of professional football was still non-profit-making. Until 1961 there had been a maximum wage for professional footballers which gave even the best of them not much more than good industrial earnings. Stanley Matthews, who had played from 1933 until 1965 and always put thousands on the gate, did not make his fortune from football. Great stars played for a fraction of their market value. Most of them took the bus to the ground or walked from club houses rented nearby.

This old world of spectator sport, of which Winterbottom had been a part, was in decline in the post-war decades. Professional football attracted over 41 million spectators in 1948–9 at the height of the post-war boom but this had fallen by a third to around 27 million in 1964–5, and to 20 million in 1980.[4] The heavy industries remained true to the old spectator traditions but the service sector had no such loyalties. A survey of Tyneside shipyard workers in 1968 showed that 11 per cent played sport but 32 per cent watched it, cramming into St James's Park to make Newcastle United one of the best supported clubs.[5] But the shipyards were closing, and so were the mines. The number of miners, perhaps the most loyal of all football fans, more than halved between 1957 and 1967, as they migrated to other industries like motor vehicle production where the money and conditions were better. By 1990 there were only 74,000 miners left – enough to fill one big stadium – where once they could have filled dozens.

Into this vacuum came the hooligans, working-class youths from the inner cities, freer than ever before of adult control and able to indulge old habits of territoriality through new rituals of aggression and violence. For a while in the 1980s it looked as if football was in real danger of collapse as the dominant British spectator sport. However, a combination of government regulation of stadia after the Hillsborough disaster, better video surveillance and live satellite broadcasting, turned football around in a few years, winning it a new 'classless' (i.e. more middle class) following as Tory ministers like David Mellor, Ken Clarke and John Major vied with each other as fans, and New Labour did the same.

The decline of cricket as a spectator sport had no such happy ending. Almost two million watched county cricket in 1950 despite matches beginning when most people were at work. By 1960 the crowds had halved to around one million and fell to a mere 659,000 by 1965.[6] Even the Ashes series, for so long the most prestigious event in English sport, felt the pinch. Attendances fell by almost a third from Bradman's last tour in 1948 to the Australian tour of 1964. If England–Australia tests could not keep the crowds coming, what hope was there to staunch the steady haemorrhage of spectators from the county game? One-day cricket was one answer, which emerged in the 1960s and has proved moderately successful, but the decline of the county championship has been inexorable. In 1991 a small county like Northamptonshire received only £48,000 in gate receipts for the whole season and £31,000 of this came from one-day games. Sussex, a bigger county, took only £53,000 at the gate for the entire 1992 season (including £10,000 for parking fees) but made £315,000 from sponsorship and marketing and £110,000 from advertising boards as venerable grounds were 'diseased by the eczema of logos'.[7] The National Westminster Bank entertained 9,000 corporate guests at cricket matches in 1992. The City was still running cricket as it always had done, formerly through the MCC and latterly with the cheque book.

Fortunately, cricket was a special case. Other summer sports fared better. The big race meetings – the Derby and Ascot – remained great occasions and drew big crowds. Wimbledon was still the premier event with tickets for the show courts always at a premium but other tennis tournaments fared less well. Five Nations rugby had drawn crowds of 70,000 and more in the 1950s and continued to fill the vast arenas of Twickenham, the Arms Park and Murrayfield, though with rare exceptions like Leicester and Bath, club rugby never attracted more than a few thousand fans. The British Grand Prix was a great event for Formula One fans and crowds grew and grew over the years. Londoners who had never attended either of the ancient universities still thronged the tow path for the annual Oxford and Cambridge Boat Race.

Golf tournaments grew in number and there was a staggering increase in prize money. The big names came to British golf and the crowds came with them, spending a nice day strolling around handsome estates like Wentworth or refreshed by sea breezes. The Open Championship now draws vast galleries over the four days and practice rounds, to the great links courses of the United Kingdom, as spectators enjoy a beer in the sun or the hospitality suites of the 'tented village', sitting in the large stands erected around the greens and checking the progress of the players on electronic scoreboards. However, the Open – only foreigners called it 'the British Open' – attracted less than 25,000 spectators to Royal Lytham in 1963 when Bob Charles became the only New Zealander and left-hander to win 'a major'. When the Open was next at Lytham in 1974, 93,000 came to see Gary Player take the title and 130,000 saw Seve Ballesteros become the youngest champion of the twentieth century in 1979, famously recovering from the car park on the sixteenth hole. It was nine years before the Open returned to that famous stretch of Lancashire coastline in 1988 when over 190,000 saw Seve do it again. Total income had risen from £190,000 in 1972 when the Open was at Muirfield to £1.5 million in 1981 – and this was just the beginning of a multi-million-pound enterprise run by an amateur committee of the Royal and Ancient Golf Club of St Andrews.[8] The Ryder Cup, which was run by the Professional Golfers' Association, had a similar commercial trajectory, going from a relatively low-key biennial meeting of British and American pros to a pan-European team event of global media proportions. Not, of course, that it could match the true giants of world sport: the Olympic Games and the World Cup. But, as both of these feature prominently in the main body of the book, it seems unnecessary to explain their British significance and global 'branding' at this point.

Playing

Participation grew steadily in most sports from the end of the Second World War to the end of the twentieth century, and spectacularly in some sports revived by television: snooker, for example, attracted around half of all young men between 16 and 24 in the 1980s and 1990s. Football already dwarfed other team sports in the 1960s, especially after Sunday leagues were legalized in 1964, growing from around 25,000 clubs in the mid-1960s to over 40,000 in the mid-1980s. This made even the 6500 clubs in the National Cricket Association in 1989 seem small beer. Although rugby had grown by around 50 clubs a year from 854 clubs in 1939 to reach 1500 in the mid-1960s and rose to 2000 in the 1980s, football was truly the 'people's game'. Skilled manual workers, mainly in their twenties, were still the largest occupational group amongst the one million adult players in organized teams in England in 1987.

The range of sports accessible to the general public increased. In 1966 Winterbottom counted 80 different nationally organized sports ranging from specialist equestrian and water sports to the outdoor pursuits of climbing and rambling. The massed ranks of the office-bound, some of whom must have experienced a more active life in the war, set out to discover the joys of physical activity. The British Sub-Aqua Club, for example, founded in 1953, increased its membership from 4000 in 1960 to 28,000 in 1980. The Royal Yachting Association grew from 11,000 to 65,000 in the same period as the modestly affluent and the downright wealthy indulged in the British passion for 'messing around in boats', re-living the naval traditions of 'our island story' in their own lives.[9] Skiing spread in the 1960s with the jet and the charter flight. So did tenpin bowling, though not to the same sort of people who went skiing. Over a thousand of the shiny new American-style indoor bowling alleys were built in the sixties.

This growing diversity, especially in summer sports, may have been a problem for cricket, which hitherto had reigned supreme as the national game. Surveying nine medium-sized northern industrial towns on the eve of the Second World War, Jack Williams found more than 700 cricket teams mentioned in the local press.[10] Cricket was still very popular in the post-war decade but began to decline thereafter. The records of the Birmingham Parks Department allow us to pinpoint the critical moment: 3,663 games were played on Birmingham municipal pitches in the 1957 season. From this highpoint the number of games dropped to 2,764 in 1960 with no appreciable difference in sunshine or rainfall in the two years.[11] The number of pitches had fallen from 89 to 81 but a 10 per cent drop in facilities could hardly explain the loss of a quarter of all games. Private clubs continued to hold their own. There were between 10,000 and 12,000 in the mid-1960s. Winterbottom thought the problem lay with youth teams – an ill omen for the future of the game.

Class

Perhaps cricket was an early victim of 'the sixties' and a new permissiveness that scorned the imperial image of the sport. As cricket began to collapse, the satire boom started, fuelled by young Oxbridge undergraduates who in other times might have been out winning a blue. For the post-Suez mood cricket was old hat and stuffy, a game of the past generation, loved by such figures as Sir Alec Douglas-Home, who compared spotting a trick question in the Commons to picking out a googly in an over of leg spin. This was just the sort of thing to persuade young men – angry or otherwise – that they could do without a sport that still separated the middle and working class into 'gentlemen' and 'players'. Besides, there was more fun to be had spending money, getting a motor bike or a scooter, buying clothes and the new craze for pop records. Cricket and rock and roll were temporarily incompatible, though Mick Jagger turned out to be a big fan of the game in his later years.

For the most part the upper classes, to which well-bred or aspiring commoners attached themselves, carried on much as before during the reign of Queen Elizabeth II. The Queen herself was a great example of aristocratic continuity – a devotee of horse racing like her forebears – and her two eldest children followed in the family footsteps with Princess Anne excelling as a horsewoman. Charles played polo to a high standard and went shooting and hunting with Camilla Parker-Bowles, 'blooding' his children in field sports despite public distaste. Anne was also a keen supporter of Scottish rugby; Andrew took up golf like so many underemployed celebrities, and Edward played royal tennis. There was not a footballer among them, though Harry and William were rumoured to take an interest in the doings of Beckham and Owen. This, at least, hinted at a change from the socially determined pattern of the past. Otherwise, the social round was pursued as keenly as ever from Ascot and 'Glorious' Goodwood to Henley and Cowes week. The opening of the grouse shooting season was still observed each August and foxhunting kept a devoted following, which was given a raunchy gloss by the novels of Jilly Cooper. The dream of living like an eighteenth-century squire for an afternoon was as potent as ever. Upper-class sport pursued the even tenor of its ways, though the prospect of New Labour capitalizing on the shift in public sentiment towards the banning of foxhunting was a large cloud on the horizon. There was always 'new money' – and plenty of it in the 1980s and 1990s – which wanted to rub shoulders with 'old families', just as there had been in the days of Jorrocks, the Victorian hunting grocer. The social power of the upper class was still a constant in British society or Nigel Dempster would never have kept a column for so long in the *Daily Mail*.

Even for those below this 'leisure class', participation rates were closely linked to occupation. Two out of five households had a car by the mid-1960s. Newly mobile clerks and teachers, salesmen and civil servants could put their clubs in the boot of a Ford Consul or Morris Oxford and 'motor down' to the club as the upper classes had done between the wars. Social emulation was a potent force. Even in a more open golfing culture like Scotland, the game kept its prestige. There were about half a million golfers in the mid-1950s and a million in the mid-1960s. There were few municipal courses in England and long waiting lists for private clubs. Only a handful of new courses were built, so improved provision cannot explain the golf boom. Golf grew with the expansion of 'middle England'. There were 1878 golf clubs registered with the English Golf Union in 1999 compared with 1335 in 1986. Over the same period there was a 63 per cent increase in male golfers and a 43 per cent rise amongst women.

In 1970 a British Institute of Management survey found nearly three in five managers played sport of some kind but less than one in ten watched live sport (except on television).[12] Despite the tendency towards a greater amount of shared family leisure time in what Willmott and Young called 'the symmetrical family', high achieving men still spent very significant amounts of time on sports outside the home. Three out of five managing directors were regular swimmers, one in three played golf, and one in five played tennis or went sailing at least once a month.[13] Lower professional and managerial grades were less likely to participate at this level but were still much more active in sport than manual workers. The Civil Service Sports Association had 40,000 members in 1945 and over 140,000 in 1958. Tennis clubs, socially linked to suburban golf, more than doubled in the post-war decade, falling back from a peak of 4600 clubs in 1958 but still remaining popular.

The General Household Survey of 1996 showed that this striking pattern of middle-class participation had changed very little in thirty years. Sport was most successful in the most affluent groups. The top professional and managerial groups were almost three times as likely to have participated in sport as unskilled workers. Apart from football, the suburban trio of golf, tennis and badminton were amongst the most widely practised competitive club-based sports in the second half of the twentieth century. These sports unusually all drew participants fairly evenly across age groups. Sport is mostly for the young and it is all too easy to forget the middle aged. The most active age group in golf, for example, was 45–59 and the participation ratio for teenagers was the same as for those in their sixties.

Sport remained a defining element of male culture throughout the second half of the century. Put a few men together at a party or in a pub and as likely as not they would talk about sport. Comparing careers and politics was too risky. Unlike women, most men didn't read novels. Discussing sex was boastful – with meanness the cardinal sin amongst 'clubbable' men – and bad taste. Sport oiled the wheels of male sociability from the corporate hospitality tent to the corner café.

Football became a favourite topic of conversation, even more widely accepted at the end of the period than at the beginning. Clubs came and went, the Wolves gave way to the 'Busby Babes'; they in turn were eclipsed by Shankly and Paisley's Liverpool, who gave way to Ferguson's Manchester United. The talk flowed on, encompassing the European Cup, the European Nations Cup and the World Cup. Working-class men in Scotland appeared endlessly absorbed in whether one of two teams would win the Scottish league. The business and professional elites who ran Scotland cared passionately about Five Nations rugby and the Calcutta Cup match with England. But not passionately enough to share the game with the working man, unless he happened to be a Borders artisan or farmer. When the Scottish Rugby Union announced a 'National Pathway' to revive the sport at the end of the century, they conveniently buried in small print the proviso that independent schools and state schools kept separate fixture lists.

Styles of masculinity clearly changed in sport, especially football. Stanley Matthews was a very different looking man from David Beckham. Modern players were much richer and flaunted it. They were also better at dealing with the media. But whether these differences were any more than skin deep is questionable. Players certainly became more demonstrative and self-dramatizing as the century wore on. This applied almost as much to cricket as to football, with much grimacing and grinding of teeth. The amateur style of elite masculinity epitomized by Peter May in the 1950s, alternating between serenity and a stiff upper lip, became a thing of the past.

How much changed in the day-to-day behaviour of the average club is hard to say. Assuming that major shifts of attitude accompanied changes in consumption is unwise. The revulsion and contempt of adult men for the violent posturing of the hooligan suggested that basic standards of decency and self-control, which had been a feature of the respectable artisan since Victorian times, were still alive and well. There was a residual commitment to the rituals of sportsmanship in public school sports like rugby and hockey, and at the more exclusive end of amateur cricket. But this seemed to be vanishing elsewhere. In working-class culture teams played hard to win and masculinity had never been synonymous with polite manliness.

Women

The middle-class woman had always been a significant – and undervalued – presence in sport, especially in golf and tennis. There were 800 clubs in the English Ladies Golf Union in 1965, which grew to 1210 clubs in 1985 with 92,000 members.[14] Scotland unsurprisingly was proportionately even richer in female players, many of whom were drawn from the large bourgeoisie of Edinburgh and Glasgow. Most women golfers, of course, belonged to 'ladies sections' of men's clubs and did not enjoy full equality. Still, the trend was clear and was echoed at the professional level with the formation of a Women's PGA in 1978 and the emergence of Laura Davies as the new champion of the Women's tour in the mid-1980s.

Men still outnumbered women in golf by five to one; in badminton, however, there were two women for every three men and in tennis the numbers were even. More women watched Wimbledon than men and in local clubs women were often much more active. There were around 2500 tennis clubs in the 1980s and 1990s and tennis players often took up badminton in the winter, which attracted around 100,000 players to 2800 clubs in 1966, mostly playing on a single court in facilities rented from the Territorial Army or the local school. There were only six badminton courts provided by the London County Council in 1950–1. But then the sport took off in the most exceptional fashion. By 1964–5 this figure had risen to 529.[15] Table tennis, too, showed exceptional growth across a broad social range with an increase from 75,000 registered players in 1948 to 175,000 in 1958. Ann Jones, the leading British woman tennis player of the 1960s, had first been a national table tennis champion. Table tennis was the staple of youth club sport as boys and girls exchanged furtive glances across the dark green table under the watchful eye of a jovial curate.

With the important exception of cue sports, the shift from outdoor to indoor activities was linked to rising female participation. 'The number of adults taking part in at least one indoor sport increased by 60 per cent between 1977 and 1987 compared to a 13 per cent increase in those taking part in outdoor sport'.[16] In the following decade, aerobics, keep fit and yoga attracted 12 per cent of adult women in 1987 and 17 per cent in 1996.[17] However, these activities were far from evenly distributed across the female spectrum. They were dominated by young women and strongly skewed in favour of the office worker, who was twice as likely to take part as a shop assistant and three times more likely than an unskilled woman. In swimming, social differences were even sharper. Men and women in the same occupational group had more in common with each other than with their own sex. Graduate women were three to four times more likely to enjoy a swim than women who had left school at 16. None of this was new or even surprising, though it does highlight the problems faced by the 'Sport for All' movement in the 1980s.

Middle-class women had always been far more active in sport than working-class women and this pattern continued. A combination of factors re-shaped gender roles and relations. The impact of the pill, which became the preferred form of contraception for most younger women in the 1960s, was profound. One estimate suggested that a woman aged 20 in 1975 would spend a mere 7 per cent of the rest of her life looking after her children.[18] Female employment changed profoundly. There were almost 10 million women working in 1981 – an increase of three million in thirty years, and more changes were to come. Only a quarter of married women were in employment in the early 1970s but by the end of the century only a quarter did not do some form of paid work outside of the home. Women were significantly more employable than men and got into the habit of having a life beyond the home as men had always done. The expansion of higher education from the 1960s onwards produced large numbers of female graduates with higher expectations not only of work but also of personal fulfilment.

Microwaves, dishwashers and automatic washing machines gave working women more leisure time to benefit from the major investment in the hundreds of multi-purpose sports centres built during the 1970s. More affluent women preferred the private health clubs, which boomed from the 1980s. Exercise became fashionable, especially with younger women, as 'style leaders' like Madonna and Princess Diana linked fitness with beauty and sport with dance. Sweat was sexy, providing it was showered off with a suitably branded product. Sports clothes themselves became highly fashionable. Running shoes were bought both by those who rarely broke into a trot and by the legions of marathon runners and joggers of both sexes. In 1990 an estimated £35 million was spent on leotards, legwarmers and other essential items of the aerobic wardrobe and £25 million on shoes.[19]

Together these factors led women to take a new attitude to their own bodies and to the use of their own time. Rather than assault the male bastions of competitiveness directly, most women have preferred to redefine sport in their own terms as healthy and relaxing movement. The boundaries became very blurred as new ways of using the body arose to meet the needs of those who hitherto had felt excluded from the mainstream. The post-feminist agenda was important, stressing the rights of women to enjoy and enhance their own femininity. Exercise became a staple element of a wide range of female literature. Sport as pleasurable, physical activity gently combining effort and skill was promoted as an antidote to obesity and depression – the twin fears of so many of the readers of women's magazines. Their 'sport' was informal and uncompetitive, part of a new 'lifestyle' to help you look good and have more fun. At the end of the twentieth century only one in ten women took part in sport on a competitive basis against one in three men. Men were three times more likely to be members of sports clubs than women.

Older established women's sports like hockey and netball also grew, but at a slower pace. The All England Women's Hockey Association had 776 clubs in 1965 and 958 in 1990. Hockey was still a 'jolly' sport with a private school profile. Netball was more popular with around 3000 teams but numbers had actually fallen from a peak of around 4000 in the 1960s. Most athletics clubs had women's sections. The Olympics, for so long reluctant to permit women to participate fully, gave a new media platform for female athletes, beginning in the 1960s with Dorothy Hyman, Anne Packer and Mary Rand. No other female sport, except perhaps tennis, offered this kind of coverage. Most female sport, however, was still neglected in the press, although the broadsheet coverage in the 1990s did improve.

Competitive sport remained a minority activity for women, who were cold-shouldered in football and cricket, and openly ridiculed in rugby. Women's cricket has slowly established itself despite being rebuffed by the MCC. Women's football, which had been snuffed out after a promising start in the First World War, however, grew dramatically in the 1990s. The number of women's teams rose from 500 to 4500 from 1993 to 2000 and the FA announced plans for a professional women's league on the lines of that in the United States. Current gates for the best women's football only run into the hundreds with up to 5000 for internationals. The unanswered question is this: will the plan to tie women's football to satellite TV coverage of the men's game work? If it does, football could be on the verge of a breakthrough which was officially unthinkable ten or twenty years ago. Women's rugby, too, is starting to grow with hallowed public school clubs like Edinburgh Academicals leading the way in Scotland. Of course, sexism was still rife. Despite the 'new football' of the 1990s and the rising numbers of female spectators in the Premier League, football was still a man's game. The sudden interest in football from girls was mainly directed at star players for a few glamour teams like Manchester United's David Beckham and Liverpool's Michael Owen. Girls were eager consumers of the footballer as 'hunk'. Young women took what *they* wanted from the game, a good few adopting a 'ladette' attitude along the way, drinking lager and 'pulling' men when it suited them.

Football as a way of being one of 'the lads' was almost as strong as ever. Sport in general showed very little inclination to come to terms with any deviation from the heterosexual norm. Only a handful of professional players 'came out' in the gay rights era. For top players it was too difficult. It took courage to endure the endless taunting of a homophobic crowd. At the amateur level a few gay teams were formed, one of which appeared as a curiosity on a TV show hosted by Chris Evans, the media entrepreneur and football fan. Justin Fashanu has been the only full-time player to 'come out' amongst the 4000 professional players employed at any one time in the British game and he later committed suicide. In an effort to tackle generic homophobia in football, which was made explicit in Robbie Fowler's infamous gesture to Le Saux in a Chelsea–Liverpool game in 1999, the 'new broom' FA has announced it will co-operate with gay rights groups to try to create an atmosphere where gay men can play the game – or watch it – without fear of ridicule, abuse or even violence. A new club, the Kings Cross Steelers, took on the 'macho' world of club rugby. Research on this team in 1998 showed surprisingly little evidence of overt prejudice at the inter-club level, presumably a reflection of the polite character of Home Counties rugby. The players themselves had mixed motives for joining: some simply wanted to be open about their sexuality and left higher level clubs for that reason; some wanted to show how competitive 'macho' gay men could be; and others openly admitted playing the game in order to enhance their attractiveness to other men.[20]

But this was a drop in the ocean – a team from 'New Labour' London, sprinkled with stockbrokers and barristers. Gay sport in the 'old labour' heartlands was still unthinkable and passed over in silence. Female homosexuality, however, was a regular topic with the tabloids, from denigrating the 'ambiguous biceps' of Eastern European athletes in the Cold War era to the explicit labelling of lesbians in the 1980s and 1990s. Women's sport had a tradition of separation from the male world and of self-regulation, which meant that these issues were at least aired amongst the more progressive and politically correct in sports education. However, it would be a mistake to think that much of this permeated the ordinary world of women's sport, which maintained a stony silence much like the men. Most gay sport was cosmetic. Like heterosexual women, homosexual men have redefined sport to suit themselves, 'working out' in the gym to create muscle tone. Athleticism seems to have become more important in the gay subculture today than it was in the past.

Ethnicity

There were other excluded groups, who did not want to swim or pump their limbs to pop music. Immigrants, in particular, often found their route into popular competitive sports was blocked. There was nothing new in this. Large communities of Irish workers had settled in Britain in the second half of the nineteenth century, frequently forming their own football clubs, especially in Scotland where indigenous Protestant nationalism was strongest. Sectarianism remained a serious issue in Scottish football with Glasgow Rangers refusing to sign Catholic players until 1989 and Celtic continuing to fly the Irish flag. There had also been substantial Jewish immigration to the East End of London at the end of the nineteenth century. Jews faced discrimination in suburban sports, especially in golf clubs, which in the 1950s clearly operated an unspoken policy of either refusing entry or adopting a quota system. Jewish golfers often had to form their own clubs. Sporting anti-Semitism seems to have been in decline since the 1960s but evidence is thin.

The main wave of post-war immigration came in the 1950s and 1960s from the West Indies and the Indian subcontinent, fuelled by government propaganda and support. Unlike most previous immigrant groups, the new settlers could be distinguished by skin colour. Full employment had created labour shortages in the public services and textile industries. Non-white immigrants made up only about one per cent of the population after the war. Several black athletes, notably Arthur Wint from Jamaica and Macdonald Bailey from Trinidad, who had both served in the RAF, were successful and popular. The sons of a Guyanese father and British mother, Dick and Randolph Turpin were successful boxers after the ban on non-white boxers fighting for British titles was removed in 1948. Black boxers have played a key role in British boxing since then and from the 1980s increasingly dominated the sport, though boxing clubs never reached the levels of popularity they had enjoyed early in the twentieth century.

Non-white immigrants were regionally concentrated so that certain areas of London, the Midlands, West Yorkshire and South Lancashire had large ethnic minorities. Other areas had almost no black or Asian immigration, which made up around 3 per cent of the population in the 1970s and 5.5 per cent in the 1990s.[21] The black community, which made up around 30 per cent of non-whites and numbered around 900,000 in 1991, made a profound impact on British sport in a short time, especially at the top level. Children of first-generation immigrants often had to confront and overcome racial prejudice to succeed, beginning in the 1970s and gathering critical momentum in the 1980s. The pattern of immigrant participation was uneven, varying between different sports and different ethnic groups. The black community was over-represented as a proportion of the total population in football and athletics but under-represented in golf and tennis, where access to private facilities was important for young players. Provision of municipal facilities was important in promoting black sport as the base of a pyramid of excellence, although this did not seem to apply to swimming, which was cheap and accessible but did not produce the stars of the track. Perhaps the commercial incentive was lacking.

Black sportsmen and women of Caribbean or African descent had a sports participation rate of 41 per cent, which was close to the white level of 46 per cent by the 1990s. However, there were striking differences within the non-white community. In 1996, 37 per cent of Indians had taken part in a sport (excluding walking) within the previous four weeks but only 25 per cent of Pakistanis.[22] Cultural prohibitions on female participation by Muslims partly accounts for this but there was also grass-roots prejudice to confront. Yorkshire, for example, was a county with a great cricket tradition and a large Asian community with a cultural attachment to the game. But the county was accused of ignoring the talent on its doorstep. By refusing to budge from its traditional Yorkshire-born policy of recruitment, the county seemed to be operating for 'whites only'. This was not helped by racist chanting from parts of the crowd at Headingley as well as amongst the Leeds United fans at Elland Road.[23] The experience of prejudice led many non-whites to form their own teams and play in their own leagues.

Participation and assimilation are not the same thing. Although great strides have been taken and the Sports Councils of the United Kingdom have been firm in their support for multiculturalism, sport has only partly fulfilled its potential as a source of racial integration.

Disabled Sport

While black and Asian Britons were establishing themselves in sport, a parallel struggle was taking place to create sport for the disabled. This had first come to public attention after the First World War, primarily for the blind and the deaf. The British Deaf Sports Association had run a World Games for the Deaf since the 1920s. They continued to organize separately from mainstream disabled sport after the Second World War, which saw new categories of disabled servicemen survive, notably those suffering from spinal injury. The treatment of this group was pioneered at Stoke Mandeville hospital under the neurosurgeon Ludwig Guttmann, who saw the potential for sport to raise morale and improve health. Starting with wheelchair polo, his patients moved on to archery and netball. Disabled archers competed against the able bodied in the Festival of Sport, which preceded the Festival of Britain in 1951.

The composition of disabled wheelchair sport changed in the 1950s from servicemen to civilians, often the victims of motor-cycle accidents.

During the 1950s the Stoke Mandeville Games became international and went to Rome in 1960 where 400 athletes from 23 nations took part following the Olympic Games. State policy was significant as 'Sport for All' in the 1970s stressed inclusiveness. Amputees and the blind joined with the paraplegic in 1976 and the International Year of Disabled in 1981 provided a platform for disabled sport. The growth in marathon running in the 1980s allowed wheelchair athletes to share routes and events with the able bodied. Stoke Mandeville had its first marathon in 1984 and the Paralympics were held for the first time in Seoul in 1988. By 1992 Britain had several world-class paralympic athletes, including Tanni Grey who won four golds in wheelchair racing at Barcelona. The top performers in this field wanted to be treated as serious, commercially sponsored athletes but found themselves hamstrung by public sentiment. 'No matter how many times you tell them a racing chair is a piece of sporting equipment like Steve Backley's javelin', as Tanni Grey noticed, 'they still respond with the patronising attitude about how brave and wonderful you are.'[24] These star performers represented the apex of a pyramid that had over 120,000 disabled sportsmen and women at its base. Much remained to be done to provide accessible facilities but the achievement of the disabled sports movement was a remarkable success of post-war British sport.[25]

Finally, there is the question of the education system. This book does not deal with physical education, which is a subject in its own right, but some brief discussion of school sport is obviously needed. The British, after all, had pioneered games in the Victorian public schools. This tradition was alive and well in private education and continued to prosper throughout the century, though with less of an ideological flourish than before. High status schools had high-achieving parents, who believed in sport as physical and moral training, insisting their hefty fees were invested in good facilities and plenty of competitive games for boys and girls. Universities varied enormously in sports provision from the exceptionally endowed colleges of Oxbridge to the ex-polytechnics. The day of the don who trudged the tow path and never published – a species still occasionally sighted in the sixties – has gone forever, although sport at university is thriving as both an academic subject and a student activity.

The Butler Education Act of 1944 raised the school-leaving age and brought the public school cult of games to the mass of children. In his 1966 survey Winterbottom noted that the provision of school sport was still something that set Britain apart from the rest of Europe, which tended to rely more on private clubs and municipal initiatives. Over 4000 schools were members of the English Schools Athletics Association, and the English Schools Football Association had 13,000 schools enrolled. In the sixties it seemed that the Victorian public school traditions were being successfully grafted onto the state system. The grammar schools, of course, had long copied their private counterparts with house games and the moral agenda of 'fair play'. But the cult of fresh air and sportsmanship now spread to the technical and secondary modern schools.

Then it all fell apart. Comprehensive education did not make sport a priority. Some radical teachers didn't like it at all, complaining that traditional games were sexist and aggressively competitive. Of course, there were also plenty of state schools with excellent facilities and enthusiastic staff. However, school sport bucked the trend towards rising participation in the 1980s as industrial disputes led teachers to withdraw the good will upon which extra-curricular sport depended. The new national curriculum made matters worse as did the widespread sale of school playing fields. A survey of 1582 schools in 1990 by the Secondary Heads Association and the Central Council for Physical Recreation found that weekend sport had declined in 70 per cent of schools and lunch time or after school sport in 62 per cent.[26] The picture was patchy but the trend was downward. Ten years later even curriculum-based sport had taken a pounding with Sport England's finding that the percentage of nine- and ten-year-olds taking two hours or more of PE per week had fallen from 42 per cent in 1994 to 21 per cent in 1999. 'It is nothing short of a scandal', as David Hart of the National Association of Head Teachers remarked, 'that PE and sports facilities in too many schools are not much better than those in a banana republic.'[27] Public figures like Hart had to be skilled in the snappy remark to get themselves noticed. All the same, he did have a point. The school was giving way to the club in teaching sport to the young – Welsh rugby was particularly exercised about this – and a distinctive strand in British sport was under threat.

At the other end of the age range, the elderly were taking up physical culture with a vengeance. The fit pensioner was a late twentieth-century phenomenon throughout western society. People were living significantly longer and were more active than they had been in the era before hip replacements and heart by-passes. Smoking had become a sin for the health-conscious middle classes, whose inflation-related pensions took them off to the sun and maintained their golf club subscriptions. The state helped in other ways, too, by providing more facilities for the elderly to exercise. From 1987 to 1996 the proportion of those in their sixties who went swimming doubled to 10 per cent of the age group and those who did 'keep fit/yoga' rose from 5 to 8 per cent.[28] Of course, this percentage was lower than younger people but still a major change in behaviour. If walking more than two miles is taken into account, those between 60 and 69 had participation rates similar to the rest of the population. Walking round the golf course was no exception. Some clubs were veritable gerontocracies where the honoured position of P. G. Wodehouse's 'oldest member' could almost mean waiting for a telegram from the Queen. Individuals were redefining age, spurred on by their doctors and the state, who saw exercise as one way of reducing the enormous medical costs incurred by an ageing population.

To conclude, there have been major changes to the pattern of watching and playing since the Second World War. The balance has swung strongly towards active participation. Of course, if televised sport is included the position is very different. Armchair sports fans abound. Still, a huge growth in participation is undeniable, even if part of it comes from activities like aerobics, which some still do not consider as sport. The trend away from physical culture to competitive sports, which had begun in the 1880s, was reversed in the 1980s. Physical culture was making a come back. Football, however, went from strength to strength, and so did golf amongst the middle aged and middle class. Occupation was still the single most important determinant of participation – frequently more important than gender, race or age – and in this sense, if in no other, there was an underlying continuity to sport in Britain from 1945 to 2000.

2 Reconstruction

Churchill did not like to hear talk of the reconstruction of Britain when the war still had to be won. For his Labour partners in the Coalition Government, however, the war was an opportunity to start thinking about a better Britain and to show ordinary people that their wartime sacrifices would not go unrewarded when the war was over. There must be no repeat of the disappointments which followed the end of the First World War. A Cabinet Reconstruction Committee was set up in 1941 and a Ministry of Reconstruction in the following year. All the political parties set up committees of their own on reconstruction. It became the leitmotif for a cross-section of radical opinion stimulated in part by the Agenda group at the London School of Economics who produced their own quarterly journal of reconstruction[1] dealing with a wide range of proposals on almost every area of national life. Sport was excluded, perhaps because it was still too crude a taste for the palate of most intellectuals in the early 1940s, though that did not mean that it entirely escaped the ethos of the hour.

Sport, of course, was not a single thing but organized by many independent, voluntary associations each concerned with its own particular competitive, physical activity. There was no single body which clearly represented sport although there were two which had some claim to speak for it. The Central Council for Recreative Physical Training had been set up in 1935 largely to encourage and promote organizations and activities to improve the nation's fitness, especially among the post-elementary school young. It soon became a focus for the representatives of sporting bodies and youth associations to discuss common problems. Moreover it was accepted by government as the source of advice and expertise in the sphere of physical education, receiving small grants from the Board of Education before the war and playing a decisive part in the physical conditioning of young people for their role in the war effort via its wartime 'Fitness for Service' campaign.[2] This work took up most of its energies before 1945.

The British Olympic Association (BOA) was a self-selecting body of the rich and powerful whose main purpose was the organization of and obtaining of financial support for British participation in the quadrennial Olympic Games. On the whole it was a conservative grouping clear about the need to keep politics out of sport though anxious to enhance British sporting performance and prestige. Wartime paper rationing meant a very austere looking four issues a year of its journal *World Sports*, but it took up the whole of its front page at the end of 1942 to chide Beveridge that in his report on Social Insurance and Allied Services he had failed to find a place for sport.[3] 'Social amelioration schemes' such as his were all right in their way but they would fall short 'without provision for national participation in all branches of health-giving sport . . .'. There ought to be Exchequer grants for more playing fields, coaches and sports equipment. Business should be encouraged to provide facilities adjacent to factories. 'This great country should reward its fighting men and women, its factory workers, its school boys and girls with readier sports facilities and national fitness through sport should post-war be a cardinal national policy.' The magazine kept returning to the same theme throughout 1943 advocating 'a Minister for Sport or a Department of Sport attached to or under the direction of the Ministry of Health, not to make sport a state monopoly but rather to give it state assistance in every direction where the nation's well-being is concerned'.[4] It also invented one of the less memorable wartime slogans: 'Make the golden rule More Players for the Games' Sake rather than crowds of Players for Promoters' Profits.' Participants were better than lookers-on especially among the young males in the fourteen to twenty-five age group.

Right and left had no disagreement about this. The Trades Union Congress was also thinking about the world after the war and in particular about the increased leisure time which the workers were going to have and what they were going to do with it. They should not be 'merely passive recipients of provided entertainments and pastimes'. Suspicion of popular ways of enjoyment ran deep in the Labour movement because they often seemed to be associated with 'mental inertia, the greatest enemy of trade unionism and democracy'.[5] But the TUC was keen to reduce the 'exclusive character of certain recreations or sports'. This ambition was apparently shared by the BOA who urged sports clubs, again 'through some system of state grant', to open up their membership, so that 'the sons of the poor could have equal opportunity with the sons of the middle or richer classes'.[6]

With the state so omnipresent in wartime it is hardly surprising that sport should look to it for support particularly in the context of thinking about the future. Early in the war Stanley Rous, Secretary of the Football Association and a Central Council for Recreative Physical Training activist, and Arthur Elvin, Chairman of Wembley Stadium Ltd, proposed that the government should set up an independent Pools company, half of whose profits would go to football. But all the government would agree to was an amalgamation of the existing companies for the duration of the war, so giving birth to Unity Pools.

Rous returned to the problem with even more radical proposals in 1943. Part of the proceeds from football pools should go into a centrally administered fund, out of which could be taken money for capital investment in sport, particularly stadiums, gymnasia, recreation rooms and sports centres. Rous's ideas came from his knowledge of state-run football pools which flourished in several European countries in the 1920s but even in the relatively propitious atmosphere for reconstruction and reform of 1943 the opposition of the Pools companies and a government with its mind on other things were sufficient to prevent any progress. Rous tried again after the war when, in alliance with the football associations of Scotland and Wales, he presented the idea of a non-profit-making football pool controlled by the government in his evidence to the Royal Commission on Betting, Lotteries and Gaming in 1950. But they were not persuaded either.[7]

It is not surprising that sport did not feature on the government's list of reconstruction priorities. Industrial production for dollar-earning exports was the main requirement of an almost bankrupt Britain after the war ended in 1945 and after that it was housing, urban rebuilding, health and education, key pillars of the welfare state, which took precedence. But these reforms were accompanied by benefits for sport. Wartime concern for the physical and social development of youth, for example, had led some opinion formers to identify a role for sport in checking the dangerous growth of juvenile delinquency. The Youth Advisory Council, reporting on *The Youth Service After the War* in 1943 stressed the part to be played by sport and physical recreation and the need for the adequate provision of facilities.[8] The McNair Report on the supply of teachers and youth leaders emphasized the value of sport and recommended that teachers of physical education should be trained in the same way and have the same opportunities for promotion as other teachers. Finally the 1944 Education Act was an important landmark. Abolishing fees for all state secondary schools opened up secondary education for all at least up to the age of fifteen and Section 53 of the Act compelled all local education authorities to provide adequate facilities for recreation and physical training. The Act also established a Ministry of Education and transferred to it the functions of the National Fitness Council and Grants Committee which had been set up by the Physical Training and Recreation Act of 1937.[9] Its most important consequence was the new Ministry's offer of 80 per cent of the salaries of qualified national coaches in sports and similar assistance in organizing local, regional and national schemes to train coaches to operate at all those levels. Only the Football Association and the Amateur Swimming Association had serious coaching schemes before the war. This new initiative led to the appointment by the Amateur Athletic Association of Geoffrey Dyson in 1947 as the first national athletics coach, and four more soon followed. They spent much of their time training teachers and volunteers to coach in youth and athletics clubs. The All England Women's Hockey Association, British Amateur Weightlifting Association, Amateur Fencing Association and Lawn Tennis Association also submitted coaching schemes which were supported by Ministry of Education grants.

These schemes had been vetted by what had become in 1944 the Central Council of Physical Recreation (CCPR). Also in receipt of a state grant from the Ministry of Education, the men and women of the CCPR were very much in the backroom of sports development in the war and immediate post-war years, encouraging sports' national bodies, helping LEAs (local education authorities) to implement the provisions of the 1944 Act, training teachers and youth leaders and in general acting as a source of promotion and propaganda for participatory and recreational sport. In 1946, for example, the CCPR presented a National Festival of Youth at Wembley Stadium at which 70 organizations were represented, and repeated it as a National Festival of Youth and Sport in 1948 when 15,000 people witnessed displays of archery, basketball, formation dancing, gymnastics and indoor football while 800 women from all parts of the country demonstrated how to keep fit.[10] The CCPR had drawn up an ambitious post-war programme in 1944. This included the setting up of national physical recreation centres in accessible but beautiful parts of the country where young people could go for intensive training weeks in one, or more, physical activity. The first, at Bisham Abbey, was opened in 1946. The CCPR 'also promised a weekly journal with a circulation of 50,000' and did deliver, in 1949, a quarterly entitled *Physical Recreation* which managed a circulation of 7000.[11]

These were real innovations in the running and structure of British sport. It needs to be stressed that few sports had even one salaried or full-time official, which made planning for post-war reconstruction out of the question. Several sporting organizations, the Women's Amateur Athletic Association, for example, set up War Emergency Committees but these were only designed to keep things going until peacetime normality was restored. The bigger and better-off more spectacular sports could do more. The Jockey Club set up a Racing Reorganisation Committee which reported in 1943, suggesting a greater role for the totalisator and the concentration of racing on a reduced number of courses, simultaneously taking steps to improve racecourse management. Not much of this was achieved in the immediate post-war years, partly because of the Jockey Club's reluctance to incur local resentment by taking fixtures away from inefficient courses.[12]

The two most popular and powerful national sports were association football and cricket. How did they face up to the problems of post-war reconstruction? English football had two masters: the Football Association responsible for the amateur and recreational side, the FA Cup and the English team, and the Football League running an 88-club professional competition from a little office in Preston. The League management committee set up a post-war planning committee in 1943 and even co-opted half a dozen non-members to help widen the discussions. It did produce an agenda for post-war football, which partly reflected the reformist spirit of the times including proposals for a British League, a League Cup, a reduction in the size of the majority needed for change, even the removal of the headquarters from the north-west to somewhere more central. The AGM turned them all down. As a representative of Liverpool said, 'what was wrong with the Football League before the war . . . were the public dissatisfied?'[13] Of course they were not and just to show the nonconformist conscience was alive and kicking within the Football League there would definitely be no competitive football on Sundays and no truck with the Football Pools Promoters either. Their offer of £100,000 every year for the use of the match fixtures was turned down in April 1945. Not that the League was against all constructive change and three years later it formed a joint committee with the Football Association to consider matters of mutual interest.[14]

That body, meantime, had an ambitious secretary, who believed in planning and who had a real awareness that there was a world outside football which should not be ignored. Stanley Rous saw the war as an opportunity to bring the Football Association more into the mainstream of the cultural life of Britain. His work at the CCPR, the National Playing Fields Association and the BOA, together with his pre-war and wartime contacts with government had put him in touch with influential people not previously sympathetic to football. He was a reformer who thought that history was on his side. In 1942, Rous drafted a memorandum on post-war development for the consideration of the FA Council in which he drew their attention to the fact that reconstruction must mean more than buildings and administrative machinery: 'there must be a courageous review of motives and methods so that new plans may be carried out in the spirit of real progress', and that applied to football as much as anything else. Like many of his contemporaries he hoped to see the wartime spirit of a more reigned-in individualism developed in the post-war peace. He even felt that he had detected a change in the attitude of the players during the war, which he hoped would carry over into peacetime, a kind of footballing citizenship, in which the balance between friendly co-operation and aggressive rivalry had shifted towards the former. Football had to contribute its quota to the welfare of the nation.[15]

The rhetoric was impressive but what was he actually trying to do? He was anxious to fight the tendency, especially among grammar and public schools, to reject football in favour of rugby. There must be more and improved coaching and training programmes which made use of the most up-to-date technologies such as film. Football should be promoted among all sections of the community but particularly among youth who had left school at fourteen but were not yet old enough to join senior clubs. Football had to be taken into the youth clubs rather than drawing young men away from them. More staff would be needed and the FA should appoint a full-time Director of Coaching to organize courses, assist with the selection of international teams and act as manager for FA and England sides.

Rous looked forward to the extension of international football and retained a strong belief in its power to unite people from all classes and cultures in a shared enthusiasm. In the short term that meant the organization of victory internationals between the four home countries, the funds to go towards restoration projects; sending teams overseas to help the rebuilding of football there; strengthening contacts with the Dominions and the Colonies; and opening negotiations with a view to rejoining FIFA, the world governing body of football.

Rous also felt it important to improve newspaper coverage of football, notably to discourage the lust for the sensational. Newspapers should be provided with regular information about all FA authorities, 'correct in fact and appropriate in character', and a press agent and public relations officer should be appointed to act under the direction of the Secretary. He also recommended that the FA should publish its own periodical and a textbook on club management written in consultation with the Football League.

The subcommittees which considered these and other issues also came up with other ideas such as helping old professionals by providing those who had the aptitude with coaching opportunities at home and abroad; a university scholarship scheme for the children of those players 'who have contributed considerably to the game', and even an accelerated promotion scheme for ex-pros who wished to become referees. Older ideas were revived. For example, the agreement signed between a club and a player under the age of 21 should permit him to undertake vocational training for a trade, business or profession. Wartime experience had brought more sympathy for those who played organized recreational football on Sundays. Although opinion was divided about whether Sunday play should be encouraged, there was a recommendation to Council to delete the sentence in rule 25 that any 'person who takes part in Sunday football in the UK shall not be recognized by this Association'. But there was to be no truck with Football Pools and no changing the name of the FA to the 'English' Football Association.

Of course many of these ideas for change did not impress the FA Council. But it is often forgotten just how much of the Rous reconstruction plan was implemented. A Director of Coaching and England team manager was appointed in 1947; Walter Winterbottom got the job. More staff were taken on to cope with the expansion of coaching at all levels. This was linked with some serious publishing, first the *Bulletin* in September 1946 which became the new and improved *FA Bulletin* in 1948 and in turn the grander *FA News* in August 1956. The benefits of coaching were stressed in both and also in the annual *FA Book for Boys*, first published in 1948. The commitment of Rous away from parochialism and towards internationalism was signalled by his enthusiasm for the staging of the tour of Moscow Dynamos in 1945 and even more tellingly with the resumption of FIFA membership by the four UK football associations in 1946. Reconstruction was more than a process of 'getting back to normal'. This was understood by some football people, in the FA if not in the Football League.

Reform may have been in the wartime air but cricket was suspicious of it. *Wisden*'s failure to welcome the Beveridge Report was probably due to lack of space but in general, like Sir Pelham Warner, the venerable cricket annual believed that there was nothing wrong with the modern game except perhaps too many first-class counties and over-prepared pitches.[16] The MCC did have a Select Committee investigate problems which might confront county cricket after the war but its main purpose was to get the game going again in what might be an awkward transitional period. The other major concern was to persuade the government to exempt cricket from the Entertainment Tax by redefining it as a 'living performance'.[17] They were keen to differentiate it from other games in which 'sensationalism, money prizes, [and] betting on pools are a dominant feature', as distinct from cricket, which was 'played solely from the point of view of arousing interest in an essentially English institution'.[18]

But in November 1948, the county clubs asked the MCC to set up a committee of inquiry 'to examine the problems concerned with the learning and playing of cricket by the youth of the country between the age of 11 and the time of their entry into National Service. To consider how best to foster their enthusiasm for our national game by providing them with wider opportunities for reaping its benefits' and to make recommendations to the MCC. It is not entirely clear what provoked this activity. There was concern that the standard of cricket had declined due to the war, a fact which successive heavy defeats by Australia appeared to confirm, but there was also anxiety that coaching in the public schools was failing to produce the requisite number of leading amateur players in the county game. Both *Wisden* and the *Cricketer* published stern criticisms of public school coaching which produced batsmen who could defend but not attack and few bowlers of any class at all. The context of these concerns also included the modern coaching schemes set up by the FA, AAA and LTA, all of whom were consulted by the committee of inquiry, which was unanimous that a national organization, sponsored and controlled by the MCC, should be set up 'to promote facilities and co-ordinate the training of the youth of the country in the game of cricket'. Trained coaches had to go out and teach the fundamentals, not only to the 'over 1,000,000 young persons' in England and Wales who would be really interested in cricket but also to the 5000 teachers who would welcome and benefit from training. The result in 1952 was the MCC Youth Cricket Association, 'the most comprehensive effort in the history of the game to take cricket to the youth of England'.[19] Modern coaching for cricket had arrived with its training courses, examinations and Youth and Advanced certificates.

Neither football nor cricket saw the need for radical change but the FA seemed to have a clearer picture of the way ahead than the MCC, whose preferred first move was to look back. The immediate post-war years were confusing and difficult to interpret. On the one hand shortages and rationing persisted, but on the other hand more people were prepared to watch the elite performers in both sports than ever before. The country at large may have still been in the grip of wartime austerity but cricket and football prospered as never before. There was no need to demand state aid though they did welcome any reduction in Entertainment Tax and the footballers would have liked an increase in their bread ration from the Ministry of Food. But the government did have sport on its mind. In 1946 it was about to embark on a policy which, if not facilitating directly the reconstruction of sport, would certainly consolidate its important place in British popular culture.

When Arthur Lewis, Labour MP for West Ham and an enthusiastic sportsman, asked Prime Minister Attlee in the House of Commons in February 1946 whether he would consider appointing a Minister of Sport and Physical Culture Attlee replied 'No, Sir'.[20] The reconstruction of British sport with state support was never part of a Labour Government programme which had many more pressing problems on its slate. Neither could the BOA have been optimistic about hosting the next Olympic Games. It had been conducting a modest campaign through its journal *World Sports* since the Autumn of 1944 when three influential members of the IOC, the Lords Aberdare and Burghley, together with Sir Noel Curtis Bennett published a statement advocating the idea, partly based on the fact that London had already been chosen as the host for the games which had been scheduled for 1944.[21]

There was some anxiety that in a period of reconstruction we might not be able to produce champions worthy of upholding British prestige and that we would need four years to bring our talent up to standard. But pressure was maintained by the visit of the Hon. Secretary of the BOA to the convention of the Amateur Athletic Union in New York who also pressed London's claims.[22] High-level IOC meetings between the most important players, Aberdare, Sigfrid Edstrom of Sweden and Avery Brundage, took place in London in August 1945, and an IOC postal ballot confirmed London as the preferred location. But in a London still short of accommodation, food, fuel and transport no international sporting festival as big as the Olympics could be held without the help and support of the British Government. So it was to the Foreign Secretary, Ernest Bevin, that the Chairman of the BOA wrote in January 1946 proposing a meeting to discuss the IOC's proposal that the Olympic Games should be held in the British capital.[23] Bevin had no reputation as a sports fan but his Minister of State was none other than Philip Noel Baker who had run for Britain in the Stockholm Olympics of 1912 and in Antwerp in 1920, and was a co-founder of the Achilles Club for Oxbridge athletes and one of the leading propagandists for amateur sport in the country. It would be surprising if he had failed to throw what weight he had behind the pro-London lobby and he was present at the meeting between BOA chiefs Lords Burghley and Portal with Bevin which took place on 10 January 1946.[24]

Bevin welcomed the proposal to hold the Games in London with a warmth that was as surprising as his justification was optimistic: that in only two years' time Britain would have put the war and its aftermath behind her, got into her economic as well as sporting stride, and would be ready to welcome to London large numbers of tourists. It was this latter aspect that Bevin stressed in a letter which he sent to Hugh Dalton, and copied to the Prime Minister, advocating government support for the Games.

As his biographer has stressed, Ernest Bevin was the first minister to urge the Cabinet to see the development of tourism as another way, besides the drive for exports, of earning the dollars needed to pay for imports. As early as November 1945 he had circulated a paper to the Cabinet asking if it was possible to promote visits to the UK by Americans in the summer of 1946. 'The more people we can get to Britain, the more it helps the F.O. and the Board of Trade.' He was very irritated by the scepticism of Treasury officials who were probably amazed at a Foreign Secretary who concerned himself with the promotion of exports and tourism, particularly at a time when the importance of the tourist industry was not widely recognized.[25] The Cabinet was apparently persuaded by these arguments, together with that stressing the honour attached to staging such an internationally prestigious event. There were some second thoughts, in a Cabinet meeting in March 1947, for example, after the terrible winter and associated economic and industrial dislocation. Should the country host the Olympics in such circumstances when the government was actually imposing restrictions on mid-week sporting events in order to avoid losses of industrial production? Could the use of scarce materials, notably steel, timber and labour, be justified for such a purpose? Anxieties such as these regularly surfaced through the summer of 1947, sometimes led by newspapers like the *Evening Standard* who thought a revival of the Games inappropriate with 'much of Europe on the verge of starvation. Should athletes be well fed while children go hungry?' while of the British the paper wrote:

> A people which has had its housing programme and its food imports cut, and which is preparing for a winter battle of survival, may be forgiven for thinking that a full year of expensive preparation for the reception of an army of foreign athletes borders on the excessive.[26]

But these criticisms were too little and too late. It would have been publicly damaging to withdraw in 1947 and anyway by then it had been estimated that the Games would bring in £1 million towards restoring the balance of payments.[27] These arguments swayed what few Cabinet doubters there appear to have been.

Government support for the BOA and its Organising Committee had begun earlier with the grant of a licence for the incorporation of the Committee under the Companies Act of 1929. Office space in London was also released and building licences worth £91,000 came later. But the most crucial help of all came under the three headings of accommodation, rationing and, of course, tourism.

Accommodation meant two things. The first of these was provision for the four to five thousand competitors who were expected. This was a responsibility of the national Organising Committee and it had been discharged in 1932, in Los Angeles, and 1936, in Berlin, by the construction of what had been known as an Olympic village. Given the shortages of labour and materials in the building industry there was no possibility of such a special project being allowed and briefly a range of ideas about how to solve the problem were floated. Billeting competitors with British families was rejected when the peculiar temperaments of athletes were taken into consideration. Other suggestions included schools, liners on the Thames, new housing estates prior to their first occupation by tenants, and refurbished prisoner of war camps. Even Butlins was considered but as the games coincided with the height of the holiday season the consideration must have been brief.[28]

The Royal Air Force eventually provided a solution although there is some evidence that high-ranking air marshalls had to have their arms twisted first. Two RAF stations were offered, at West Drayton and Uxbridge, together with a camp in Richmond Park which had been built for RAF convalescents. This latter had room for 1500 competitors together with a range of facilities including sick quarters, a cinema and the essential telecommunications. Most important was the fact that all were within reasonable reach of Wembley.[29] The Army also did its bit by providing shelter and accommodation for grooms and horses engaged in the equestrian events at Aldershot, signals personnel to man the telephone exchanges, and other equipment such as tarpaulins and tents. The cost of bringing the camps up to date was about £720,000 of which the bulk was spent building new barracks at Uxbridge which it took 306 men a year to complete, from May 1947. The labour and materials, including 600 tons of steel, were given one of the highest priorities and this is a further illustration, if any were needed, of the crucial role of the Labour Government.

Accommodation also had to be found for the officials of the various competing sports and countries and the spectators, particularly those expected from overseas. Although providing rooms for these was not the direct responsibility of the Organising Committee it was clear that in the abnormal circumstances of post-war Britain, government help would again be essential. One of the most interesting initiatives was taken by the British Tourist Board, which realized that there was insufficient hotel space for all visitors and appealed to householders living in the vicinity of Wembley Stadium to help. Five thousand offered to do so and almost all these offers were taken up.[30]

The BOA Organising Committee also received important help from non-governmental sources, most crucially from Wembley Stadium Ltd. Not only was the stadium itself provided rent free for the duration of the Games but the Stadium company agreed to lend the Organising Committee up to £60,000 interest free and to guarantee any loss up to £100,000. The Organising Committee offered the *quid pro quo*, profits permitting, to compensate Wembley for the losses suffered in shutting down the greyhound and speedway tracks during the course of the Games. Wembley also loaned the services of its permanent staff immediately before, during and after the Games.

Without Wembley it is difficult to see how the London Olympics could have taken place.[31]

There were other useful gifts, most notably timber from Finland and Sweden, and 100 tons of fresh fruit and vegetables from Holland. It should be remembered that in 1948 most of Britain's leading sports administrators and even some of the participants adhered to definitions of amateurism which made it difficult to obtain commercial sponsorship. Lord Burghley, for example, was reluctant to approach the government about the possibility of a surcharge being made on the commemorative stamps because it was 'against British principles'. Gifts from business for the British team were accepted only on the understanding that the donor could not describe them as 'Olympic' nor use in his advertising the names or pictures of any competitors, nor suggest that the items had helped in their victory. They *could* say – like Horlicks – that they had supplied the drink to the team for use during the Games and the BOA agreed to acknowledge in their publications any equipment that was used.[32]

If the most important help provided by the government was in the matter of accommodation for the athletes, another valuable concession came with exemption from some of the rationing restrictions, especially in clothing and food allowed for both British and overseas competitors. The President of the Board of Trade, Harold Wilson, announced that twelve clothing coupons would be issued to all overseas competitors, officials, press and their wives and families. This was in addition to a new tourist voucher scheme and the pre-existing and rather more cumbersome personal export arrangements.[33]

But it was the relaxation of some of the food restrictions that fascinated and obsessed a nation still on rationing three years after the end of the war. Each individual, each week, was entitled to thirteen ounces of meat, one and a half ounces of cheese, six ounces of butter or margarine, one ounce of cooking fat, eight ounces of sugar, two pints of milk and an egg. Queuing was embedded in the culture and a points system was in force for the many other foods which, although not rationed, were in short supply. Even bread had been rationed since July 1946 but, coincidentally no doubt, it came off the ration four days before the official opening of the Games.

Competitors were given the maximum food allowances available, which was the Category A industrial scale which *daily* comprised six ounces of meat, half an ounce of bacon, one ounce of cheese, two ounces of sugar, one ounce of preserves, two ounces of fats, one-third of an ounce of tea, one ounce of dried egg, one pound of bread, one and a half pounds of potatoes, one point in value of canned food, two pints of liquid milk per day plus eight ounces of chocolate and sweets for a week.[34]

Of course, a good many teams brought their own food (and wines), on which no import duty was paid. Special precautions were taken against the black market. The Americans shipped most of their foodstuffs before the team actually sailed and American food quotas applied. A Los Angeles bakery apparently sent fresh bread daily, by air, to the US team headquarters at Uxbridge. It was announced that any surplus food would be distributed to children's homes and hospitals and doubtless this placated some critics. But there were several mischievous newspaper reports like the story about a chef with the Argentine team who made an omelette for all ninety-four of them with thirty-six dozen eggs in it.[35]

As we have already noticed, government support for the Games was based largely on the premise that it would help rejuvenate the tourist trade thereby bringing in much-needed dollars; it certainly streamlined customs regulations to mitigate irritating delays at ports and airports. Three other major concessions were made to overseas visitors. One was the issue of Tourist Voucher Books (TVB), obtained through banks on presenting their passport and cashing £25 worth of overseas currency. Each TVB contained six vouchers permitting the holder to make one purchase, without coupons, of rationed clothing or footwear for delivery anywhere in Great Britain.[36] Generous petrol allowances were made to overseas visitors either bringing their own cars or hiring without petrol coupons, on production of a TVB. Finally visitors resident in boarding houses or hotels were not required to produce a ration book for stays of less than twenty-eight days. Even if staying at one of those Wembley private homes, you could obtain a temporary ration card after showing your passport or travel documents. Every visitor to Britain received a copy of the British Travel Association tourist guide. That must have been a lot of guides as numbers visiting Britain in July 1948 reached record levels – estimated at 90,000, excluding Empire countries. This was 25 per cent above the pre-war July average and 40 per cent more than in July 1947.[37] It is impossible to say what proportion actually came for the Games but it must have been a major factor. Harold Wilson said in response to a parliamentary question in June 1949 that 505,000 people had visited Britain on business and pleasure in 1948: 147,000 came from Canada and North or South America and earnings from them amounted to 50 million dollars, a major contribution to British foreign currency revenues in 1948 and *the* most important source of US dollars, exceeding even cotton and whisky.[38]

What of the Games themselves? The British expected to be underdogs given the closeness of war and continuation of austerity afterwards and were clearly not too disappointed at the outcome. Three gold medals, two in rowing, one in yachting, was about par for the course at the time and equalled the achievements of 1928 and 1936. There were no British victories on the track or in the field although the British four were placed first in the 4 × 400 metres relay after the winning Americans had been disqualified (they were subsequently reinstated). Silver was also won in the marathon and by four women, in the 100 and 200 metres, 80 metre hurdles and high jump. Tebbs Lloyd Johnson, aged 48, won bronze in the 50 kilometre walk and reasonable accounts were given in the equestrian events and in the football where it was not clear that the Swedes who defeated Great Britain in the semi-final nor the Danes who won the play-off for bronze were amateurs in the British sense. America dominated as everyone knew they would.[39] But there were many memorable moments untouched by American success. A Czech called Emil Zatopek finished second in the 5000 metres but almost caught the Belgian winner in the last 100 and then went on to win the 10,000 metres. Gailly of Belgium staggered into the stadium first in the marathon but was then overtaken and Cabrera won Argentina's first ever track and field gold medal. But the real star, as the *Daily Mirror* headline cried out, was the Dutch housewife and mother of two, Fanny Blankers-Koen, who won four gold medals in the 100 and 200 metres, 80 metre hurdles and 4 × 100 metre relay. As she was the world record holder in the long jump and the high jump she would probably have won those too except that the Olympic rules limited the number of events in which an individual could compete to four. Avery Brundage, not entirely convinced of the wisdom of women competing in top-level athletics, was moved to talk of a new type of woman, lithe, supple, physically disciplined, strong, slender, efficient but then could only think of comparing them to the Goddesses of Ancient Greece.

When the Olympic flame reached Britain in 1948, at Dover, it went out. This could have been a moment of the most postmodern symbolism but it was not, because in spite of the somewhat austere context the Games were a success. Apart from some eccentric decisions in the boxing tournament there was much less acrimony among the competitors than when the Games had last been in London in 1908. The notorious cartoon by Osbert Lancaster – 'You think international relations are in a bad way. Wait till the Olympic Games starts' – was not borne out at the London Olympics.[40] Crowds were big, so much so that in spite of £5,000 worth of tickets returned by the US Olympic Committee, the Games made a modest profit of about £30,000. This did not happen again until business had its way, finally, in Los Angeles in 1984. Crowds were big and appreciative but not particularly chauvinistic. Contemporary commentators were struck by how 80,000 people inside the stadium at Wembley stood for the Marseillaise for a victory ceremony in the fencing competition that had actually been fought out elsewhere. It was a minor triumph of organization that such an event was put on at all given the relatively short time available and the economic difficulties that the British were experiencing. Much of it was the work of the sporting volunteer, though it could not have been done without the support of some of the bigger battalions.

Of course there were complaints. The total experience was not festive enough for some, like the man going to the opening ceremony on a bus up the Harrow Road who saw few flags but a sign saying 'Welcome to the Olympic Games. This road is a danger area.'[41] Visitors did have criticisms – the monotonous food, the poor standard of public cooking, slow and dirty trains, inadequate street lighting, the red-tape binding anxieties about the black market, even the commemorative stamps were too big to lick.[42] Not everyone enjoyed it, notably the seven Henley parishes which protested at Nye Bevan's decision to allow the local council to levy a special rate to raise money for the local Regatta Entertainments Committee. The programme inside the stadium was not as skilfully put together as it might have been. Some of the very few viewers who saw the events on television thought the overriding impression given was of a shoddy, shabby, muddled production, one critic rather insensitively comparing it unfavourably to Leni Riefenstahl's *Olympiad*.[43] It is true that there were no open-air cafés on the Mall and the drabness of the British Sunday in particular still grated, provoking one frustrated Labour MP to declare that he felt the introduction of the Folies Bergères, with appropriate modifications, would liven the place up a bit.[44] The government were generally satisfied: after all, if the Games had not gone on in London it would have been the United States who played host and sending a British team would have been costly in dollars.

Ernest Bevin wrote a piece for the official programme extolling the revival of international gatherings such as the Olympics and offering a simple but doubtless sincere piece of labourism that 'one of our great objectives is to get people to meet and to know each other and in this way to establish friendship between the nations'. The sporting bureaucracy and the sporting public were happy although it is perhaps worth remarking that of the six most favourite sports of the British in 1948, football, cricket, tennis, horse racing, rugby and greyhound racing, only football was on show at the Olympics. The press and radio welcomed the opportunity to describe this sporting festival to the world. And for the rest, it was probably a small sign that things were improving.

But the backdrop to the Games was the start of the Berlin Crisis. As several serious people pointed out, it was 'idle to pretend that such successful gatherings can do much to induce a better spirit of international unity' and anyway the Russians were not even there.[45] War brought benefits as well as costs for British sport. Servicemen and women received regular physical exercise training, often through competitive sport. Some were introduced to sports they might otherwise never have known such as sailing, skiing and mountaineering, which could be taught for military purposes. The fact that a squash court was built on every operational RAF station shows how new sports might reach a new public. Even rugby union and rugby league players were on the same sides in wartime. Watching others play could stimulate interest and although difficult to measure it does not seem too fanciful to say that the war created more widespread interest in many forms of sport and physical recreation.

Of course there were costs. Clubs had lost premises as drill halls previously used for badminton or basketball were monopolized by the Army. Playing fields were ploughed up as part of the dig for victory campaign and swimming baths, gymnasia and other sports arenas were damaged by enemy action. Clubs had lost many of their most active members to the services. But in general sport survived the war well, unsurprisingly as it was so useful to the authorities. The London Olympics signalled the recovery of sport, replaced on its peacetime pedestal. It was also a little noticed staging post on the road to closer relations between government and organized sport. But it did not herald sport's reconstruction. As we have seen, sport was not a single thing and it lacked clear leadership. Someone like Stanley Rous or Arthur Elvin might have provided it if they had had the means. But they lacked resources. A nationalized football pool could have acted like a national lottery. In fact to the public the Pools *were* the lottery save for that minority who regarded them as a game of skill. The government refused to get involved, partly because few people accepted that sport was something which the government ought to be responsible for and partly because social and physical reconstruction just had to have other priorities: put crudely, housing and industry had to come first. As for resources from the private sector the CCPR's experience was telling. When a Special Purposes Fund was launched in 1946 to finance projects like the National Recreation Centre at Bisham Abbey the big five banks gave only £670 between them and a National Sports Development Fund with a target of £100,000 had only raised £11,000 by the end of its first year.[46]

So British sport, no doubt thankfully and with relief in many cases, went back to its pre-war ways, run by a largely volunteer force inspired by an amateur ideology. There was no shortage of ideas about improvement. The *Architects' Journal* published a project for a sports centre for London; others advocated more physical training colleges on Loughborough lines; there were plans to convert football grounds into health and recreation centres to be used throughout the week and earnest suggestions that British sports administration could derive inspiration from Soviet parks of rest and culture.[47] Coaching schemes became as fashionable as 'the new look'. The reconstruction of sport had to wait. What accelerated the hesitant steps towards it, was the quickly emerging post-war fact that other countries were better at it than the British. As Britain searched for a new role in the post-war world, it seemed, at least to the popular press, that to lose our alleged pre-eminence at sport was nearly the last straw.

3 Amateurism

The term 'amateur' came into general use in the second half of the nineteenth century to indicate someone who played for the love of the game rather than for the purposes of gambling or financial reward. Britain was famous for its privately-educated middle-class idealists, who had wrested control of sport from aristocratic gamblers and lower-class professionals. They stamped it with a distinctive moral vocabulary of 'good sports' and 'straight bats', of gentlemanly spirit and voluntary organization. Amateurism was a marriage of honour and competition, of an upper-class ideal of chivalry and a new middle-class belief in the moral value of strenuous effort. These values and structures had a major part in shaping British cultural identity and remained tenacious and influential in the post-war years. Lord David Burghley, sixth Marquess of Exeter, who won Olympic gold in the 400 metre hurdles in 1928, was President of the AAA for forty years and a member of the IOC for forty-five, retiring in the 1970s after a career in sports administration which he combined with a lifelong passion for foxhunting. 'He minded terribly that people shouldn't take part in sport for profit or gain,' his daughter recalled, 'what he really loved was the fact that everybody was joining in just for the pleasure of racing each other . . . Nothing mattered, just the taking part.'[1] That less fortunate competitors did not have the means to take part on an equal basis – or would have to struggle financially to do so – never seemed to occur to him or to most of the ageing administrative elite of British amateur sport.

Amateurism was popular with a broad cross-section of the general public. With the exception of some of the leading performers themselves, who resented the restrictions and irrationality of the amateur system, most people seemed happy enough to accept the peculiar patchwork of British sport. The public and politicians hardly questioned the fact that professionals and amateurs could play side by side in cricket but not in rugby, or that tennis players could claim expenses but athletes and swimmers could not. From its seemingly impregnable position in the 1950s, however, amateurism collapsed as the guiding principle for serious competitive sport, beginning in the 1960s and gaining momentum in the 1970s and 1980s. Although it still operates at the lower reaches and in less commercial sports, the age of the amateur is over. The beliefs of a body like the Rugby Football Union – one of the staunchest supporters of amateurism in the past – now bear little or no resemblance to its former values. What was so recently a source of pride is now an embarrassment, which only a few 'old farts' – to use Will Carling's phrase – believe in.

Just as amateurism went into terminal decline in the 1980s, the Olympic heroes of the Paris Games of 1924 were the subject of a film that sought to capture the essence of amateurism. *Chariots of Fire*, the phrase came from Blake's 'Jerusalem' rendered into a rousing Victorian hymn, was an enormous success. It came at a time when the performances of Ovett, Coe, Cram and others meant Britain could look back on the 1920s without a feeling of inferiority. Athletics was once again a national passion. There was a whiff of glory in the air, of the commercial innocence and gratuitous exertion of an earlier generation. All this was a comforting conceit for traditionalists wedded to the old values. But the reality was rather different. Athletes were setting up trust funds and taking appearance money. As recently as the 1950s there had been amateur batsmen like Peter May and Colin Cowdrey, who could take on the best in the world, and undergraduate athletes who could break world records. Thirty years later amateur sport was more like amateur dramatics: good fun for the participants, their friends and relations but not to be taken seriously by anyone else.

In those sports where amateurism still ruled, often the more obscure Olympic events, public interest was minimal except for a bald swimming gold medallist like Duncan Goodhew or the great rowing pair, Pinsent and Redgrave. Such performers were in any case no longer amateurs in the familiar sense of the word. Their whole approach was increasingly professional; they had – and needed – sponsorship and subsidies to train full-time and get the best scientific back-up. Excellence and ordinary participation drew further apart. There *was*, of course, a role for amateurs in late twentieth-century Britain. The club and county structure of most sports would have collapsed without them. Even in an era of hugely increased state intervention, the role of the unpaid enthusiast is crucial to British sport. In 1985 the Sports Council estimated the annual amount of voluntary labour at 22 million hours for coaches, 21 million for administrators and 0.6 million for referees. Rising participation rates meant more humdrum work for unpaid officials in many sports. But theirs is not the dominant role. The state, the media and the performers themselves now have far more power than they enjoyed in the past. Amateurism no longer sets the agenda.

It is this diminution of amateur authority rather than the routine administration of the thousands of clubs which concerns us here. These quiet harbours of casual exertion and sociability continued relatively undisturbed. It was on the open seas of high performance that the old structure was increasingly challenged as individual sportsmen and sportswomen, their agents and the media stepped up the attack. 'In this country to change the rules of a national game in any serious degree is a task almost of social revolution,' *The Times* had written in 1946.[2] Fifty years later it was promoting the massive commercialization of formerly amateur sports through the power of another part of the Murdoch media Empire: Sky television.

The decline and fall of amateurism was not simply a product of the market value of sport to the new media, although this was undoubtedly the most important reason. Amateur authority was eroded by a range of factors, combining together in different sports in different ways: the growth of international competition; the expectations of the public and the state for success; the changing work and educational pressures of the 'meritocracy'; a decline in deference to established hierarchies and a shift to more individualistic, market values under Thatcherism. Different sports were influenced by different combinations of these and other factors at different times. The following short case studies of cricket, athletics, rugby and tennis show how the tenacious amateur grip on sport was gradually loosened.

Cricket

For the 'men in blazers', who took up the reins of power in British sport after the Second World War, it was a case of business as usual. There was no transformation of sport as there had been in welfare or employment policy. The Labour Party had little interest in sport, inheriting that lofty Fabian contempt for the body and for popular culture combined with a tacit acceptance of amateur values and control where it had existed previously. Hence there was no serious challenge to the status quo. British sport continued to be run on a voluntary basis by amateur committees composed of the middle and upper strata. The ingrained distinctions of rank that struck foreigners so forcibly were relatively undisturbed.

All this was music to the ears of the Marylebone Cricket Club, the private gentleman's club which had governed the game since the late eighteenth century. County cricket was still divided into 'gentlemen' and 'players'. Some counties still had separate changing facilities and different entrances. All scorecards still placed an amateur's initials before the surname and the professional's initials after, to indicate their respective status. 'Your cards show, at No. 8 for Middlesex, F. J. Titmus,' announced a loudspeaker at Lord's. 'That should read, of course, Titmus, F. J.'[3] This was 1961 and Fred Titmus – a test cricketer – was a much loved figure. Yet Middlesex, which often still fielded amateurs, was anxious there should be no confusion. Denis Compton, a professional and the son of a north London lorry driver, who thrilled the country with his cavalier centuries against South Africa in the summer of 1947, claimed he 'never felt or minded the distinction, though it was there quite precisely'.[4] Compton said professionals resented amateurs who took jobs as club secretaries but did no real work, although he had no objection to those who actually did the job retaining amateur status. He thought that great amateurs like Peter May or Colin Cowdrey should be able to accept commercial propositions without losing amateur status. Peter May duly endorsed cricket bats manufactured by his amateur predecessor as Surrey captain, Stuart Surridge.

Unquestioned acceptance of social traditions was widespread and considered natural, although it was probably a lot stronger in southern teams like Middlesex than in the northern counties, especially Yorkshire. The habit of deference was deeply ingrained in the south and west. Men who had played together in wartime service teams, had to readjust to the old order in civilian life. Some captains like Basil Allen at Gloucester were 'determined to reassert the traditional values of amateur leadership . . . and believed professional newcomers, however talented, should be kept in their place'. When David Sheppard made a century for Cambridge University against Gloucestershire and the young professional Tom Graveney congratulated 'David' on his innings, his skipper snapped 'He's Mr. Sheppard to you' and later apologized to the future Bishop of Liverpool for his young player's 'impertinence'.[5] Conservatives were determined to preserve the social hierarchy, especially in those areas of national culture like cricket where they had long enjoyed unquestioned supremacy. The prominent amateur captain Wilf Wooller had argued privately for abolition of the gentleman–player distinction immediately after the war. But his arguments fell on deaf ears at Lords.

The captaincy of county cricket teams remained in amateur hands even though it was often hard to find an amateur good enough for the job. This was justified in terms of encouraging entertaining cricket – professionals were thought too unwilling to take risks or show leadership. What was really at stake was deference. Cricket was held to be more than a game. It had a cultural centrality in England that no other sport could approach, especially in relation to the middle and upper classes. If the tradition of amateur captaincy was undermined, another plank in the social order would be removed. Society worked best, it was claimed, when each knew his place and assumed his particular responsibilities; the 'university men' looking after 'the lads'; the professionals looking up to the amateur with his knack for leadership and getting the team to pull together. The older professionals who had played before the war tended to accept the established order of things more readily than the younger ones. Jim Laker, the great Surrey and England off-spinner and a Yorkshireman, was well known for his hostility to the class distinction of cricket. 'Errol Reginald Thorold Holmes was my first captain at Surrey,' he recalled, 'and quite frankly he was the biggest snob I ever met.'[6]

Hence the significance of the decision to appoint Len Hutton as the first professional captain of England in 1952. In fact, this was a strategic move rather than a decision of principle by the MCC. Hutton himself said he was just keeping the seat warm for a suitable amateur. All the same, it was a major change and the first serious crack in the amateur façade. Len Hutton was the senior English professional batsman, whose record innings of 364 against Australia in 1938 had made him a national hero. He was the natural choice, especially as he headed the batting averages against Australia in 1951 with 88.83 when the next best was 38.77. Yet there were great reservations about the appointment, which came as a surprise to Hutton. He was asked if he would become an amateur to take the captaincy – as Wally Hammond had done earlier – but he refused. At one level he stayed true to his origins in Yorkshire professional cricket and could put on the accent when he wanted. But at another he was becoming a 'gentleman', polishing his vowels, sending his son to Repton and Cambridge and settling in Kingston-upon-Thames. He captained England 23 times, never lost a series and was rewarded with a knighthood, only the second to be awarded to a professional cricketer. The 'player' was formally created a gentleman.

Cricket was slowly starting to change. But this was not in response to muted and intermittent criticism from Labour papers like the *Daily Herald*. There was plenty of quiet resentment amongst the players about travelling third class when amateurs went first or staying in pubs when the gents got the best hotels and better food. But there was a marked reluctance to mobilize opinion to change these divisive arrangements. Individual players had too much to lose. They risked their jobs and their benefit matches by taking a stand. There were always enough of those who accepted the status quo to replace any dissidents. Cricket had no equivalent of the Professional Footballers' Association with a Jimmy Hill to threaten strike action. Although he said 'the removal of the distinction between the gentlemen and the players remains the best thing that has happened in my lifetime', Laker was a Conservative and reluctant to rock the boat in public.[7] He even played as an amateur for a few seasons at the end of his career.

It was not so much pressure from below as the increasing difficulty finding enough good amateur players, which finally pushed the MCC to change the system. Fewer and fewer pubic school boys were coming into first-class cricket and staying there. Assembling a good amateur team for the Gentlemen vs. Players became difficult. The percentage of amateurs had gone down from around 40 per cent before 1914 and 30 per cent between the wars to around 20 per cent after 1945 and this figure continued to decline. Despite the flowering of a few great amateur batsmen in the 1950s, the 'rise of the meritocracy' meant that exams had to be passed and promotions earned. Denis Compton told the Wolfenden Committee that 'the amateur cricketer was dying out because he was not able to afford the time involved. Only men with well-established parents were able to take part: it had become an economic problem to be an amateur.' Careers could no longer be constantly interrupted by mid-week cricket, which continued to be organized at the county level as if young gentlemen had leisure and private means. Amateurs had to be in the office more often. As John Arlott remarked, 'there is no room for the amateur because people simply can't afford to play without pay and shamateurism has become increasingly objectionable'.[8] So the system was changed in part to allow amateurs to play for pay without losing social status.

Arlott's point about 'shamateurism' was well made. Ever since the days of Grace it had been common knowledge that top amateurs could make more in expenses than some professionals. The press, however, were now less willing to tolerate hypocrisy or class distinction. Laker let it be known he was thinking of changing status from professional to amateur to earn more money. Social attitudes were changing amongst younger amateurs. David Sheppard recalled his acute embarrassment at having to defend the distinction on BBC's *Sportsnight*. When this was combined with the practical problem of providing a better way for amateurs to stay in the game, the argument became overwhelming. Cricket crowds were falling and there was a clear case for modernizing the game to attract income and spectators. Almost two million spectators watched county cricket in 1950. By 1960 there were scarcely one million. Even the England–Australia series, the jewel in the crown of English cricket, had seen numbers fall from the 520,114 for Bradman's last tour in 1948 to the 388,533 for Richie Benaud's 1961 side.

The old guard put up stiff resistance. As late as 1959 a committee of the MCC rejected 'any solution to the problem on the lines of abolishing the distinction between amateur and professional and regarding them all alike as cricketers'. However, this was widely seen as simply delaying the inevitable and in 1962 the decision was finally taken. The Gillette Cup was introduced the following year to provide income from one-day games on the lines of Lancashire League cricket. Another plank of amateur orthodoxy had been removed.

There was a delicious irony in this. Never since the Edwardian 'Golden Age' had England produced such a crop of gifted amateur batsmen: men like David Sheppard and Trevor Bailey, Peter May and Colin Cowdrey, Mike Smith, Subba Row and Ted Dexter. England had not only won but retained the Ashes when the great West Indian side of the three Ws came in the summer of 1957. Weekes, Worrell and Walcott faced an England team in which star professionals like Godfrey Evans, Jim Laker and Fred Trueman were joined by May and Cowdrey who made 411 in a famous partnership. Combining amateur batting and leadership with professional bowling and guile still seemed to work.

Peter May, the Charterhouse, Cambridge and Surrey batsman with a job at Lloyds, was the key figure in English cricket in the 1950s, leading England 41 times in six years, to be followed as captain by Cowdrey and then by Dexter, who had played rugby, rackets, and was a scratch golfer as well as playing cricket at Radley and Cambridge. Driving majestically through the covers, never going to a lecture in his three years at Cambridge, Dexter was the embodiment of the amateur age. The legend of the gifted gentleman lived on. From the 1960s onwards England tended to oscillate between the tough 'old pro' as captain like Brian Close, Ray Illingworth or Mike Gatting and the more refined amateur style of Mike Brearley and David Gower, the stylish left-handed batsman from the King's School, Canterbury. Gower's whimsy and refusal to take training schedules too seriously, especially the harsh regime of his dour 'professional' captain, the half-shaven Graham Gooch, led to him being dropped. This in turn prompted a prolonged controversy in the pages of *The Times* over what kind of cricketer England really wanted to represent them.

Despite the ending of formal social distinctions, the divisions within cricket lingered on. Administrative changes meant that the MCC no longer controlled cricket as it had done. In 1968 it surrendered effective power to the Test and County Cricket Board. There had been a quiet revolution in cricket. Yet the MCC continued to thrive not simply as a gentlemen's club in the Long Room at Lord's but in the sense that much of the old culture of cricket survived. For all his records as an all rounder, Ian Botham – the supreme player of the recent past – seemed to fulfil the old amateur fears of a professional captain who could not conduct himself in public with the self-control required. The spectacle of Mike Gatting, who hailed from humble origins in Neasden, verbally abusing a Pakistani umpire – not without provocation it must be said – seemed to confirm amateur fears. Mike Atherton of Manchester Grammar School and Cambridge took over in due course. The residual expectation that the England captain should behave like a gentleman gradually disappeared during the 1990s to be replaced by a supposedly tougher and more competitive professional approach to winning. Ironically, winning was something which England teams had not done consistently since the Indian summer of amateurism in the 1950s.

Athletics

Cricket was an old sport, patronized by the eighteenth-century aristocracy and played by their servants and tenants, which permitted mixed teams providing the social rules were observed. However, this did not apply to other sports such as rowing, rugby and athletics. Here amateur purity banned any contact between amateur and professional, opposed the formation of leagues and punished gambling with the utmost severity. Amateurism was not simply a way of separating the social classes, it was a moral code which filtered down to the respectable lower middle classes and to skilled workers.

Athletics, unlike rowing, had never formally excluded participants on the grounds of occupation. There had been several working-class amateur champions like the railwayman Albert Hill, who won the 800 and 1500 metres in the 1920 Olympics, though they had never seemed to get the recognition accorded to middle- or upper-class medallists despite the greater sacrifices required. Athletics was run by an executive committee appointed from those who had risen through the ranks of club and regional committees over many years. Only those who could afford the lengthy investment of time and money to climb the ladder ('or put something back in', as they preferred it) could enjoy the power and prestige of running British athletics.

For all that, most officials were dedicated individuals who sincerely believed in amateur ideals formed earlier in the century. Hence the Amateur Athletic Association maintained a fierce opposition to any payment of athletes, refusing to reimburse training costs, the cost of equipment, even the entrance costs to facilities and postage to reply to fan mail. In the cold war era with athletics drawn into a global struggle for prestige between the West and the Soviet bloc, the standards of international performance rose inexorably, leaving the British behind. The gap between the British purist and the subsidized American or German competitor had been evident in Berlin in 1936 and was again apparent after the war with mediocre results in the London Olympics of 1948 and worse at Helsinki in 1952. In fact, Chris Brasher's victory in the steeplechase at Melbourne in 1956 was the first British individual track gold since 1932. The public expected better, especially now that television was starting to bring these events into the home.

Gordon Pirie, Britain's leading long-distance runner throughout the 1950s and a silver medallist in the 5000 metres in Melbourne, was scathing in his criticism. 'Amateurism in British athletics is a sham and a hypocrisy which prevents us from competing on equal terms with athletes abroad,' he wrote in pent-up fury on his retirement, denouncing 'out-of-date ideals which prevent our athletes from dedicating their whole lives to their chosen careers without endless humiliating worries about money and their future'.[9] No one thought the less of Stanley Matthews or Denis Compton for being professional sportsmen, so why should athletes be considered morally polluted for taking money? Pirie calculated he needed twenty pairs of shoes a season for which he got no allowance from the AAA let alone any other expenses. Competing cost him at least £500 a season, which was a year's income for an average man. Athletes were expected to have benevolent employers or families with deep pockets. He retired at 30 'a married man with no job and no prospects' who felt he couldn't 'honestly advise youngsters to do what I have done'.[10]

Yet Pirie did not favour the payment of large amounts of prize money or appearance money – what he called 'gross professionalism'. Nor did he favour Soviet-style state employment for athletes or American sports scholarships. The answer was simply to give athletes enough support to allow them to develop their full potential through a properly funded training and expenses system and to remove the barriers to them making money from the media once they had got to the top. Dorothy Hyman, the daughter of a Yorkshire miner, had a hard struggle to pay for her training and travel before winning her silver medal in Rome in 1960. She took a similar view of the obstacles amateurism placed in front of the serious competitor and the right of the athlete to get some reward for the sacrifices involved. She prepared for the Olympics in a deprived area where there was no cinder track, no floodlights, no indoor facilities, no showers, no training partners and coaching only once a month. Despite all this she became one of the leading female athletes in the world, almost beating the great Wilma Rudolph. Yet she found herself unable to publish her life story before the 1964 Tokyo games on the grounds that she would profit from her athletic success. Like Pirie, Hyman did not want full professionalism. 'I would never want to earn money by winning; only from commercial undertakings outside . . . appearing on TV, writing, modelling, endorsing sports equipment, advertising, selling and so on. I don't believe for a moment such earnings would interfere with the spirit of athletics.'[11]

This, however, was precisely what the amateur establishment did believe. In the face of mounting criticism of poor British performances, the President of the AAA, the Marquess of Exeter, used the 1958 AGM to restate the difference between the professional for whom sport was 'a vehicle for earning his daily bread' and the amateur who regarded it as a 'happy recreation'. John Disley, a leading hurdler who was there, remarked that 'it was quite obvious that the actual athletes present did not agree with a word of it, but their objections were disregarded as being unworthy'.[12] Disley admitted that some athletes took appearance money to cover their expenses and equipment. Like Pirie and Hyman, he opposed professional athletics but thought athletes should be free to profit from the spin-off from their sporting success. It was 'better to alter the amateur rules than to make it inevitable that many people should break them'. Chris Chataway, an Oxbridge amateur and future Tory MP, went even further. 'Olympic athletes may have been gentlemen amateurs before the First World War,' he remarked on the eve of the Rome Olympics, 'today, they clearly are not,' and added that athletics should be made into an open sport forthwith.[13]

Amateur officials consoled themselves with the view that it was better to stay true to their principles than to be drawn too far into the battle for medals. The United States was prepared to throw its vast resources behind sport and use the college scholarship system to produce the best. No one at the AAA thought of combing the country for talent and sending them off to Oxbridge. Still less did they consider following the example of the Soviet Union and its satellites. The British, of course, wanted to break records and win medals but they still wanted to do so on their own terms. And they could always point to the events of 6 May 1954 at the Iffley Road stadium in Oxford to prove that the true amateur could still excel.

When Chris Brasher and Chris Chataway made the pace for Roger Bannister's four-minute mile, they also made a rod for the back of all those who wanted to change the system. This was a triumph for the amateur spirit of British athletics, a team effort with a touch of undergraduate innocence. Even the running style was distinctively amateur with long graceful strides and a relaxed, trance-like expression which contrasted sharply with the 'puff-puff' motion and contorted facial expressions of Pirie, who modelled himself on the great Czech runner, Zatopek. Coming on top of Sir John Hunt's gentlemanly management of the successful Everest expedition, it seemed as if the pure British amateur could still compete at the top level. 'The officials,' according to the shot-putter Geoff Capes, 'thought all the athletes were students on a summer vacation with a family stipend. They still thought in terms of Lord Burghley and Harold Abrahams.'[14] There was a generation gap in amateur sport of all kinds. Those who had grown up in the post-war world of greater affluence and better education were increasingly reluctant to be dictated to by men who had been reared on ingrained notions of status and privilege.

Crowds, however, were starting to decline sharply in the 1960s. It was only the biggest meetings that drew more than a few thousand and television rapidly replaced gate money as the main source of income for athletics. Ironically, the AAA were happy to accept press and commercial sponsorship for their own purposes in the 1960s. The formation of the Sports Council in 1964 augured well for a positive government input but the large number of different national bodies involved and their entrenched interests and rivalries made it extremely difficult to reform the structure. Hence when athletics in Britain was booming in the 1970s with the spread of marathon running and jogging, the British Amateur Athletics Board, which supervised the national team, was almost bankrupt. The Sports Aid Foundation was set up to attract commercial sponsorship in 1976 and athletes benefited significantly. But it was not until 1989 that a unified national structure came into being in the form of the British Athletics Federation.

The 1960s saw the emergence of female athletics as a major force. This was to prove the last flowering of the old variety of pure amateurism. Dorothy Hyman had led the way. When she brought home her Olympic silver medal to the small Yorkshire town of Cudworth, there were 15,000 to greet her with brass bands, baskets of fruit, and all manner of tributes including a poem from a thirteen-year-old girl called Dorothy Goose. Hyman was voted BBC Sports Personality of the Year in 1963. Anne Packer won the Tokyo Olympic 800 metres in 1964 and Mary Rand became the first British woman to win an Olympic field event with her victory in the long jump, following Hyman as BBC Sports Personality of the Year. This crop of brilliant young women athletes injected a new energy into the staid amateur cause. Rand, a working-class girl from Somerset, had won a scholarship to Millfield and circumvented the funding problems that handicapped others. She was soon followed by Lillian Board, who took a silver medal in the 400 metres in 1968 at the age of 18 only to die of cancer at 22 in Munich where she had hoped to win gold in the next Olympics. Her early death brought a sense of loss that had not been felt since Duncan Edwards had died of his injuries fourteen years earlier, also at Munich. Women's athletics had become major news. This continued with Mary Peters, who won the pentathlon in the 1972 Games, and was a much loved figure but lacked the glamour of 'the golden girls' which had drawn the press, especially the new tabloids, whose interest in these young blondes was not confined to their athletics. In the decade when George Best took the headlines, there was clearly a market for attractive female athletes to exploit their new fame. Amateur rules stopped that. But the ground was being prepared for the obsessive interest in the female athlete as woman which came to the fore in the 1980s and 1990s.

There were, of course, also important male athletes like Alan Pascoe, Lynn Davies, who won the Olympic long jump in the same year as Mary Rand, and David Hemmery who won the 400 metres hurdles in 1968 and 'left earlier than he might have done thanks to the absence of sponsorship or financial reward'.[15] These were the last generation of pure amateurs. For all their fame and television exposure, they earned very little from sport. Hemmery, Pascoe, Davies and others published an open letter of protest to the AAA in 1972. The next generation was to benefit both from more generous support as well as from new forms of payment. From the late 1970s Sebastian Coe, Steve Ovett and then Steve Cram achieved a dominance of middle-distance running which was even more emphatic than the Olympic successes of the 1920s celebrated in the film *Chariots of Fire*. This was accompanied by Daley Thompson's decathlon triumphs in 1980 and 1984 and the success of the sprinter Alan Wells. The nation was agog. Ovett and Coe were the BBC Sports Personalities in 1978 and 1979 respectively, and Daley Thompson and Steve Cram in 1982 and 1983.

Daley Thompson was invited to appear on Radio 4's *Desert Island Discs*. Daley's choice of music, which appeared to distress his highbrow host, caught the popular mood perfectly, commercial, transatlantic, multicultural. Daley Thompson seemed to enjoy sport whilst also making money and he was a key role model in promoting serious athletic competition amongst younger black men. Tessa Sanderson, who won the Olympic javelin in 1984, provided a similar example to black girls. During the 1980s there was a remarkable increase in top-level black competitors, who quickly became a crucial element in the national squad. Without the rolling back of amateur restrictions it is hard to see how some of the poorer black athletes would have found the resources to compete in what was an ever more expensive and complicated process of preparation.

These remarkable 'amateur' achievements were in fact the product of the payment of top athletes through advertising, sponsorship and appearance money. The 'éminence grise' of this complex system of double standards and public hypocrisy was in fact a police sergeant from Bromley: Andy Norman. Norman, an athletics enthusiast with a vast knowledge of the sport, saw the growing television appeal of top athletes and set about helping them – and himself – to reap the material benefits. During the 1970s appearance money was not large – David Bedford, the world 5000 metres champion, got around £500 to run in big new meetings such as those at Gateshead organized by Brendan Foster, the Tyneside distance runner turned TV pundit and athletics promoter. Norman managed Ovett's affairs and was also helpful to Coe, who credited Norman not just with making the sport lucrative but with paying big money to get the best athletes in the world to Britain and raising the standard of domestic performance.

The achievements of Coe, Ovett and Cram are especially important. This was partly because of the exceptional drama of their races and partly through the media fascination with their rivalry. Ovett surprisingly took the 800 metres in the 1980 Moscow Olympics only for Coe to come back a few days later to win the 1500 metres. Then there was Coe bursting past Cram, the world record holder, to take another gold at Los Angeles four years later. The period between these two Olympics marked an exceptional moment in British athletics and the point at which amateurism in the old sense finally collapsed under the pressure of television and advertising. The Coe–Ovett duel grabbed public attention. Stoked by a patriotic popular press wallowing in the reassertion of British power in the Falklands, athletics assumed a new importance and a series of head-to-head races were set up between Coe and Ovett, who had avoided each other in the 1981 season. 'The big show down begins' trumpeted the *Radio Times* in July 1982 with a cover showing an artist's impression of the two men battling shoulder to shoulder for the line, in plain white vests and shorts, straining every muscle, staring into each other's eyes.[16]

Appearance money and other payments were firmly established on a legitimate footing when the International Amateur Athletics Federation ruled in favour of the setting up of trust funds for athletes in 1982. But the market is a tough place and only the top athletes really benefitted from the vast increase in money that was openly available for the first time. Coe, for example, had no time for flat-rate payments for all participants. Top money was for top men – and women. Being a 'top' athlete was not just measured by the stopwatch. It was more a question of what grabbed the public imagination or who was thrust into the public eye by the press. Hence a highly promising young white South African runner, Zola Budd, was picked up by the *Daily Mail*, briskly turned into a British citizen and offered a staggering £90,000 – the highest sum ever offered for a race in Britain – to run against the American champion Mary Slaney, who had fallen in the Olympic 3000 metres when they met at the Los Angeles Games. The lure of such rewards naturally pushed younger athletes to make the sacrifice of time and effort – or the 'investment' in talent as it was perceived by agents like Mark McCormack or the former athlete Alan Pascoe. These opportunities proved important in attracting outstanding young black athletes like Linford Christie, Colin Jackson and Denise Lewis. The rewards for those who got to the top were high but the public was only interested in the very best. Those just beneath the top of the pyramid could expect little more than help with their training. Unlike football, the benefits of professionalism did not extend very far.

Rugby

What happened in athletics in the eighties hit rugby union in the nineties. Rugby union had always been militantly amateur. The very division of the sport into the union and league forms had arisen over the issue of allowing 'broken time' payments to players. This amounted to a class division of the sport which expressed itself in regional terms. The southern clubs were largely composed of members of the liberal professions and business elite who had played the game as part of their private education or in grammar schools emulating the public school ideal. No public school boys played in the Lancashire and Yorkshire bastions of the League. Professionals and amateurs had observed a temporary wartime truce, sometimes finding themselves side by side in service teams when brightening up the Home Front and bolstering troop morale. But all this came to an abrupt end in 1945. J. A. Gregory, who had played for the Army, was banned from playing rugby union simply because he had played once for Huddersfield in the wartime Rugby League. The fact that he had not received any payment and had reported the matter himself made no difference. To play beside professionals in service teams washed clean by patriotism was one thing; to cross the social divide out of uniform was quite another.

No money except the bare minimum in expenses was paid to those who played by the union code. This rule was firmly applied in England and Scotland, where the game was predominantly middle class, but less strictly enforced amongst the miners of Wales. The rewards of playing rugby for famous sides like Harlequins or Wasps came in different, and in many ways more lucrative, forms. Playing rugby at a good level – there were no leagues before the 1980s as clubs liked to arrange their own fixtures – was a route to a good job. Long before rugby entered the world of commercial sport, business 'networking' was strongly entrenched. When players came off the field to mingle socially with the opposition, there was plenty of opportunity to mix business and pleasure.

Big clubs like Bath, anxious to establish themselves at the top, were known to have powerful figures who could tailor a career to fit the player. Malcolm Pearce, chairman of Johnson's News Group, a successful businessman and a keen Bath supporter, was able to arrange jobs within his organization and enlisted the help of other businessmen to find work for the right players. Gareth Chilcott was 'an itinerant french polisher' who was turned into the director of a limousine hire company while Ben Clarke's training at agricultural college made him a natural candidate to run Pearce's dairy herd. Chilcott was a useful reminder that rugby union players no longer had to be gentlemen. One of the most prominent England players of the 1970s, Fran Cotton, came from a big mining family near Wigan and idolized the town's rugby league star, Billy Boston. It was the expansion of higher education which turned him into a rugby union man. He won a place at Loughborough University to train as a physical education teacher and developed his rugby union there before going on to run a sports clothing business on his retirement from international duty. Top quality rugby union became less socially exclusive in England. Barking's Jason Leonard, the son of an East End carpenter, was England's most capped forward in the 1990s.

In Wales rugby union was a (genuinely) popular game, played by the miners as well as the products of local grammar schools, whose schoolmaster rugby coaches were part of the folklore of the Principality. 'Gwendraeth Grammar . . . was one of the legendary nurseries of Welsh rugby. Every decade a great outside half emerged from its playing fields. Carwyn James in the Fifties, Barry John in the Sixties, Gareth Davies in the Seventies and Jonathan Davies in the Eighties.'[17] One of the men behind the legend was a former international winger, Ray Williams, who recalled how they would hold trials of hundreds of boys to get a representative local side. But the world moved on. The grammar school went comprehensive and in a series of confrontations with the Thatcher government many teachers withdrew cooperation. There was 'a growing diversity of interests' amongst the boys according to a new Gwendraeth headmaster whose enthusiasm for rugby went no further than 'watching a game now and then'. Before long there wasn't even a First XV any more. 'That's the most heartbreaking thing in rugby I've heard for years,' commented Cliff Morgan, a gifted product of those post-war valley grammar schools and an influential voice for the old values on national radio.[18]

Along with changes in education, the collapse of coal mining and steel making in South Wales set the scene for a sharp decline in Welsh rugby from the glory days of the 1970s when the likes of Gareth Edwards, Phil Bennett and J. P. R Williams carried all before them. Their great period coincided with the advent of colour television and the new appeal of the Five Nations championship to a mass British audience. From such a height, there was a long way to fall. It has been especially hard for Wales to face defeat at the hands of teams from Romania or Western Samoa. Wales had always been less strict in its interpretation of amateurism than the English or Scottish unions and historically this had helped them to keep their best players in Wales, apart from those who chose to 'go north' to Rugby League. Top players like Jonathan Davies were still being lured away to the League game by offers of big money in the early 1990s but the new professionalism of the union game itself has posed an even greater threat in recent years, especially from the big English clubs.

Rugby union as a televised spectator sport, especially the Five Nations championship, enlivened the early months of the year and became a fixture in the BBC sporting calendar, complete with Bill Macleren, the rugged Scottish schoolmaster, a much loved enthusiast and gift for impersonators. Rugby now had its media voice. Sponsors saw that rugby was popular, especially with the upper-income bracket, and advertisers followed. At the same time the pressure for greater inter-national events led to the setting up of the Rugby World Cup in 1987. The Home Nations had lost a veto over changes to the sport when France was admitted to the International Rugby Football Board in 1978 alongside Australia, New Zealand and South Africa.

The success of the World Cup in 1991 with a profit of over £5 million kept up the commercial momentum, culminating in the signing of a $550 million deal between the Murdoch Empire and the three big southern hemisphere nations. This was concluded in June 1995 on the eve of the World Cup in South Africa, which made a profit of £22 million. The game was awash with money but the players were not supposed to touch it. A professional game in the southern hemisphere cut off from an amateur one in the northern hemisphere was unthink-able. The best Europeans would go south and world rugby would be ruined. The pressure from top players was simply too great and the 'shamateurism' too shameless to continue on an amateur basis. This led to the final historic decision of the International Board meeting in Paris in August 1995 that the game should be 'open', effectively making British rugby professional overnight. Not surprisingly it was the Mur-doch-owned *Times* that urged the Home Nations along the professional road, backed up by its populist stable mate the *Sun*, which saw amateurism as plain daft and snobbish.

New forces moved in. Almost all the top clubs shifted to company status from being membership-based in the old amateur tradition. The Tyneside retail and building magnate Sir John Hall acquired Newcastle United as a soccer flagship for the 'Geordie nation' and then proceeded to buy a local outpost of rugby union and hire a bunch of star names to go with it. The economics made no apparent sense as crowds of 4,000 or so watched players like England's World Cup star Rob Andrew, who signed a five-year contract for £750,000. Newcastle duly became national champions in May 1998 but almost bankrupted themselves in the process.

Leading clubs who had rarely paid their players more than travel expenses suddenly faced escalating wage bills. The low overheads of the amateur era had meant the major clubs were financially secure and the provincial businessmen in charge had fostered a cautious attitude to investment. Suddenly such men had to think commercially or accept that their clubs would be marginalized. Paying high salaries for stars made clubs reluctant to release players for international duties and tours. This led to a head-on conflict with the RFU which rumbled on through 1997–8. There were strong rumours of a split between the RFU and the top clubs until a compromise was finally hammered out in May 1998, which involved the departure of Cliff Brittle, the chairman of the RFU's management board and a defender of the old order of country over club.[19]

The assumption was that Sky television would bankroll the new clubs. The logic of American spectator sport was coming to Britain. Old established teams like Saracens and Richmond moved in order to share facilities with Watford and Reading football clubs. Rugby clubs copied the 'new football' and aggressively marketed themselves with the help of powerful new backers. But an amateur sport could not be turned into a mass commercial spectacle at the drop of a hat. There was simply not enough interest in going to these games in large numbers or watching them on satellite television to justify the investment. Sir John Hall pulled out from Newcastle, and Richmond, one of the oldest rugby clubs in the world, went bankrupt. But there were also benefits. Taking money for playing no longer denoted social or moral inferiority as it had done for a century. Moreover, the standard of play, especially at club level, was relentlessly driven up as players were expected to train as professional athletes instead of talented enthusiasts.

The advent of professional rugby has not destroyed all the old traditions. The Five Nations has become Six but the festive side of the event for spectators appears unchanged. The Welsh still love to travel to see their team, gathering in little groups in Edinburgh, Paris or Dublin on the Wednesday or Thursday before a match, swelling to mighty proportions by the Saturday, roaming the pubs, renting every bed and breakfast for miles round. When the French, Scots or English came over, their contingents were more middle class but with the same emphasis on a cheerful, boozy weekend with the boys, escaping domestic surveillance before resuming their respectable lives. Some 'amateur' traditions hadn't changed and probably never would.

At the grass roots, however, there had been a major shift in amateur rugby away from schools, whose role in the game declined sharply. The Welsh case was the most dramatic but the Welsh were not alone. As Gerald Davies, the celebrated international winger, remarked in a letter to *The Times*, 'famous state grammar schools have disappeared, been amalgamated or have had their names and responsibilities changed without anything as remotely successful put in their place. A tradition, however flawed, was ruined, a rung in the ladder of excellence removed.'[20] There was a similar trend in Scotland where the 'Scottish Rugby Union recorded a drop from 15,000 to 6,000 of regular players in schools' rugby during the 1983–7 period'.[21] The focus of youth rugby shifted from school to club and with it came a further decline in the traditions of sportsmanship that had been a part of the old amateur ethos of school sport.

The clubs, however, benefitted and enjoyed a modest expansion in the 1980s after the boom period of the 1970s: the RFU, for example, grew from 971 clubs in 1965 to 1769 in 1975, settling around 2000 in the 1980s whilst Scottish rugby had 110 clubs in 1965 and 207 in 1975 with around 250 in the 1980s. Wales, where the game had always been relatively popular, had less room for expansion, with 162 clubs in 1965 and around 200 in the 1980s. Most of these clubs were relatively untouched by the sea-change at the top. Boys played rugby competitively within their area, passing from youth teams to First XVs and then on to the senior sides where sociability and recreation were more important than results. Amateurism, at the grass roots, was about preserving male traditions and relationships which were expressed through loyalty to a particular code and the values associated with it.

Tennis

Just as rugby was important to middle-class men, tennis was a key sporting activity for middle-class women. Rugby clubs were segregated areas but tennis clubs made a point of mixing the sexes socially and on court. Many a young romance began at the tennis club dance in the post-war years before discos and night clubs proliferated. Wimbledon was at the heart of the polite world of British tennis and was probably the most widely followed amateur sporting event. The Lawn Tennis Association (LTA) was steeped in the traditions of genteel recreation and firmly established in the leafy suburbs. Tennis was the most popular summer game for girls, who often received some coaching at school. In clubs there was also a strong female presence and a tendency for members to carry on into middle age. Two in five club members in the 1990s were over 30.

In this respect tennis closely resembled golf with the important exception that golf clubs had a resident professional. In golf the amateur governing body, the R&A, organized the 'Open Championship'. The LTA, however, rejected 'open tennis'. Golf, like cricket, had its origins in the eighteenth century and professionals had always had a place in the game. Lawn tennis, on the other hand, was a Victorian invention and adopted the prevailing values of amateur purity. From dominating the game in the late Victorian and Edwardian era, the British were supplanted successively by the French, the Americans and Australians. British women fared better than the men. Fred Perry's success in the thirties cast a long shadow and no one was able to repeat it. Yet even in the women's game there had been no British champion since Virginia Wade in 1977.

Why was this? Was it the weather? This was a favourite excuse before the Swedes and Germans emerged in the 1970s to disprove it. Or was it something more fundamental to do with the social structure of amateur tennis itself and the special place of Wimbledon within it? As time passed, the search for talent was carried on by all kinds of enthusiasts such as the Christian pop singer Cliff Richard. Attention turned from climate to sociology. Perhaps British tennis was too English and too middle class? It was an elite sport based around private clubs whose purpose was to provide congenial recreational facilities for members. The LTA, it was argued, had let Britain down. The profits of Wimbledon had been squandered. They had done little to promote school tennis and less to improve municipal provision. Sagging nets and lumpy tarmac were the order of the day in public parks where new talent might have been found if there had been proper coaching for ordinary players. There was some truth in this, though the actual picture was more complicated. Private provision for tennis was extensive with a boom in the 1950s from 2061 clubs in 1948 to 4603 in 1958 – a figure which declined thereafter but remained at around 2500 through the 1970s and 1980s. In this sense amateur tennis was alive and well. But looking at municipal provision in a major city like Birmingham reveals a different picture. In 1955–6, 71,544 tickets were issued to play on the city's 290 courts; only eight years later, in 1963–4, 31,631 tickets were sold for 305 courts.[22] Lack of facilities was not really the issue. It was lack of use and lack of coaching, especially in state schools.

As Fred Perry himself remarked much later, Wimbledon, which clung on to its claim to be the world's top tournament, was part of the problem. 'People here aren't interested in anything else except Wimbledon and there isn't the sort of club system they have in Germany and Holland . . . so you struggle to establish roots.'[23] There were plenty of clubs in Britain but they did not play competitively and recruit widely. Playing tennis in Britain was a pleasant amateur pastime with an allocation of tickets for Wimbledon via the clubs as a reward for voluntary service to the sport. In 1992 these cosy arrangements hardly broadened the pool of talent. There were only 240 clubs in the Boys' Schools Lawn Tennis Federation as against 4351 for athletics and 13,000 school football clubs.

The problem varied between men and women. But even girls' tennis was relatively restricted with only 700 clubs in the Girls' Schools Tennis Association most of which were private schools. More women watched Wimbledon than men and for many it was the climax of the sporting year, curtains drawn against the evening sun, Mum and the family peering at a black and white TV, passing the salad cream and the Kraft cheese slices. Tennis was really more of a female than a male game in England; girls, for instance, still learned it in school – in private and grammar schools at least – without the distraction of cricket. Tennis was one of the few amateur sports which genuinely welcomed women, giving their best players respect and a place on the Centre Court. Women's tennis – like most other female sports – was more thoroughly amateur than the men's game. British amateurs did relatively well. There was an all British Wimbledon final between Angela Mortimer and Christine Truman in 1961 but the new star was a young table tennis player, Ann Jones, who won the French Open in 1961 and 1966 and was twice runner up in Paris. However, her great triumph came in 1969 beating both Margaret Court and Billie Jean King to take the Wimbledon title. Eight years later Virginia Wade also won Wimbledon and was voted BBC Sports Personality for 1977.

By the time Ann Jones finally conquered Wimbledon, the tournament had accepted professionalism. The writing had been on the wall for some time. The LTA's rules on expenses were far more generous than the Rugby Union's. In his confidential evidence to the Wolfenden Committee in 1958, John Barrett admitted that most of the top players were 'shamateurs' and felt 'that the day must come when tournament players would have to be called professionals . . . and would have to be paid'.[24] He went on to say that foreign 'amateurs' like Drobny and Patty 'made a living from the game'. Tennis was a 'money-spinner' as Jack Kramer had shown and amateur stars would continue to join the ranks of Gonzales, Sedgeman, Hoad and Rosewall. 'Whatever rules were made to keep the game amateur would fail so long as the public were prepared to pay to watch tennis. The only logical move for the governing body was to recognise a situation which existed already.'[25]

The LTA had a divided duty. On the one hand, they wanted to protect the social status of their sport. On the other, they had to maintain Wimbledon's reputation as the top world tournament. Social elitism and sporting excellence were drawing further apart. Crowds had been declining since the fifties and it was clear tennis was not making the best of itself with amateurs controlling the prestige venues and Kramer, a genial man and a former Wimbledon champion himself, handling the players the public really wanted to see. 'The craziest thing about tennis during these years', as Kramer recalled, 'was that the fans continued to be attracted to the traditional amateur fixture, even though they knew the pros had the best talent.'[26]

Public loyalty to an event which excluded some of the best players in the world was starting to wear thin. For all the 'strawberries and cream' and trappings of the social season, the numbers attending Wimbledon were declining. With the departure of the 1961 and 1962 grand slam winner Rod Laver for the professional tennis 'circus' in 1963, the credibility of the top amateur events was badly shaken. A tournament that didn't include Laver didn't look serious even if it was a gorgeous social event. The Soviet satellite states of eastern Europe were starting to produce players who wanted to compete at Wimbledon as amateurs but in effect were state employees. Cricket had dropped social and pecuniary distinctions between players in 1963 and the Lawn Tennis Association, which had close links to Lord's, followed suit in 1967, risking expulsion from the international amateur body in the process. However, the following year international tennis went open, which paved the way for the Kramer-inspired Grand Prix circuit in 1970.

Wimbledon was immediately rewarded with the return of Rod Laver as champion. The willingness of the tournament committee to keep up with the prize money on the international circuit combined with the value of the event in terms of advertising and sponsorship for leading players has ensured its viability and prestige. Prize money and profits have grown at a staggering pace. From a figure of under £300,000 in 1980 prize money rose to over £5 million in 1993 and the profit to the LTA went up from a mere £20,000 in 1980 to £16.4 million. Between 1980 and 1993, the LTA benefitted from almost £100 million for the development of the game. Clearly money alone is not the answer to raising the domestic game.

The price that tennis has paid for global commercialization is massive appearance money, deals between players over exhibition matches, and pressure on umpires from tournament directors whose livelihood depends on attracting the top players. 'Appearance money is a response to the laws of supply and demand,' observed Arthur Ashe, the respected black American 1975 Wimbledon winner, 'tournaments know the top players are worth more than the prize money they're offered . . . there's collusion between some tournament directors and some umpires (who) . . . are ordered not to discipline stars.'[27]

This was the state of affairs the old guard had dreaded. It was one thing to have accepted commercial logic, it was another to throw out the values and etiquette of the former amateur system. The advent of an enormously gifted but verbally abusive young American John Mc-Enroe at Wimbledon set the scene for a clash of sporting cultures both on and off the court. McEnroe simply had no time for the conventions and trappings of Wimbledon, its cosy superiority, ex-army types running the show. 'I'm Irish, you know', he announced on the jacket of his biography, as if to explain his lack of deference to tradition or royalty.[28] The point here is that Wimbledon had only abandoned some of its amateurism. Professionalism was allowed – even welcomed – providing due respect was paid to the wider cultural significance of the event. Wimbledon remained a carefully orchestrated national ritual in which royalty played an important part. The Duchess of Kent still presented the singles trophies, congratulating the winner and consoling the loser after keeping both of them waiting while she walked between lines of ball boys and girls, stopping for a brief word before passing on.

Players were expected to bow or curtsey to the Royal Box before leaving the court. Wimbledon was seen by the amateur establishment as a microcosm of all that was best and traditional in British life, ranging from the benign influence of the monarchy to the quality and independence of the unpaid officials who adjudicated and organized. Hence the appalled reaction to the sight of McEnroe screaming at a linesman or stalking up to the umpire's chair to complain about a call, muttering angrily or smashing his racquet on the ground. Nastase, of course, and even Borotra before him had thrown the odd tantrum. But this was more frequent, more calculated and by no means confined to McEnroe.

Exasperation with English stuffiness was one thing. Flagrant abuse of an opponent was another. The brat element in professional tennis was gradually contained and 'The Brat' himself began to mellow. But what if the brat turned out to be British? When a rising young player, Tim Henman, smashed away a ball in anger and injured a ball girl, public condemnation was swift. But it was soon forgotten as he began to look like a winner. Even McEnroe said so. The stockbroker belt was gripped with 'Henmania' as Britain found a new tennis hero. Part of Henman's appeal was his amateur pedigree; both his grandmother and mother had played at Wimbledon. Ironically, the long awaited successor to Fred Perry – pent-up expectation far outran performance – came not from the northern streets or school yard but the family tennis court of a country house in the Home Counties.

There was no need for a newly knighted benefactor to sweep this talented youngster off to Florida. He had most of what he needed at home. The cradle of amateurism had supplied the best chance of professional success as Henman showed just what the amateur elite could do if they used their privileges in conjunction with the greatly improved practice and coaching facilities now available. Alternately, of course, we could adopt someone who had learned the game elsewhere but was technically qualified to play for Britain. Canada's Greg Rusedski fitted the bill perfectly.

Survival: Varieties of Amateurism

Of all the amateur sports, rowing had the most strongly elite image. The Amateur Rowing Association (ARA) was alone among amateur bodies in having a social definition of the amateur, excluding anyone who was 'a mechanic, artisan or labourer'. This formal social segregation dated from the late Victorian era and had led to the setting up of the rival National Amateur Rowing Association (NARA), which welcomed all who did not compete for cash. Hence there were different amateur bodies with different entry requirements. For all its manifest elitism, the ARA with its Leander and boat race crews was a formidable competitive force which performed brilliantly between the wars. Jack Beresford won three gold and two silver medals in five consecutive Olympic Games during the inter-war period. Criticism of the treatment of the Australian police crew from Henley before the Berlin Olympics of 1936 eventually led the ARA to drop its manual labour clause. This prepared the way for a post-war amalgamation of the ARA and NARA, which finally came about in 1956. Fusion had been hastened by the emergence of the Soviet Union as a great rowing country whose oarsmen were starting to snap up the glittering prizes at an alarming rate. The cold war had a way of concentrating the amateur mind wonderfully.[29]

The new ARA made piecemeal efforts at reform and incorporated female rowers in 1962. However, it was not until a further reorganization and reduction of the power of the old clubs that amateur rowing reasserted itself at the top level. This came about through a new 'professional' approach with the creation of a national rowing course near Nottingham and the appointment of a national coach, snapped up from Czechoslovakia after the Russian invasion. A social revolution in rowing ensued: the formerly unthinkable fusion of the supremely exclusive Leander Club and the Thames Tradesmen to form successful teams. Since then British rowing has won a clutch of Olympic golds and world championships culminating in the remarkable achievement of Steve Redgrave winning four consecutive Olympic golds with a fifth in sight. He was the nearest thing Britain had to an amateur sporting hero before he effectively became professional in the 1990s. It was left to less famous Olympic sports like yachting and shooting to provide amateur competitors who really were amateur.

The changes in amateur sport have been so striking it is easy to overlook the continuities. One of the most remarkable survivals is the annual Boat Race between Oxford and Cambridge. Not only are there large crowds on the towpath and the bridges of the Thames but the BBC pays around £300,000 a year for the privilege of broadcasting a single race that is also sold to over 160 countries around the world. It cannot be an interest in rowing that creates this audience. Rather it is the thought of watching one of the oldest continuous sporting events in the world (the year 2000 was number 146), which offers a convenient opportunity to observe the English elite (liberally sprinkled with Americans and others) and the London landscape. In other words this is a 'heritage' event as well as a serious athletic contest; a chance to sell England to the world, giving foreigners a conveniently packaged piece of sporting history. Presumably this is why 'Beefeater Gin' was willing to spend £225,000 a year sponsoring the crews.

Even the sacrosanct world of rowing has now accepted professionalism with the nice reservation that oarsmen who earn money are not to be called professionals but 'fundholders' like athletes and rugby players before them.[30] Watching the 1997 race – a neck and neck affair with oars touching as the Cambridge cox held unswervingly to his course to win by a little over a length – the intensity and drama of the spectacle was all too obvious; so, too, was the odd mixture of amateur sportsmanship and the fierce triumphalism of victory. The Cambridge President punched the air repeatedly before adding, almost as an afterthought, a ritual acknowledgement of the efforts of the other team. The Oxford eight collapsed, utterly deflated and demoralised, seemingly inconsolable after having put up a marvellous fight which thrilled the large crowds on the bank and the huge television audience. Amateurism, albeit of a new and very different kind, was alive and well. When Oxford finally broke the Cambridge run in 2000, the Oxford President never even mentioned Cambridge in his post-race remarks.

Sports varied greatly in their commercial appeal. Swimming was the Cinderella of the major sports with a huge recreational following of almost five million in the mid-1980s but limited professional potential. Swimming was a sport open to women and it was women who made the bigger impact in the post-war years, especially Judy Grinham who won the 100 metre backstroke at the Melbourne Olympics of 1956. Although she approved of the amateur principle, she objected to the stringency with which it was applied to top competitors in the same way as to athletes like Pirie and Hyman. She had to train for five hours a day and was only able to work part-time. All her earnings went on swimming. Her parents had even sold their house to help with her coaching costs. After winning her gold medal, she had to buy clothes for public appearances without being able to take any fees. Whilst she did not wish to race for money, she felt it was wrong for promising youngsters to have to pay their own entrance fees and travel expenses.[31] She retired at 20 instead of defending her Olympic title. To recoup some of her costs and her parents' investment she had to try her hand – without much success – at modelling and acting.

What Judy Grinham seemed to want, like Hyman, Pirie and others, was a looser form of amateurism. So did Anita Lonsborough, the daughter of a Regimental Sergeant-Major from Huddersfield, who followed Grinham as the star British swimmer. She worked for the local council and had her pay stopped when she was competing. She recalled how she 'had to pick cockroaches out of the water' before she started her morning training: '. . . when I warmed up I kept thinking: "have I missed any? Is there another one? Am I going to swallow it?"'.[32] When she won the 100 metre breaststroke in Rome there was a collection in the town and she was presented with a silver tea service. She had to make a speech. As she spoke she realized several of the older women in the audience were crying with pride and joy. Amateurism had its own emotional rewards which professional celebrities could not know.

As Olympic swimming became more widely televised, there was clearly more potential for profiting from amateur fame. Duncan Goodhew, for example, turned his 100 metre breaststroke gold at Moscow to good account, advertising eggs, beer and even shampoo. Sharon Davies was determined to exploit her swimming talents and her looks by becoming a media personality. For all that, swimmers are mostly unsung heroes. Neither David Wilkie nor Adrian Moorhouse, both breaststroke gold medal winners, have achieved the public recognition which similar achievements might have brought in other sports.

This seems surprising. Given there are more than five million swimmers, why does the sport have so little commercial potential? Why are the great swimmers still amateurs? Perhaps the answer lies in the sharp division between recreational and competitive swimmers and the fact that many of the best of them were young girls who were willing to accept the amateur system. Then there is the relative lack of media appeal in the spectacle itself. Membership of the Amateur Swimming Association has remained more or less stable, rising only from 1585 clubs in 1965 to 1709 in 1990. Recreational swimmers clearly take relatively little interest in those who excel competitively.

Of course, the same argument could be made with even greater force about walking. Apart from Don Thompson's 50 kilometre gold in 1960 in Rome, race walkers are among the unsung heroes of British sport. Yet according to the Sports Council, which considers walking two miles or more a sport, walking is by far the most popular sport in Britain with over two in five of the population taking part. Walking is five times more popular than playing football as a participant sport but who knows – or cares – about the heroes of race walking. What rewards do they get from their gruelling sport apart from the inherent pleasure of competition and the chance to excel? It is in such corners of the competitive world that the old values survive.

The discrimination against female sport has meant amateur values have survived more strongly in women's sport than men's. Hockey, for example, like rugby, is a largely middle-class team sport. Why has hockey remained amateur when rugby has gone professional? Clearly, historically hockey was never as popular a spectacle as rugby. Part of the reason was surely that hockey was identified by the public as a female sport. In 1965 there were 1126 clubs in the Hockey Association and 776 in the All England Women's Hockey Association. By 1985 there were only 796 men's clubs to 943 women's. As media coverage of sport grew, hockey became more female and suffered accordingly. Even winning the gold medal in the Olympics of 1988 brought only temporary media attention. The star of that team, Sean Kerly, began an internet campaign to get television coverage and a results service for hockey. But without much success.

Gymnastics is another old-established sport with a high level of female participation which lacks the media exposure to create a professional elite. So, too, does the All England Netball Association, which has over 3600 adult clubs and 3000 affiliated school clubs. Netball has a traditional set of amateur values. This middle-class image has alienated some of the newer inner London-based black clubs such as the Queens of the Castle, 'whose long term aim is to get the game recognised as an exciting, forward-looking sport that will be given television coverage and sponsorship rather than a sport which is played out of the public eye and in a school girl atmosphere'.[33] In other words what some of the younger non-traditional recruits want is to turn netball into a kind of basketball with commercial potential and media appeal. The question, however, is whether any sport which is entirely female will be able to attract the kind of public interest and media income to sustain professionalism. Given changing attitudes and new television channels, there seems no reason why women's sport should not blossom. Australian and New Zealand netball have shown what can be done with the sport as a competitive spectacle and one of its leading proponents has announced her intention of transforming the British game.

From its pinnacle of influence in the 1950s, amateurism as a set of beliefs about how sport should be played and what it means has collapsed. Amateurism at the top level is mainly to be found in a few female sports. However, top women involved in activities where men are also prominent like athletics, tennis and golf can earn very large amounts as professionals. From its lofty moral high ground, amateurism has almost disappeared as an ideology for serious competition. Yet it still rules the world of ordinary club sport. After all, even organized sport at the lower levels is really just a way of making and keeping friends as well as staying fit and competitive.

At the end of the twentieth century 'amateur' meant little more than 'participant'. The word itself seemed to be used less and less. The long amateur century had come to an end and with it the moral values attached to sport, the stress on fair play, mutual respect and enjoyment even at the highest levels. Yet amateurism had meant indignity as well as idealism. The value system that had stressed modesty, loyalty, self-restraint and sacrifice as part of a wider ideal of sportsmanship had also been a source of snobbery, humiliation and resentment. In terms of performance, the stress on style and pleasure could not conceal the lack of financial support, which meant our competitors sometimes failed to give their best at the highest level. The end of the amateur age brought feelings of liberation and of loss, a new freedom alongside a sense of nostalgia for a world where vanity and greed were less evident than they are today.

4 The Professionals

When Charles Harvey published his *Encyclopedia of Sport* in 1959 he was able to list 67 sports which were played by the British. Admittedly, he did count Fives at Eton and Fives at Rugby as two, split rifle shooting between the real thing and the world of small-bores, and also included game shooting as a separate sport. Nonetheless it is a salutary reminder of the variety of British sporting life. From angling to water skiing, badminton to weight lifting and croquet to wrestling, the British played the game and most of them because they enjoyed it. Very few did it for a living. Perhaps twenty sports had a professional sector and several of those were relatively obscure and hardly thriving in the new affluence of the late 1950s. Professional athletics, for example, or 'pedestrianism' as it was often called, had a summer circuit of sports mainly in the north-west and north-east of England and the Highland Games of Scotland. It also had a two-day winter meeting at a shabby football ground near Edinburgh. But attendances fell off at the famous Powderhall sprints in the 1950s and it was temporarily wound up in 1957. The Powderhall event was resurrected, however, in 1965 and is still going. There were about 2000 active pedestrians in the early sixties, semi-professionals who had full-time jobs.[1] It was a sport which the media largely ignored. Billiards and snooker were pub and club games but there were few professional billiard players left: indeed between 1952 and the mid 1960s there was no professional billiards championship. Snooker had a small number of professionals of which Fred Davis was the most celebrated but its growth was in the future. The same was true of flat-green bowls. There was a small panel of professional crown-green bowlers in Lancashire and many pounds were won and lost on spectacular events such as the Blackpool (Talbot) Sweepstakes and the Waterloo Cup but few bowlers made it a living.[2]

At the other end of the country rackets had a few pros, enough to stage amateur-professional matches in the late 1950s but the pros were really teachers in private clubs like Queens and the RAC or in the public schools. Few of them were young any more, so when they did meet the best amateurs they usually lost. There was a professional squash championship of the British Isles, which was dominated by overseas players like the Khans, Hashim and Azam in the fifties, so much so that a separate tournament for those born and working in the United Kingdom was instituted in 1954. In 1962, the professional championship of the British Isles was discontinued due to lack of entries. There were very few British tennis professionals before the 1970s although lawn tennis was one of those sports where shamateurism thrived. The racing of motor cars and motor cycles supported a professional elite of works drivers but their numbers were small. In ice hockey, the number of paid players was even smaller as it slid down the sporting popularity table until there were only five teams in the British league. It is unlikely they provided jobs for more than 60 pros and most of them were Canadians. Rugby League was a commercial sport whose matches had been watched by seven million people in 1948–9 but the vast majority of its players, in 30 clubs located in Lancashire, Yorkshire and what we now call Cumbria, were part-time professionals who had other jobs. Finally speedway was also a commercial sport which had been very popular in the 1930s and 1940s with 30 clubs in three divisions during the post-war sporting boom. By the late fifties it had subsided to a national league of nine clubs with another five in the southern area league. In all of these ten activities the number of people actually making a living from sport alone must have been well under a thousand. If you were looking for a representative British professional sportsman he was not to be found here.

Where *was* he to be found? Basically in six sports, boxing, cricket, cycling, golf, horse racing and football. There were about 1700 professionals licensed by the British Boxing Board of Control in 1958 but the growing prosperity of post-war Britain had not been kind to the 'noble art' and the number of professional tournaments had fallen from around 900 in 1948 to 306 in 1958.[3] Cricket offered a variety of opportunities to the professional player. The 17 members of the county championship provided jobs for about 300 players and league cricket in Lancashire, Yorkshire, Staffordshire and Birmingham probably gave opportunities to another 50 or more although many of these were taken up by overseas players. The number of full-time professionals in cycling in the first two post-war decades was probably small. In 1964 about 7000 cyclists took out racing licences from the British Cycling Federation. Some of them made up the sponsored teams in the annual tour of Britain, known colloquially as the Milk Race following its revival and sponsorship by the Milk Marketing Board in 1958. But few of these would ever make a proper living from the sport, though many would probably have liked to. In golf the professional cadre was becoming increasingly divided between the club professional, who taught the game to the members and made most of his money by selling equipment to them, and a growing elite of tournament professionals. Although still attached to a club these men would increasingly devote their time to the tournament circuit. It would be from among this elite group that the demand for reform of the PGA would come in the 1960s. In 1948–9 there were 1425 professional golfers of whom 325 were assistants. About one in five professionals took part on tournament golf in the 1950s, though only a dozen or so with any sustained success.

In horse racing the equivalent of the professional player in other sports was the jockey. Flat racing had the greater status and produced the greater rewards for its 170 jockeys. National Hunt racing over the sticks was the poor relation but about 100 jockeys tried to make a living at it during each autumn to spring season. But it was association football which was the most popular sport both to play and to watch in all four of the countries which made up the United Kingdom. There were probably around 4000 professional players working for the 92 clubs in four English divisions and 350 in the three Scottish ones in the 1950s. There were also probably another 2000 semi-professionals scattered throughout non-league football. These figures would decline in the early sixties as a consequence of the abolition of the maximum wage.

The 1951 census for England and Wales listed 'persons professionally engaged in entertainment and sport'. Racehorse and greyhound trainers, jockeys, stable lads, kennel attendants: male 4813, female 642. Cricketers, footballers, golfers etc.: male 5468, female 321.[4] This total is not that far away from the Sports Council's 1996 estimate of 8406 – a striking degree of continuity over time.[5] It was also made up of a relatively small number of champions, a significant group of steady performers and many who were not so successful. Moreover many were called but few chosen. Careers were generally not long. It was a largely white, overwhelmingly masculine world. And the professionals were mainly young men from the working class not only excited by the fact that they could do something well, but also that it might, given some luck and good health, provide them with a better life than that of the vast majority of their class contemporaries. How did they get into it, what was this 'job' like, what special qualities did it demand, what were the occupational hazards, what money could be earned, what was the status of the professional sportsman, what was it like for his family and what did he do when his body finally signalled it was time to stop?

Most sports were learned by doing. Games such as football and cricket were played at school. Professional clubs would send scouts to watch school matches and local recreational football. Some football league clubs adopted junior sides as nurseries. All professional clubs relied on the local area to a much greater extent than today. Wolverhampton Wanderers ran seven teams in 1956 when Ted Farmer signed for them as an amateur after being spotted in local football. After scoring 86 goals in the Wolves junior team he turned professional on his seventeenth birthday in 1957.[6] There was no formal apprenticeship until 1960. Before that young boys were given groundstaff jobs which did not necessarily involve much football but almost certainly meant a good deal of cleaning baths, sweeping dressing rooms, painting woodwork and cleaning the boots of the senior players. Even after the apprenticeship scheme was introduced there was often little formal teaching and no preparation for what might happen if the boy either was not thought good enough for professional football or had to give up the game due to injury.

Racing also had an apprenticeship programme but nine out of ten young hopefuls failed to join the professional ranks. Again it is not clear how the skills of the jockey were supposed to be learned. Some stables taught riding, but in many, apprentices were little more than cheap stable labour although the weight allowance probably meant that the best or most favoured got a few rides. Apprentices could not switch stables in the fifties. Many top jockeys such as Sir Gordon Richards and Lester Piggott came from racing families.[7] Professional golfers like Peter Alliss or John Jacobs were often the sons of club pros. Knowing the trade and its people and having access to training and practice was an advantage. Families were important in other ways. Brian Robinson, the first Briton to win a stage in the Tour de France, had been introduced to cycling by his father who was an enthusiastic club cyclist. They actually biked down to London together to the 1948 Olympics where Brian saw his first cycling road race. A successful amateur career led first to independent status, riding in the 1953 Tour of Britain for a local bicycle shop which provided the bike and spares together with his food and hotel expenses and £50 for a win. He did well enough to be recruited by the Hercules team for a £500 retainer and the chance of doubling that with prizes and bonuses.[8]

Jobs could also occasionally lead to taking up a particular sport. Reg Harris was to win three amateur national sprint cycling championships in 1944 before becoming World Amateur Sprint Champion in 1947. He would turn pro after the 1948 Olympics. His first job after leaving school in 1934 had been as an apprentice motor mechanic. He moved to work in the showroom where he found the garage was an agent for cycles as well as cars. That began his interest in cycling and enabled him to buy a cheap secondhand racing machine.[9]

Most British professional boxing champions had come up through the amateur ranks, often having trained alongside professionals, but others, like Freddie Mills for example, were products of the fairground boxing booths, which were in rapid decline by the later 1950s, soon to be followed by small hall promotions. Until 1962 it was possible to take out a professional licence at sixteen. Successful amateurs could, and did, turn professional in all of these sports. This meant that they had to provide repeated demonstrations of their individual skills to promoters, managers and a public all less forgiving of professional failure.

Professionals had to be fit as well as skilled and that meant training to build a body of strength and stamina, as well as practice. Training meant different things in different sports. Leading boxers aimed to peak for their fights but were still bound up with a regular training programme often involving six miles on the road most mornings and workouts in the gym on two or three evenings or afternoons. Skipping, the punch bag and sparring were punctuated by circuits and press-ups. Those who were not contenders and never would be, probably had too many fights to do much work outside the gym. Boxing was the one professional sport which had no close season.

Cricket, cycling and golf, on the other hand, were still largely summer sports in the fifties. After pre-season, cricketers played six days a week for almost five months. Time for either training or practice was limited, which was just as well, for some of them had little interest in either. There were still a few professionals who played football in the winter and cricket in the summer in the fifties: Ian Hall and Ian Buxton at Derbyshire and Derby County; Arthur Milton at Gloucester and for Arsenal and Bristol City; Henry Horton for Hampshire and Hereford United; Stuart Leary for Kent and Charlton; Ken Grieves for Lancashire and Bolton Wanderers; Ken Taylor for Yorkshire and Huddersfield Town; and Willie Watson for Yorkshire and Sunderland, who was a double international playing 23 times for England at cricket and four times for the national football team. But the pressure to specialize made them a dwindling band. Some golfers spent many hours practising but there were only a dozen tournaments in the season before the late 1950s.

Football training, on the other hand, was a three- to four-week pre-season binge of lapping, running and physical jerks followed by a nine-month slog of training sessions for five days every week. Some clubs only organized morning sessions for a couple of hours: a few trained both mornings and afternoons. Ted Farmer found going from three, two-hour nightly training sessions a week while an amateur at Wolves to five days full-time a real shock to the system. But the grouse of some players was that it was all so monotonous and unimaginative. Danny Blanchflower was very frustrated by the managerial regimes he found at Barnsley and Aston Villa. At the former, he wanted to come back in the afternoons for ball practice but the trainer refused saying that if he allowed one all the others would want it.[10] Blanchflower was disappointed by the lack of preparation for the games and the failure to plan. Partly this was due to a particular British disease. Most British footballers had been born into a working class which saw few of its sons and daughters educated beyond the age of fourteen or fifteen. It was not surprising that most professional footballers were not interested in the tactics or theory of the game. Even Stanley Matthews, non-smoker, teetotaller, obsessive about diet, and a dedicated trainer and enthusiast for ball practice, was suspicious of coaching because he thought you could not tell an experienced professional how to play.

In individual sports like cycling some of the training regimes were ferocious, especially by those with the will and ambition to be a champion. The sprint cyclist Reg Harris was only 17 when he gave up his job for the summer cycling season so that he could train. He did not have much idea how to go about it but put in 30- to 50-mile rides most mornings, practising starts, which were particularly important for the handicap races. He was slipstreaming lorries on the public roads on bikes with no brakes. He changed clubs from Bury to Manchester Wheelers because the latter had better training facilities at their Fallowfield headquarters. He was one of the few people to be demobbed from the army in the Second World War who emerged from the service less fit than when he had gone in. His preparations for an indoor race in Brussels early in 1946 are revealing of his determination as well as his strength and stamina.

> I developed quite a useful technique for training in these evening sessions: I paced out the distance between the lampposts on the road and found the intervals to be about eighty yards. I reckoned three of them was a useful sprinting distance . . . I would crawl along slower than walking speed and then on coming level with a particular lamppost . . . I would explode and do the 240 yards absolutely flat out . . . maintaining maximum effort for the whole distance. Often I did this with hoar frost glistening all around me . . .

After some pacing about to 'warm down' he would repeat it all again. No wonder that when he trained with the professionals later in Switzerland they were pleased he wasn't going to race with them. As we saw earlier he turned professional after the 1948 Olympics and became the first man to win a world professional sprint title in his first season as a pro. He had been a professional in all but name before.[11]

Flat-race jockeys had to keep their bodies at artificially low weights if they were to make any kind of a career in the sport. Eddie Hide used to go running wearing a sweater and a mackintosh and calculated that he sweated off the equivalent of 18 stone in a season. Many jockeys, including champions such as Lester Piggott and Pat Eddery, chose to eat very little – in their cases conquering the craving by smoking, cigars and cigarettes respectively. In racing, if you were strong enough you were old enough: Piggott was twelve when he rode his first winner at Haydock Park in 1948, Eddie Hide had his first ride at thirteen and Josh Gifford rode his first national hunt winner at only ten. The minimum age was not raised to fifteen until the sixties.[12]

In professional sport, as in the rest of British industry, the employers held the whip hand. In horse racing, for example, the stewards of the Jockey Club could refuse a licence to any jockey without having to give a reason. A jockey called before them to answer a charge of infringing the rules of racing would have no representative to speak for him. He would be addressed by his family name and have to call his masters 'Sir'. This was the language of the classroom and the 'big house', bound up with the snobberies of class and the expectation of deference. There was no Flat Race Jockeys' Association until 1966.

Some football clubs still issued bye-laws and training rules for players, forbidding them to enter pubs after Monday in each week during the season or attend any dance after Tuesday 'unless in [the] charge of a responsible official of the Club or with permission from the Manager or (in his absence) the Trainer'.[13] Some clubs stipulated that players should be at home by 10.45 p.m. on the night prior to a match and some refused to allow their players to ride motor cycles. The Football Association was almost as patrician as the Jockey Club when it came to meting out justice for offences committed both on and off the field. And if all else failed, the retain and transfer system enabled clubs to keep a firm hold on their players by retaining their registrations while offering the same contract terms as in the previous season and refusing any transfer unless it suited them.

Young county cricketers and golf club professionals had also to watch their Ps and Qs with the members who essentially employed them. At the Stanmore Golf Club in 1952, for example, the Committee made clear that the club professional and his wife were not entitled to attend dances or other entertainments in the club house but might be invited at the discretion of the Committee. It is clear that social distinction mattered and playing with pros was different from mixing with them in the world outside the sport.[14]

If discipline and social segregation were occupational hazards for some, there were worse ones for others. Boxing and motor sports carried the greatest risks of personal injury and even death. Evidence given by a leading neurologist in 1963 suggested that being 'punch drunk' was not a condition only to be found at the base of the profession in the small halls. A conference between representatives of the British Medical Association, the Royal College of Physicians and Surgeons, the Ministries of Education and Health and the two main boxing organizations, the British Boxing Board of Control and the Amateur Boxing Association, did lead to some improvements. A boxer would now be automatically suspended for 21 days if he was knocked out, beaten inside the distance, or deemed to have had a particularly hard fight. Before this his licence would have been suspended only until he had been passed fit by a Board of Control doctor. He could have been back in the ring within four days.[15]

Reg Harris had had his fair share of injuries while an amateur cyclist and he suffered several more as a professional. Preparing for the world championship in 1953, for example, he and his opponent collided at more than forty miles an hour. Harris fell onto the rough concrete of the track. Apart from the crash helmet he had no protective clothing. As he sprawled on the track parts of his hands, arms and legs had their skin removed. His knee was badly bruised and swollen. Following penicillin injections twice a day he was back racing within two weeks. He would probably have won the World Championship again in 1955 but for another 45-miles-an-hour crash while training in Milan.[16]

As Wray Vamplew has pointed out, serious injury at work for a jockey is 'not a possibility or even a probability: it is inevitable'.[17] In the fifties and sixties, a jockey could have a bad fall but if showing no signs of distress would be allowed to ride in the next race. Several former national hunt riders were diagnosed as suffering from a condition akin to being 'punch drunk' following head injuries sustained on the track. Broken bones, dislocations and cracked ribs were common. Terry Biddlecombe, champion National Hunt jockey three times in the sixties, had concussion more than one hundred times.

Injuries could end careers prematurely. In many cases they were inadequately diagnosed, delaying proper treatment. Employers did not always take them seriously and could show an insensitive haste in ridding themselves of a player who had become a wasting asset. Ted Farmer looked like a future England centre-forward in 1960–1 but he had already begun to incur the injuries which would force his retirement from the game at the age of 25. A broken leg and ankle, a four-month lay off with a wrongly diagnosed back injury and finally a serious knee ligament injury received in a second eleven vs. first eleven practice match in January 1964 ended a career which had looked destined for glory. The lack of sympathy of management was graphically illustrated when Farmer came off at half-time in a match against Manchester City feeling ill and passing blood in his urine. The club doctor told the Wolves manager, Stan Cullis, who replied, 'wait till it comes through his backside before you take him off'.[18]

There was not only the physical challenge of professional sport but a mental one too. Professional sportsmen were like actors: they had to put on regular performances. It would not be surprising if, also like actors, they got stage fright or forgot their lines. Moreover professionals often performed in front of audiences half of whom at least might want them to play badly and lose. Their performance might be criticized in the press and with the coming of radio and television they might be asked potentially embarrassing questions about it. As we have seen, sports like boxing, cycling, National Hunt steeplechasing and motor sports involved considerable risks. The nerve that was required to fight, ride and drive could be lost. Confidence was an important factor in all sports and in part depended on continued success. But even the successful might not always escape an attack of 'nerves'. The cyclist Reg Harris admitted to being tense and short-tempered before races. Jackie Milburn, the Newcastle United centre-forward, was so anxious about the coming cup final in 1951 that he was left out of the previous league game. A year later his legs were too shaky to take a penalty in a replayed FA Cup semi-final. Even Stanley Matthews had what he called 'butterflies in the stomach' before most games although he recognized it as helpful in providing the necessary sharpness and concentration. Professional cricket was a sport whose long drawn out rhythms could produce exceptional excitement: it also provided a lot of worrying time. Roly Jenkins, a legspin bowler who played successfully for Worcester and England, seemed to have no problems in the first innings of a match against Scotland but in the second he sat down in the middle of the pitch, tears streaming down his face, saying that he couldn't bowl any more. He had to return home and did not play again for a month.[19]

Being a professional sportsman was not only about the money. But as Tommy Simpson, the cyclist who finished sixth in the Tour de France in 1962, noted, 'when you're a professional, this is what you've got to think of . . .' and he rubbed his thumb and index finger together.[20] By the beginning of the sixties some pros were making very good money indeed. About a dozen jockeys were earning in excess of £10,000 a year, a useful yardstick as it was Harold Macmillan's salary in 1960 and he was Prime Minister. But it was not until 1969 that the Jockey Club decreed that jockeys should receive a guaranteed percentage of the prize money. On the other hand, most stable workers or apprentices were probably earning between £10 and £12 a week and most jockeys would not have managed enough rides to earn five figures.

Motor racing could also be lucrative, again for the twenty elite drivers. Stirling Moss almost certainly earned more than the Prime Minister in 1960 and when Graham Hill became the first ever World Motor Racing Champion to drive a British car, in 1962, his five-figure salary was based on a retainer from the manufacturer, a percentage of the starting and prize money which by that stage of his career had risen to 50 per cent, and bonuses from the motor accessories firms involved with BRM. To that should be added income from the promotional work he did for Shell, articles for the *Daily Herald* and other business activities.

Golf was also beginning to make a small group of tournament professionals rather well off. Nicholson estimated that in 1963 one player won over £7000, another over £3000 and eight more between two and three thousand. Twelve won between one and two thousand pounds. To this would need to be added sponsorship, advertising and media work and the retainer which most tournament professionals received from their clubs. Top players might earn as much as £2000 a year from Sunday exhibition matches.[21]

The club pro made his money partly from selling and repairing golf clubs in the club shop, partly from the fees he could earn from giving golfing lessons to members, and partly from the club retainer, all of which could provide a steady living without the anxieties and excitement of tournament play.

Boxing was another sport where a small number of champions might do well and the lumpen proletariat of the trade could find themselves in a never ending struggle to earn more than a thousand pounds a year. Managers and promoters, who after all took one kind of risk, did rather better than most of the boxers who took another. As for cycling, as we have seen, there were few British professionals but the champions did well. Reg Harris, who certainly did not seem in any need of an agent, claims to have made about £12,000 a year from racing in the early 1950s.[22] From 1949 Raleigh cycles were paying him what he thought a modest retainer of £1000 a year with a £100 bonus for winning the world sprint championship, £50 per Grand Prix victory and £25 every time he broke a British record. He still felt that he was providing his employers with plenty of free advertising. Tommy Simpson realized the importance of playing the market as hard as he could.

> All through the summer of 1963 he had a friend with a stopwatch looking in at Eurovision, and totting up the minutes that Simpson appeared alone on the TV screen, riding in the lead, with the names of his trade sponsors, BP and Peugeot, displayed on his shorts and jersey. When I spoke to him in August the score was 270 minutes, a persuasive argument for a better contract the following season. 'Just work out', he said, 'what that would have cost them at peak time.'[23]

County cricketers had no maximum wage. Indeed they had no agreed wages structure at all. All agreements were individual and local which often meant that players of equal service or merit but playing for different county clubs received very different earnings. Until 1969 there was no Professional Cricketers' Association. There was also the semi-feudal relic of the county cap, awarded by the team captain when he felt a player had merited it. It was an honour accompanied by three important practical results: a feeling of relative security as capped players were rarely dropped or not re-engaged, a pay rise and, after ten years' service, a tax-free benefit. For a summer season of five and a half months in the late fifties a salary of between £700 and £800 might be paid, which was probably about £1000 by the mid to late 1960s. Jack Bannister earned £1100 in his last season as a Warwickshire professional in 1969.[24] An England player would have received £100 per match plus expenses in the sixties. Most players had other jobs in winter. In the Worcestershire side of 1956, for example, Bob Berry delivered cars, Don Kenyon worked for Dudley Iron and Steel, Laddie Outschoorn in Smithfield Market and Martin Horton in the county's new indoor cricket school.[25] A favoured few went coaching overseas.

There was, of course, a considerable disparity between the earnings of those at the top of a sport and those at the bottom. There was a maximum wage in English football, but by no means all the players were paid it. The National Arbitration Tribunal in 1947 had raised the maximum to £12 a week during the season but also fixed a minimum of £5 a week for all those over the age of 21. Further rises were negotiated through the fifties until in 1958 the maximum reached £20 during the season and £15 in the summer, but only about 30 per cent of professionals received it.[26] Eddie Firmani, on signing for Charlton Athletic in the First Division in 1951, was paid £7 a week during the season and £6 in summer. John Charles at Leeds earned £15, and £12 in summer, in 1957, an established first team player in a team just promoted to the first division. Ted Farmer was just beginning his professional career at Wolves in that year and he was paid £8 a week during the season and £6 in the close season. As a second team player in 1959, his pay had risen to £14 a week and £10 in the close season. The bonuses for wins and draws had risen from ten shillings and five shillings respectively to £2 and £1. By the time he broke into the first team in 1960–1 he was receiving the maximum wage of £20 a week during the season with bonuses of £4 for a win and £2 for a draw, and £16 per week in the summer.[27] It is worth remembering that by this time the average weekly earnings of adult males in manufacturing were £15 a week, which suggests that the differential between the top footballers and industrial workers was being eroded. The leading players could increase their earnings by advertising but such opportunities were not widespread in the fifties. There were few with the articulate intelligence of a Danny Blanchflower who wrote regular columns in the local press while at Aston Villa and Tottenham, and published articles in the *Observer* in 1957–8 when its coverage of football was scanty. He even appeared on BBC Television's *Panorama* programme in 1959.[28]

Professional sportsmen spent a good deal of time away from home, which may have increased the strain on marital and family relationships. Cricketers, cyclists and jockeys travelled a lot during their summer seasons. In the fifties much of this travelling was by train or coach. It was 1953 before Bristol Street Motors provided three sponsored cars for Worcestershire's senior players. It was even tougher for professional jockeys, whose place of work changed almost every other day or two. Both the jockeys and cyclists could travel up to 50,000 miles in a season. Motor sport and tournament golf also involved long absences. It must have been particularly difficult for wives and families at weekends and on public holidays when their husbands or fathers were away at work while most others were at home. Footballers, for example, could play on three successive days at Christmas if 27 December was a Saturday.[29]

On the other hand, footballers didn't spend too many hours training, in fact they often had a lot of time on their hands. Boredom and associated mischief could be problems. Managers liked their players to be married but in such a masculine world a wife was expected to know her place. If the wives themselves had sporting backgrounds it was easier for them to understand and manage the absences, food fads, the alternative bouts of training and sleeping of the racing cyclist, the mood swings that might accompany the very visible and often spectacular successes and failures. It was a job; Margaret Horton did not tell her children that Daddy was a cricketer but that 'Daddy's gone to work'.[30] The lifestyle of most families remained that of the traditional working class. When Eddie Firmani played for Charlton in the early fifties his wife kept the money for clothes and holidays in two envelopes. Until he signed for Sampdoria in 1955 and received the first instalment of a £5000 signing-on fee he had never had a bank account nor a cheque book. Audrey Bowen's family did not have a television set in 1958 to watch husband David lead Wales in the World Cup in Sweden.[31] But it was not quite like other jobs. At any level there was the excitement, the acclaim of the crowd, the camaraderie of dressing or weighing room. Most professionals never find anything to equal it and they don't like giving it up. That explains why Stanley Matthews played until he was 50, Lester Piggott spent almost fifty years in the saddle, and many other jockeys, cricketers and golfers continued well into their forties. It is true that their skills were not easy to take elsewhere: but it is also true that they did not want to take them elsewhere, which explains why so many wanted to be coaches, trainers, managers, umpires, groundsmen, anything to stay not only in the only world which they had known but one which they had mastered. No wonder Danny Blanchflower quoted Scott Fitzgerald on his retirement in 1964 that it was 'like the blow that comes from within – that you don't feel until it's too late to do anything about it, until you realise that in some regard you will never be as good a man again'.

But many had long lives ahead of them. Most professional sportsmen had finished by their late thirties. In the fifties and early sixties their opportunities for social mobility were restricted. As we have seen, staying on in some job in the sport was often the preferred option and there were slowly expanding media opportunities for the articulate and successful. Motor sport might lead to running a garage or showroom; cycling, for the 'also raced', may also have meant a cycle shop on retirement. Former footballers and cricketers were often to be found behind the counter of a shop or, perhaps more likely, the bar of a pub. Some found adjustment difficult, like soldiers returning from the war. Even those who had put by some capital might lose it via unwise business ventures or addictions to drink or gambling. Tommy Lawton, for example, after a playing career which began at Burnley in 1936 and ended at Kettering in 1956 after more or less undiminished stardom at Everton, Chelsea, Notts County, Brentford and Arsenal could make little of life without football. Most of the rest of his life was spent in straitened circumstances with a string of court appearances for petty theft and deception.[32] But as we have seen, apart from professional boxing, there was no falling off in the numbers who wanted to join the sports professionals. And a clutch of already seductive jobs were about to become even more attractive.

The late fifties and the sixties were largely prosperous years, part of the long post-war boom as a result of which, as Harold Macmillan famously said in 1957, Britons had never had it so good.[33] Certainly in material terms this was true if a touch complacent. Consumer spending grew, especially after 1957 and especially on durables such as cars, refrigerators, television sets and washing machines. The expansion of secondary and tertiary education and the growth of better paid white-collar employment had begun that broadening of the middle which would eventually change the nature and state of Britain. But alongside this there developed some dissatisfaction that we were not doing as well as we ought to have been, that Britain remained an essentially conservative, traditional culture. Ordinary people were allegedly being prevented from attaining the full material and social benefits of the modern age by a ruling group which had a vested interest in obstructing change.

Books like *The Establishment* (1959) whose essays provided a sharp critique of those British institutions engraved on the hearts of most conservatives, such as the public schools, Parliament, the Army, the Civil Service, the City, and the BBC; books like Michael Shanks's *The Stagnant Society*, and Anthony Sampson's *Anatomy of Britain*, both published in 1961, were part of a growing literature of modernization designed to persuade the British to look forward rather than back. It was a position with which some professional sportsmen could identify.

There were few radicals among the three hundred or so professional cricketers but their traditionally deferential attitudes were changing. They could still admire the contribution of the amateur but what they were increasingly unwilling to accept was the hypocrisy and deceit that was used to maintain his position. Shamateurism meant that a young cricketer could have all the privileges of the amateur, to be called Mr or 'Sir', to have a separate dressing room, to stay in separate hotels, not on the basis of an independent income but by being given a fake job such as assistant secretary or assistant to the treasurer of a county club and paid lavish expenses. The amateur Trevor Bailey upset Frank Tyson during the 1954–5 tour of Australia by telling him that he could not afford to be a pro. Three years later Jim Laker asked one of the doyens of the cricket establishment, Gubby Allen, how he would feel if Jim 'turned amateur as he would earn more from the forthcoming tour of Australia in expenses than salary'. Powerful voices among the amateurs, including Peter May and David Sheppard, began to talk about the need to reform cricket. The abolition of the amateur–professional distinction was usually high on their list of essential changes.

Yet when the MCC appointed a special committee to consider the role of the amateur in 1959 it reiterated the value of the independent leadership he provided and suggested no change. The mystique of the amateur captain remained powerful; only five out of seventeen counties had appointed professionals. Yorkshire appointed their amateur second team captain, Ronnie Burnett, to captain the first team in 1958 and 1959 to the disgust of some of the senior professionals, one of whom, Johnny Wardle, was sacked mid-way through the 1958 season. He was always one of the awkward squad and he went public in the *Daily Mail* over an article headlined 'We're Carrying the Captain'. Yorkshire's first twentieth-century professional captain, J. V. Wilson, was appointed the following year.

The Lancashire Committee put the club in a worse mess. They had appointed Cyril Washbrook as their first professional captain in 1954. He retired in 1959 and was replaced by a young public school and Cambridge amateur, R. W. Barber, who was apparently told not to stay in the same hotels as the rest of his under-achieving team. Barber was sacked at the end of the 1961 season. The Committee then appointed a 33-year-old amateur batsman, J. F. Blackledge, over the obvious senior professional Ken Grieves. Poor Blackledge presided over the worst season in the county's history, in which they only won two matches. Blackledge was sacked and Grieves appointed for 1963.

By this time, the MCC had changed its mind, accepting that in modern Britain they could no longer expect young men to play a season of first-class cricket without pay. The 1961 Cricket Inquiry Committee was told by H. S. Altham, the club treasurer, that it was too difficult to work out broken time payments for amateurs. He also persuaded the traditionalists that cricketers from the public schools and ancient universities would take up the game if the money was right. In 1983, 15 per cent of professionals playing at least ten county matches had public school or Oxbridge backgrounds. The last Gentlemen vs. Players match, dramatic symbol of the amateur–professional divide, was played in 1962. The centenary edition of *Wisden's Cricketers' Almanack* in 1963 was resigned, but warned: 'by doing away with the amateur, cricket is in danger of losing the spirit of freedom and gaiety which the best amateur players brought to the game'.[34]

Cricket sought reform partly from a position of weakness but golf was booming by the sixties. Golf benefitted from those social changes, expanding access to secondary and tertiary education, the growing number of managerial jobs, and increased opportunities for leisure, which were transforming post-war Britain. The Professional Golfers' Association had been founded to defend the interests of those workmen who earned their living by mending golf clubs and teaching the better-off how to play. It was bound to face difficulties when a generation of young professional golfers saw opportunities for earning *their* living without having to work in a club shop, indeed without having to be club pros at all.

Golf was already one of the few sports regularly featured in the press and on the radio when television opened up new possibilities. Professional tournaments increasingly became both spectator sport, reflecting increased participation, and a vehicle for advertising. In the 1960s unattached pros were still rare. Geoffrey Hunt, for example, would be playing tournaments from Wednesday to Friday but would be expected back for club duty at the weekend. Hunt was one of a new breed of professional golfers including Peter Alliss, John Jacobs, both the sons of golfers, and Dai Rees who wanted to scrap the deferential, hierarchical and, as they saw it, old fashioned and inefficient way in which the PGA was run by retired old pros with an ex-naval officer as secretary. So far as they were concerned Jack was not only as good as his master but better. Golf was a game for the better-off and it needed to establish better links with business, just as the Americans were doing. Golf at the elite level was becoming big business and international business.

A reform programme emerged stutteringly through the late fifties and into the sixties. The younger generation must be adequately represented on PGA committees. Most of the PGA funds came from tournaments so it was essential to have tournament players on the tournament subcommittee. The highest rewards should go to the best players. The justification was that tournament golf was the shop-window of the sport. If it thrived, then club pros would benefit from the equipment sales and publicity generated by the top players. Dai Rees argued that golf equipment manufacturers got their tournaments too cheaply. If the search for sponsors was spread wider to include car manufacturers and especially the drink and tobacco producers, then prize money could be increased. In 1960 the tournament professionals got four players elected to the PGA committee. British golf also had its own star by the end of the sixties. Tony Jacklin, once an apprentice fitter in Scunthorpe earning £5 a week, won the British Open in 1969, the first Briton to do so for eighteen years, and won the US Open in 1970.

In the background, most of the time, was the threat from the tournament players to withdraw from the PGA and go their own way. In 1971 this powerful pressure group forced the appointment of a tournament director, John Jacobs, who hoped to have the British and Irish circuit worth £200,000 of prize money within three years. In fact, such was the interest that he was able to conclude a television agreement with BBC and ITV to show eight tournaments. The cigarette manufacturers and drink companies flocked into a sport which offered professional media exposure at relatively little cost, and in 1972 the prize fund was half a million pounds. In January 1975 a tournament players' section was set up with full control of all tournaments in Britain and Ireland.[35] This was the modernization of professional golf with a vengeance! Golf's reformers produced a rejuvenated tournament structure which included Europe, and greatly increased sponsorship and prize money. This in turn generated a more robust competition which enabled the professional golfers of Britain, with a little help from their European friends, to make something of a comeback against those Australians, South Africans and Americans who had regularly upstaged them.

The changes in tennis were prompted by different circumstances and motives. Like cricket and later athletics, the reform was designed in part to deal with appearance money and the expenses world of shamateurism. It was not so much an attempt to embrace the logic of professionalism as to control it in the interests of maintaining the traditional power structure in this elitist international sport. It was also necessary to protect Wimbledon as a major world tournament.

After a collection of Pro-Am tournaments in wartime to raise funds for the war effort the segregation of amateurs from professionals resumed after 1945. Various Lawn Tennis Association regulations tried to cope with the shamateur. Between 1947 and 1951 they could only receive travelling and hotel expenses for eight weeks in the year, about the length of the British summer. The regulations were liberalized in 1956 but toughened in 1958 to the extent that expenses would only be paid for 240 days, not more than 150 of which could be spent abroad.[36]

By this time the Jack Kramer professional circus was beginning to have some impact on the leading players. Of the fifteen men who at one time or another had occupied the number one ranking in the world between 1946 and 1967 ten had turned professional, most famously Rod Laver, the last man to win the Grand Slam of Melbourne, Paris, Wimbledon and New York, in 1962. The professional circuit was not only tempting the best players but showing that there was another way to run the sport.

Anxious to protect both the status of Wimbledon and the traditional structure of control over tennis, the LTA pressed for reform, against the wishes of the International Lawn Tennis Federation (ILTF). In December 1967 the LTA announced that the distinctions which existed between amateurs and professionals were to be removed. A compromise was negotiated with the ILTF. There were still to be two categories of player: players who accepted the jurisdiction of the national LTAs and through them the ILTF; and contract professionals who signed with a tour promoter. Most of the top male players signed up with the American entrepreneur Lamar Hunt and his World Championship Tennis (WCT). Their Grand Prix circuit began in 1970. By the early seventies the WCT was demanding money in return for the participation of its players in the major championships. In 1972 WCT players were barred from the official circuit including the grand slam tournaments of Paris and Wimbledon. This led directly to the foundation of the Association of Tennis Professionals, which would in future represent the interests of the players on the reformed governing bodies of the sport. The LTA and the ILTF had hoped to avoid this: their own reforms had made no provision for player representation. But elite tournaments needed all the best players. The ATP responded to the ILTF ban by organizing a boycott of Wimbledon in 1973. Seventy-nine players followed their Association's advice and the tournament lost thirteen out of the sixteen men's seeds at a stroke. A devastating smash indeed. By 1973 the women had their own players' association and a major sponsor, Virginia Slims Cigarettes, which enabled them to play their part in the wider women's movement. Their slogan was 'you've come a long way baby'. Open tennis meant a shift in power away from 'the blazerati' and towards the professional player: they were soon to have not only more money but more individual autonomy, more say, more power. Perhaps it would benefit British tennis and satisfy Dan Maskell who in 1959 had told the Wolfenden Committee that 'he could no longer appeal to young players by demanding courage and "guts" from them: a far more materialistic approach was needed'.[37]

In a working-class sport such as professional football the players had always appreciated the value of a materialistic approach and in Jimmy Hill they had found the man who could provide it. The son of a baker's roundsman, he had won a scholarship to a London grammar school and trained in insurance before playing for Fulham for nine years. Moreover he was already something of a familiar figure due to the beard he began to grow in 1957. As he later wrote:

> In two weeks I turned from being just Fulham's inside right to a personality plus. I became the only footballer with a beard and had changed myself from being the ordinary to the extraordinary. Advertisers became interested in me. The beard photographed well on television. People wanted to hear what I had to say about things . . .[38]

The world outside sport was changing. A less deferential spirit was providing the impetus for a challenge to traditional hierarchies of power. Professional football was one such area of conflict. There was some dissatisfaction among leading players that the differential between their pay and the average industrial wage had narrowed during the fifties. The earnings of players in the Third Division had actually fallen below this figure. Yet more money was coming into the industry following the abolition of the Entertainment Tax in 1957 and the ten-year deal done with the Pools companies in the same year.

A few players began to look abroad. John Charles, the Welsh International centre-half of Leeds United, joined Juventus of Turin in 1956 for a then British record fee of £65,000. He said that he went to Italy not only because he would earn more money but also because he would be treated better and live a more comfortable life. He seems to have achieved all these goals, becoming the head of a two-car family, living in a club-provided flat, having a villa on the Mediterranean coast, a share in a restaurant and a larger salary, including much bigger bonuses than any player in Britain.[39] Charles also did something else that was extremely rare in the fifties but was to become as common for the professional footballer as it was for the actor – he employed an agent. Edward Sommerfield, with the help of broadcaster Kenneth Wolstenholme, helped negotiate the move to Juventus. It was transfers such as this, together with the rash of moves in the spring of 1961, which helped to build up pressure against the maximum wage.[40] But most players accepted it with varying degrees of contentment. For one thing collective action was difficult with the players' union more of a gadfly on the flank of the Football League than a guided missile.

Then, in 1957 Jimmy Hill became President and the next year the union's name was changed to the Professional Footballers' Association, which was much less resonant of the workers' movement and more evocative of middle-class aspirations to material comfort and respectability. Hill's union career was launched by having to deal with the Sunderland affair. The club was fined and the directors banned for making illegal payments to players. Five players, Ray Daniel, Billy Elliott, Willie Fraser, Johnny Hannigan and Ken Chisholm, were also banned and they appealed to the union for help. Hill demanded an inquiry into the whole issue of illegal payments and claimed that the union would collect the names of a thousand players who would admit to having received them. This was no easy task at the end of the football season and Hill later admitted that it was impossible. However, the legal adviser of the union had discovered that under existing rules the joint commission which had considered the Sunderland case had no standing in law.[41]

The Sunderland affair, followed by investigations into several other clubs, merely emphasized the hypocrisy of both the maximum wage and the level of it. It also encouraged the union to demand its abolition and from June 1960 to declare an official dispute with the Football League. The negotiations were long and unfriendly with the employers very reluctant. Indeed the League only finally agreed to abolish the maximum wage in January 1961 three days before a players' strike was due to begin.

The retain and transfer system remained. But its legality was about to be tested in the courts. George Eastham, an England international playing with Newcastle United, asked for a move to London. Newcastle refused but kept his registration, which meant that he could not play for anyone else. One Newcastle director said he would see Eastham shovel coal before he left Newcastle. But Eastham refused to play, and took a job in London, and in November 1960 Newcastle transferred him to Arsenal. The PFA persuaded him to issue a writ against his former employers alleging that they had deprived him of the opportunity to earn his living by playing football. The case was heard before Mr Justice Wilberforce in June 1963. He famously found in favour of the player, his judgement emphasizing that:

> The system is an employers' system set up in an industry where the employers have established a monolithic front and where it is clear for the purposes of negotiation the employers are more strongly organized than the employees.

The retain and transfer system was in restraint of trade, although full freedom of contract would have to wait until 1978. What were the results of all this? In the short term, it produced the first £100 per week footballer, the Fulham and England captain Johnny Haynes. His £5000 a year represented seven and a half times the average annual wage. Danny Blanchflower was paid £3000 a year by Tottenham. But he was an opponent of the free market in football, arguing that wage ceilings could have been raised considerably without removing the roof. Nor was he a supporter of freedom of contract.

Hill, on the other hand, claimed that football had been sold too cheaply to workers who, in the affluent sixties, could afford to pay more. Football was a commodity and, Hill insisted, the footballer was a professional entertainer rather than an artisan. Eamon Dunphy's *Only a Game?* broke new ground as a real footballer wrote about the realities of life in the lower divisions and what it was like to play in a losing team in the 1970s. Hard grind and glamour still co-existed uneasily in football. Hill, however, compared the professional footballer with actors in television, the theatre and the cinema. They should be paid, and respected accordingly, as professionals. That word was to be used a lot in future years as an adjective to qualify nouns such as attitude, determination, responsibility, even foul. A professional foul may have been an infringement of the rules but it was a justifiable infringement to protect the position of the team. In the medium term, the number of professional players would decline but wages, transfer fees and the costs of admission would rise faster than inflation. It could be argued that in all four of the sports we have considered, the balance of power has shifted away from the employer towards the professional player, the full consequences of which are still working themselves out.

How has the world of the professional sportsman changed in the nineties? There are certainly more of them. The 1991 Census included a 10 per cent sample of the occupation and employment status of managers and administrators which included professional athletes and sports officials. The total for males was 1507 of which 766 were full-time and 150 part-time. For females the figures were 829, 221 full-time and 340 part-time. This suggests an overall figure of around 8000 males and about 2000 females earning a living from sport.[42] In 1996 the Sports Council estimated that there were about 8400 professional sportsmen and women in twelve sports but they excluded athletics, badminton and squash and included 1500 Rugby League players, over half of whom were almost certainly part-time.

The increase in the numbers of sports containing serious full-time practitioners is underlined by the Lottery funded World Class Perform-ance Programme which began in November 1996, managed by Sport

Table 4.1   Professionals in British sport, 1996

Basketball	70
Boxing	40
Cricket	450
Cycling	70
Darts	20
Horse Racing	600
Football (England and Wales)	2000
Football (Scotland)	450
Golf	3000*
Motor Racing	20
Rugby League	1500
Snooker	128
Tennis	60**
Total	8408

* Includes club as well as tournament professionals
** Only those with world rankings
Source: Sports Council, *Career in Sport Compendium* (March 1996), pp. 24–5.

England with Lottery funding contributed by each Home Country Sports Council. It was designed to support the training and preparation programmes of athletes who have the potential to win medals at Olympics and Paralympics, and achieve top places in significant events. In 1999 it was paying out £38 million to 2234 UK sportsmen and sportswomen in 33 different sports from bobsleigh to weightlifting, canoeing to water skiing, netball to squash, and judo to table tennis.[43] The largest numbers were in track and field, Rugby League and rowing. Lisa Mason is a top gymnast, a member of the Huntingdon Olympic Gymnastic Club. An England international with Olympic medal potential she currently trains seven hours a day for six days a week. World Class Performance gives her an annual grant of £8500; she is also sponsored by Barclaycard.[44]

On 1 July 1999, the UK Sports Council became a Lottery distributor in its own right, and became directly responsible for a UK World Class Performance Programme and Major Events Programme. Each Home Country Sports Council contributed to provide Lottery funding of about £18.5 million pounds in 1999–2000. Currently the UK Sports Council supports 24 sports and about 730 athletes with a budget of about 20 million pounds in 2000–01 for its World Class Performance Programme. Sport England continues to run its own Performance Programme and is developing its World Class Potential and Start Programmes.

Flat green bowls is a sport which used to be characterized as an old man's (and old woman's) game with no potential for professionals. But young players took it up in the sixties and it became more competitive at the elite end. It also began to move indoors as new sports centres and bowling rinks were opened in the seventies. In 1976 BBC Scotland recorded the international singles tournament at Coatbridge. Here was a sport for television with no weather problems and with personalities to focus on such as David Bryant who won the first of his World Indoor Championship titles in 1979. When the sport went open the next year, he became its first professional at the age of 48, soon to be followed by a much younger Tony Alcock. The son of a Leicester bowling family, he signed a contract with a local shoe firm to promote their products and became a full-time pro in 1987. Product endorsement, personal appearances and prize money tempted others to join the professionals. But the boom did not last. Although the English Bowling Association has over 2500 clubs and a quarter of a million members it does not have the competitive strength in depth at club level that is a feature of the sport in Australia, for example, where many clubs have their own pros. Perhaps twenty British bowlers are making a living out of the sport in one way or another, like Gary Smith, Secretary of the Professional Bowlers' Association, who has won eleven English national titles but earns most of his income as marketing manager for Botra Bowlswear. Mary Price, a leading woman player, runs a bowls shop.[45]

If it was a surprise when bowls went open in 1980, it has been a much bigger surprise to see two of the leading regiments of amateurism lower their colours and succumb to the lure of the pound. Perhaps the graffiti was on the goalposts for Rugby Union when it established a national knock-out cup in 1971 to which many followers had been opposed. The organization of leagues and their sponsorship by the brewers Courage in 1987 was another move towards the money. Yet Rugby Union continued to turn a blind eye to shamateurism in Wales and France, for example, where, as the former New Zealand scrum half Chris Laidlaw said, 'any rugby player worth his salt . . . who does not accept payment is considered a fool and a rare one at that'.[46] Rebel tours to South Africa defying the Gleneagles agreement also made money for those who went, hardly surprising as the top players in the southern hemisphere were increasingly professional in all but name by the late eighties. Yet the Rugby Football Union was still upholding the rule which branded anyone a professional who made money out of past effort, by writing or broadcasting on the sport after their own playing career was over. Bill Beaumont, a former England captain, was barred from a coaching role until enough good sense was discovered in 1990 to change a few minds.

The 1991 Rugby World Cup in England was another potential turning point. No turn was made but with 13.6 million viewers for the final the marketable nature of the international product at least was underlined. Moreover players such as Will Carling, Jeremy Guscott and Gavin Hastings may not have received salaries from their clubs but they obviously had very lucrative careers which reflected their image and status as rugby icons. The decision of the International Rugby Board to turn professional in August 1995 has already been examined in the previous chapter. The precise timing was influenced by the moves of Rupert Murdoch's News Corporation. Early that year it had financed Rugby League's new Superleague in return for the sole television rights in both Great Britain and Australia. Old fears about mass migrations to northern Britain from the southern hemisphere were revived.

In 1997 Allied Dunbar Financial Services agreed to sponsor the 26 clubs in the top two divisions of the RFU league for three seasons. First Division clubs were to receive £500,000 each, Second Division £250,000. There are now 38 full-time professional clubs in England, Scotland and Wales providing job opportunities for about 800 professional players. A few hundred more are effectively part-time pros. One never thought one would live to hear Newcastle's Director of Rugby, Rob Andrew, say, after the home defeat by Wasps, that the performance was 'not good enough. The players ought to go and apologise to *the owner* for producing that and thank him if he is still paying their wages.'[47]

And then in December 1997 Henley ended 159 years of amateur competition by announcing that from 1998 the Royal Regatta would be open. It was a belated acceptance that many of the world's best oarsmen were now professional, including the British gold medallists from Atlanta, Steven Redgrave and Matthew Pinsent. They had a £1 million sponsorship package from Lombard Financial Services for the four years between the Olympics and would obviously earn more from appearances and other activities. Henley was unapologetic and would not pay rowers for entering nor offer any prize money. Nor did they seek sponsorship for the Regatta itself.[48]

There has been a separate Henley Women's Regatta since 1987. And that is another reflection of change in the world of professional sport. There are not only more women participating at every level but a growing number of women professionals. It took a High Court case before the Jockey Club would grant training licences to women in 1966. The Sex Discrimination Act of 1975 has been important in compelling the Jockey Club to allow women to race against male professionals, but owners and trainers are reluctant to employ them. The most successful female jockey, Alex Greaves, is the wife of a trainer and in 1998 there was still only one woman – Sophia Mitchell – riding professionally over the fences.[49] But the growth of sponsorship, product endorsement, and help from government via the Sports Aid Foundation and now the national lottery have made it less difficult for women to join the professional ranks.

Fatima Whitbread was the highest paid European athlete in 1989 after her World Championship victory in the javelin two years earlier although in general, prize money for women, in golf and tennis for example, still lags behind that for men. Feminists also say that in order to endorse products or obtain sponsorship women have to be not only competitive but also attractive, a test which no male professional has to take. Certainly success breeds success and that applies to the women as well as the men. Sally Gunnell was a relatively minor sports earner before her gold medal in Barcelona. She had won the Commonwealth 400 metre hurdles title in 1990 and had a grant from the Sports Aid Foundation together with a part-time job with an accountant. After winning in Barcelona she was a target for sponsors and marketing agents desperate to get her name on their products. It has been estimated that her earnings rose from £75,000 in 1991 to £400,000 in 1993. But Linford Christie was still paid £25,000 a race to her £15,000.[50] A few women can make a living from playing badminton and squash but – tennis and athletics apart – it is in golf where the greatest progress for female professionals has been made. The Women's Professional Golfers' Association was only formed in 1978 with an initial £80,000 in prize money. Yet by the mid-1990s this figure had shot up to £2.5 million in 19 tournaments – a large figure though still small compared with the £30 million or so available on the men's European Tour in 38 tournaments.

If more women have entered the previously masculine world of professional sport in the eighties and nineties, so have more black people. Never have there been so many black professionals. And yet they tend to be found in a relatively narrow range of sports: athletics, boxing, cricket and football. In the European Championships athletics team of 1969 there were only two black athletes. In the Commonwealth Games athletics team of 1986, 33 per cent were of Afro-Caribbean origin although Afro-Caribbeans comprised but 2 per cent of the population as a whole. In boxing, the Board of Control banned black boxers from fighting for British championships until 1947. By the recession-riddled eighties, out of 600 professionals about a third were from Afro-Caribbean backgrounds. At the same time about one-quarter of professionals with English football league clubs were Afro-Caribbean and about half of all black professional players were in the Premiership in 1992–3. There have been famous black players in Rugby League: Billy Boston, Ellery Hanley, Martin Offiah and Clive Sullivan – who has a street named after him in Hull – but not so many in Rugby Union.

But where are the black British jockeys, golfers, squash players, swimmers, snooker players, rowers, tennis players and racing drivers?

It is also notable how few Asians there are in British professional sport. The absence of Asians in the Yorkshire County Cricket team has often been remarked upon. Perhaps now that Nasser Hussain is England's cricket captain things will change. In 1989 the Youth Training Scheme football programme had 1200 clients but only two were Asian. The only Asian footballer to succeed as a professional was Ricky Heppolette who played over 200 league games for Preston, Orient and Peterborough during the late sixties and early seventies.

In spite of the growth in numbers, those black players who did succeed had to be not only good but better than the white competition. Neither Everton nor Liverpool had had many black players on their books before Liverpool signed John Barnes from Watford in 1987, this in spite of a long established black community in the city. For Emlyn Hughes, a former Liverpool and England captain, the lack of black players could be easily explained: 'they haven't got the bottle', he wrote in his tabloid column.[51] The first time Barnes played for the Reds against the Blues some of the Everton fanatics chanted 'Everton are white, Everton are white', and threw bananas. Clearly black professionals had to cope with pressures which their white colleagues and opponents did not.

There were various ways of reacting to the snubs and taunts. Daley Thompson won two Olympic golds and was master of the decathlon universe for a decade. Son of a Nigerian father and Scottish mother he was genial, fashionable and confident but when asked to help produce a book about black sportsmen he denied that he was one. Black people were often encouraged to view sport as an opportunity for economic and social betterment at the expense of education and training. But as with whites only a few could expect to reach the professional pinnacle. Moreover, there were few black members of sports governing bodies, few black secretaries or managers, chairmen or administrators. Perhaps it is a matter of generation. Of the five managers of the British team for the Sydney Olympics, two are black. Garth Crooks became PFA President in 1989; Viv Anderson, in 1979 the first black player to be chosen for England, became manager at Barnsley and is now assistant to Bryan Robson at Middlesbrough. But John Barnes found it difficult to get a manager's job because, he suggested, 'black guys haven't proved themselves as managers', they don't get appointed.[52] In 1993 the PFA and the Campaign for Racial Equality combined in a project to 'Kick Racism out of Football'. This was both an indicator of progress and a sign of how far there was still to travel.

But the biggest change in the professional's world was the money.

Fame began to be translated into fortune in the new world of satellite television and international marketing. This is most clearly demonstrated in football and golf. In 1997–8 the wage bill of clubs in the English Premier League was in excess of £100 million, and in the Scottish Premier, around £40 million; £2 million annual deals were common as were large signing-on fees for the best players. In 1996–7 the average Premier League player was earning £210,000 a year while the average Third Division player received a salary of £28,000, well in excess of the average wage, it should be pointed out.[53] A recent survey by the Professional Footballers' Association and the *Independent* showed that the average Premiership wage for players over 20 was now £409,000, 20 times more than average earnings. Over 100 players earn over £1 million a year, in salary alone. The average First Division salary is £128,000, Second Division £52,000 and Third Division £37,000. No wonder players require the help of accountants, solicitors and above all agents, who are key figures in the financial negotiations. Few footballers are without them and even some apprentice jockeys now have them.[54]

Earnings on the European Golf Tour in 1999 also showed that although few could match Colin Montgomerie with his £1.5 million plus in prize money and a range of lucrative commercial endorsements, 83 players made over £100,000 a year, which, even allowing for expenses, was not to be sniffed at. Moreover several who were not actually household names earned well in excess of £100,000.[55]

In other sports the gap between the rich stars and the journeymen pros remains clearer. In racing the top flat-race jockeys are millionaires but there are probably only between ten and twenty of them. Another 25 or so who manage to ride twenty winners a season or more will be well paid for it. Over the sticks, Tony McCoy will certainly make £250,000 a year but it has been estimated that in order to make a profit a National Hunt jockey would need about 250 rides and twenty winners, and only 30 jockeys do that.[56]

Similarly snooker has an elite of perhaps twenty players who will earn in excess of six-figures a year and twenty more will be in the financial high fives. Test cricketers can't compare with international footballers but again they will be six-figure earners. The average county professional does less well. Simon Hughes claimed that he only received £14,000 from Middlesex in his eleventh season as a professional, in 1990. Durham paid him £20,000 in 1991 and his benefit raised over £100,000, a sum which was double his total earnings for the whole of his twelve years in county cricket.[57]

In 1999 the leading earners in British sport included four footballers, three drivers, two boxers and a golfer. Of the footballers, Alan Shearer is paid an estimated £40,000 a week by Newcastle United while Steve

Table 4.2.   British sports top earners, 1999

1	Lennox Lewis	Boxing	£16.6 million
2	Naseem Hamed	Boxing	£8.7 million
3	Damon Hill	Motor Racing	£5.6 million
4	Steve McManaman	Football	£4.75 million
5	Eddie Irvine	Motor Racing	£4.1 million
6	Colin Montgomerie	Golf	£3.5 million
7	Colin McRae	Rallying	£3.2 million
8	Alan Shearer	Football	£3.1 million
9	Michael Owen	Football	£2.9 million
10	David Beckham	Football	£2.85 million

McManaman's transfer from Liverpool to Real Madrid brought him a £3 million signing-on fee plus wages of about £2 million. David Beckham's earnings were boosted by the £1 million paid by *OK!* magazine for exclusive rights to the photographs of his wedding to Victoria Adams.[58]

The list of the ten richest British sporting stars, all men, is led by Naseem Hamed and Alan Shearer, both of whom have assets worth £17 million. They are followed by the racing driver David Coulthard and then five more footballers and two tennis players, David Beckham, Robbie Fowler, Ryan Giggs, Duncan Ferguson and Steve McManaman, and then Greg Rusedski and Tim Henman.

When Johnny Haynes became the first British footballer to be paid £100 a week it was seven times the average wage. Those Premier League players earning £15,000 a week in 1995–6 were receiving sixty times the average wage. In such circumstances it is perhaps not surprising that an opinion poll conducted by the sports publishers Collins and Harvill in 1997 found that almost 70 per cent of those asked agreed with the proposition that sportsmen and women were paid far too much.[59] Perhaps there have always been mixed feelings about professionals profiting from a game. Although they themselves often characterized it as a job like any other, to most fans it was not like any other; it was being paid to do something you were good at, something you loved. Most people were paid much less for much less rewarding work.

The money has also prompted other changes. Britain has long provided opportunities for overseas sporting stars. Boxers and cricketers, jockeys and rugby players, footballers and speedway riders, ice-hockey players and more recently basketball players have come from all over the world to sell their athletic talents. Numbers have been increasing in the nineties, especially in football. It is mainly the result of Murdoch's millions but it is also the result of a change in European law which has led to the lifting of restrictions on the movement of all labour within the European Union. It is also the result of the famous Bosman judgement, which has allowed professional players at the end of their contracts to move to another club without a transfer fee. There were only ten registered overseas players in the Football League in 1966–7. The signing of the Argentinian pair of Osvaldo Ardiles and Riccardo Villa by Tottenham and the two Dutch midfielders Arnold Muhren and Frans Thijssen by Ipswich provoked a minor rush to 57 in 1980–1 of which those well-known football peripatetics, the Yugoslavs, formed the largest group. But since the formation of the Premiership the number of overseas footballers has increased dramatically. In 1992–3 there were only eleven overseas players in the Premiership; in 1998–9 there were 166.[60] Scandinavian, Dutch and French imports have been the most welcomed due not only to their high level of technical skill but also to their personal maturity and balanced lifestyles. The PFA has expressed some anxiety that foreign professionals are restricting the opportunities of the young native born. And when English professionals have been asked what they think of it, the vast majority would prefer the numbers of non-British players to be restricted. It is not without significance that there has been relatively little traffic the other way. The explanation seems to be in part a cultural one. Most British professionals have their origins in a working class for whom education was never a high priority. Language and way of life have formed difficult barriers to 'abroad'. As Ian Rush famously remarked after a sad season with Juventus of Turin in 1987–8, 'it was like being in a foreign country'. In Europe, on the other hand, football has long been an acceptable career for the sons of the middle class.

In general, channels of recruitment to the world of British professional sport have not changed much. The FA's Charter for Football of 1998 set up football academies at 34 licensed professional clubs to help not only bring on the next generation of footballing talent but also provide essential education for young hopefuls, the vast majority of whom will not join the professional ranks or, if they do, will not stay there long. Similarly the British Racing School at Newmarket and the Northern Racing College at Rossington Hall are teaching some of the jockeys of the future. Nevertheless, learning by doing remains the most common path to the professional sports world of the nineties as it was in the fifties.

Has elite sport become more competitive, the experience of it more intense? Has the term professionalism taken on new meanings? In 1988 Oxford University appointed their first professional director of rowing and this seemed a rational decision to the 'amateur' crew, for as one of them said, 'we are completely professional only there is no money in it. We're not amateurs. We're sportsmen. Sacrificing months of your life that's damn serious.'[61] It is indeed and the word sacrifice was not ill chosen. A new age of professionalism has been emerging fuelled by the findings of sports science and technology imposing a discipline on diet and lifestyle and emphasizing the importance of gaining a psychological edge by visualization exercises and analysing performance. As Edward Tenner has pointed out, technology does not just introduce new materials and techniques but develops extended networks of people to help the athlete win events which often depend on smaller and smaller margins of superiority. So they need the help of coaches, trainers, psychologists, shoe and equipment manufacturers, and financial managers. These are the invisible teammates but they come at a price: the loss of autonomy. For some professionals this has led to a brutal conformism crushing the fun out of being a pro. One cricket professional calculated that in 1990 there were half as many public-school educated county cricketers as in 1980 and the number of ex-Oxbridge students playing in the championship had fallen from 22 to 9. It had become too serious, too much like hard work. The initials FEC carved on Michael Atherton's locker at Lancashire did not mean future England captain.[62]

Many professionals have been dedicated trainers like squash champion Jonah Barrington who said in 1989 that if he failed to do two training sessions a day he could not produce what the public were entitled to expect. Real champions have to be prepared to suffer and their coaches have to set them an example.[63] Some sports people train three times a day and it does beg the question how far the body is designed to be punished in this way in order that athletes, cyclists, footballers, rugby players and swimmers can play a winning game. Part of the ever-increasing pressure to perform has led many sportsmen and sportswomen to take dietary supplements and drugs to help them get through the level of training necessary for a professional in the twenty-first century. Part-timers too suffer similar problems with a job as well as the daily training grind tempting them towards chemical assistance. There is often an element of another kind of addiction at work here. There's no feeling to match the one that comes with scoring a goal, footballers say, and the feelings expressed by the 1950s marathon runner John Tarrant will find an echo in the heart of many of today's professionals. 'When you run, you feel you can do anything – you feel like a king, a god. No one can touch you. On the good days you feel you can run for ever. I can hardly stop myself from laughing out loud sometimes, it's so good.'[64]

Moreover the dedication is not only physical. Richard Johnson was the jockey who rode 'Looks Like Trouble' to victory in the 2000 Cheltenham Gold Cup. He told the *Guardian* that he was too busy riding and travelling to read, to go to the cinema, watch television or listen to the radio. He had never read a book in his life and he did not really need things like computers as he had an agent to do everything like that.[65]

As professional sport and business have moved closer together, so the sporting values of fair play and sportsmanship have declined. The professional sportsman is 'here to do a job' and winning, or not losing, is the most important thing. And as professional sport has taken on more of the characteristics of business so advertising, marketing and media hyperbole have become its trademark. All cannot win, all matches cannot be good but in order to persuade people to pay to watch, the media machine demands that they shall be. God help the performer who doesn't come up to expectations. Yet the bigger the hype the bigger the let down. And if all else fails you can blame the referee. If you are a sixteen-year-old who really loves a particular sport, plays it well and would like to take it up as a career here is some advice from Sport England:

All professional sportspeople spend a great deal of time training and practising to become successful, and ultimately the best, in their chosen sport. In most cases they will work with trainers, coaches, nutritionists and sports scientists, and some may have managers to organise travel, accommodation and publicity. The work will often require following a strict daily routine, and usually means working at the weekends and in the evenings. Professional sportspeople often need to have a second career.[66]

5 Media

At the end of July 1956 England were playing Australia at Old Trafford. Jim Laker, the Surrey off spinner, took 19 wickets for 90 runs in the finest piece of bowling in the history of the game. Driving home from Manchester to London, he stopped for a sandwich in a pub. The locals were watching the highlights of the Test Match on a television recently installed in the bar as Laker joined them. Remarkably, no one in the pub recognized the tall, quiet Yorkshireman in their midst as the man on the screen who had just bowled out Australia single-handed. A few years later this would have been impossible. With the spread of television and the replays of that remarkable piece of bowling, Jim Laker's quiet anonymity was over. He was voted BBC Sports Personality of the Year – the only cricketer apart from Ian Botham to have won the award. From 1967 to his early death in 1986 he was a BBC cricket commentator. When he died there was a sense of loss that went beyond that which always accompanies the passing of a great player. Laker had become part of the furniture for all those who followed televised cricket.[1]

Understanding the role of the media in sport involves the complex relationship between media institutions, the programmes they make and the audience itself. How technology transformed what could be made and how such changes in production were received is the subject of a growing volume of media research, especially in North America.[2] In Britain exploring this triangular relationship requires an appreciation of how press and radio coverage provided a model for BBC television sport. From the 1950s to the 1980s BBC sport acquired a special kind of national authority through its distinctive broadcasting style and the personalities it chose to put before the nation to speak to and for 'us'. The stable of long-serving BBC commentators – a self-conscious bunch of 'characters' with a strong Oxbridge element, especially in cricket – played a central role.

Presenting sport to the people was never a simple matter of objectively reporting events. From Pierce Egan in the early nineteenth century to Neville Cardus between the wars, sports reporting involved a process of selection, dramatizing, interpretation and reflection. The same has been true of the last fifty years with one critical difference: technology has provided fans with visual access to live sport within the privacy of their own homes, removed from the communal atmosphere, the stadium compressed onto a small screen with the spectacle 'mediated' by a sports producer selecting shots and by a commentator. No longer the sole providers of match reports, the popular press took to the 'human interest' angles not covered on television. The back page was turned into a kind of sports magazine. This had begun in a modest way between the wars but assumed enormous importance from the 1960s onwards. The contemporary media, led by the popular press but with commercial radio and satellite television in hot pursuit, have turned sport into 'male soap opera'.

Before Commercialization: BBC Radio and Television

The fifties were the last decade when spectator sport was still produced for live consumption. Those who wanted to watch football went to see a game on a Saturday afternoon. The post-war crowds were immense as manual workers not yet provided with televisions, cars and other new consumer durables sought live sporting entertainment. Football, cricket and boxing matches prospered and new events like greyhound racing and speedway as well. Over 82,000 watched Arsenal play Manchester United at Maine Road in 1948 and Newcastle United won promotion to the First Division in the same year watched by an average home crowd of over 56,000 (not counting the legions of small boys who sneaked in during the 'pre-fortress' era of professional football).

Part of the boom in live spectator sport no doubt came from pent-up wartime demand but another element was growing radio coverage which whetted the appetite without weakening demand. There were eight million wireless sets in Britain by 1939 and the BBC estimated half their audience listened to football and cricket. When Len Hutton broke the record for a Test Match innings at the Oval in 1938, it was 'the voice of summer', Howard Marshall, who described the event to millions of listeners. The war itself had heightened the role of radio to raise morale. 'Giants of Sport' was a wartime series celebrating Britain's sporting heritage and the bonds of Empire with Sir Pelham Warner ('Plum') extolling 'Australia's Greatest Batsmen' and Bernard Darwin on Grace's last match when the Grand Old Man managed 31 not out at the age of 66. Sport was a handy weapon of wartime propaganda, expressing our indomitable spirit and imperial solidarity.

After the war a new commentary team for test cricket was assembled bringing in the young poetry producer and ex-policeman, John Arlott, along with E. W. Swanton, the cricket journalist, and Rex Alston, a BBC producer who was to help shape the structure of post-war sports broadcasting. Arthur Gilligan was on hand as an entertaining amateur player of the inter-war years with C. B. Fry to represent the Edwardian 'Golden Age'. From the start cricket coverage crossed over easily between radio and television with Arlott and Swanton equally at home in either medium and Brian Johnston soon joining in. Cricket required far longer than football and there were constant breaks in the action. Commentators became adept at chatting about the crowd, the ground, the weather or reminiscing over earlier games and old characters. The commentator combined technical expertise with a powerful sense of the cultural consensus around which the English ideals of sportsmanship, self-control and respect for established authority revolved. Noisy West Indian crowds were treated with amused tolerance tinged with condescension and characterized as 'exuberant' or 'colourful' whilst players who challenged the status quo were seen as bringing the game into disrepute. The subtext of much sports commentary, especially in cricket, tended to be conservative with a small 'c', stressing tradition, respectability and deference, although this inevitably varied a good deal from one individual to another and from sport to sport. Even such icons of 'middle England' as John Arlott or E. W. Swanton spoke out against apartheid when most of the sporting community simply preferred to ignore it.

Test Match Special, familiarly known to its devoted listeners as 'TMS', provided ball-by-ball commentary on Radio 3 for 33 years before switching to Radio 5. Extensive cricket coverage was promised on Radio 5 but ball-by-ball commentary in the summer when other big events were competing for time could not be guaranteed. This apparently reasonable proposal was met with an outcry from the English establishment. In the House of Commons 140 members signed a motion deploring any change in the programme's idiosyncratic format. Gillian Reynolds in the *Daily Telegraph* said TMS 'has become a national institution, a piece of radio which transcends class, age and gender'. Analysis of the actual TMS audience would probably not bear this out. But this was not the point. TMS was an invented tradition, a powerful metaphor of Englishness. 'If one national institution is proved mortal', observed Roy Hattersley, 'how many more will die a commercial death?[3]

The BBC backed off and TMS was preserved, occupying a unique slot on Radio 4 in recognition of its special place within English sports broadcasting. However, whether this can survive with the emergence of aggressive commercial radio in the 1990s must be in doubt. Talk Radio bought the rights to live transmission of the 1999 series in South Africa and will undoubtedly compete strongly for future programming. The BBC have finally been forced to realize that clinging to the past is not enough. A female commentator has been brought into this bastion of male privilege. The 'heritage' content is more of a self-parody with Henry Blofeld, a resident commentator since 1974, playing the 'old buffer' role to the younger Jonathan Agnew. Reforming to conserve, BBC sport is trying to hang on to the traditionalists and win over a newer audience more accustomed to the upbeat style of commercial radio.

Football commentary, of course, was usually more dramatic than cricket. The calm midfield build-up interspersed with frantic goal-mouth action became a distinctive feature of radio reports. From 1948 *Sports Report*, first presented by Raymond Glendenning, from 5.30 to 6.00 p.m. was a results and short match report service preceded by the rousing 'Out of the Blue', a signature tune that became instantly famous amongst the fourteen million listeners to the programme checking their football pools results. When the BBC thought about abandoning the familiar 'te-tum, te-tum, te-tum, te-tum, te-tiddly tum, te-tum', there was an outcry. Desmond Lynam, then a radio sports presenter, compared scrapping 'Out of the Blue' with knocking down Tower Bridge. *Sports Report* was 'part of the fabric of sports broadcasting'. And so it has remained, still going strong after over fifty years with a million listeners – the largest audience of it kind. It has survived a move from the Light to the Third programme in 1964, then to the new Radio 2 in 1970 and finally to Radio 5 in 1990.[4]

Since 1970 there has been a full Saturday afternoon of radio sport. As the current producers of *Sports Report* point out, there is much more sport on radio nowadays, the market is more competitive and the news service much faster. Instant post-match interviews with stars and managers are now the norm. Radio has made a come-back as television rights for big events have soared beyond the means of the public broadcaster. The 1999 Ryder Cup is a case in point. Radio 5 handled the event, which was shown on Sky, with whispered green-side commentaries, which turned out to be very effective. Despite being statistically overtaken by television, radio sport has kept a distinctive niche in the market. The Football Association and League were not worried about radio coverage. Listening to football, for all its claustrophobic thrills, was never going to pose a serious threat to match attendance.

Watching football on television was quite another matter. The BBC managed to persuade the FA and Football League to allow coverage of the England–Scotland match and the Cup Final in April 1939. But with only a few thousand TV sets this was hardly surprising. After the war, activity from sporting bodies opposed to live coverage gathered momentum as the number of television sets reached almost a quarter of a million by the end of the decade. An Association for the Protection of Copyright in Sports was formed and matters came to a head when the 1950 Cup Final between Arsenal and Liverpool was broadcast live while the League programme was still in full swing. Attendances dropped by around 40 per cent in areas receiving the broadcast. The 1952 FA Cup Final was not televised. It was only in the teeth of opposition from the Football League that the FA permitted the televising of the classic Cup Final of 1953 where Stanley Matthews at last got his winner's medal and national recognition. It was Coronation year and many families had bought a television for the occasion. Neighbours were invited in to show off the acquisition and watch the match. Around ten million are thought to have seen the game, which the Queen attended – the first reigning Queen to do so. This was a turning point. Professional football ceased to be regarded as the preserve of the working class and came to be recognized as the equal of cricket as part of English national culture. Appropriately England regained the Ashes from Australia later in the summer and, of course, a British-led expedition had conquered Everest on the eve of the Coronation. Sporting triumphs were available for mass consumption as never before and eagerly taken up as tokens of national revival in a new 'Elizabethan Age'.[5]

The arrival of commercial television in 1955 brought with it the prospect of bidding wars for live football. Yet despite the relatively large sums of money newly available, the League decided firmly against any televised coverage of the weekly programme. Gates were falling throughout football, especially in the lower divisions. There were a number of factors involved in this: rising affluence and increased choice of leisure activity, changing family structures and employment patterns as well as Saturday afternoon television. But those who ran football were disinclined to take risks. The idea that television could revitalize the game was dismissed. On the other hand, there was strong public pressure to allow the national game to appear on the new national medium. An accommodation between the demand for public access and the need to protect live attendance led to a deal permitting recorded highlights and the advent of *Match of the Day* in 1964.

During the fifties there was relatively little football on television. From the BBC viewpoint this was not a problem providing no one else got live access. There were plenty more fish in the sea. The Professional Golfers' Association, for example, was pushed by its leading players to get greater television exposure. John Jacobs, the first PGA Tournament Director, made deals with both the BBC and ITV to televise eight tournaments in 1972, including the Dunlop Masters which was taken over by Silk Cut, and a new Benson and Hedges tournament. Alcohol and cigarette manufacturers flocked to a sport that offered prolonged periods of media exposure and access to a male middle-class audience with serious spending power. The prize money available in British professional golf increased tenfold between the 1950s and the 1970s. In 1954 the total prize money for the year had been £25,000. By 1974 sponsors were paying the same figure for a single tournament – providing it was televised.[6]

Horse racing, which appealed both to the gent and to the ordinary working man, was another sport keen to offer itself to television. When off-course betting was belatedly legalized in the sixties, a TV in the corner of the betting shop came to be a common sight. Predictably the BBC did not see greyhound racing in the same light. The rapid growth of the sport after the war created over two hundred licensed tracks keen to get on to television. But the BBC governors took a dim view of 'the dogs'. Despite the BBC Sports Department's enthusiasm for televising greyhound racing, only three races per year were allowed to be broadcast – and the results were not to be read out on the *News*. Sport was no longer seen mainly as a means of moral improvement but nor was it supposed to encourage vice. Lord Reith still cast a long shadow.

Show jumping was the first sport to be reinvented by television. The English public was introduced to a new form of an old sport which suddenly appeared like a triple set of fences in the middle of the evening schedule. This was adopted for the 1948 London Olympics. The equestrian team provided the only gold medal for Britain at Helsinki in 1952. The BBC saw an exciting spectator sport with a touch of class and tradition which appealed to women as well as men. Men and women could compete on equal terms as the four 'jump-offs' between Colonel Llewellyn and Pat Smythe at the 1952 Horse of the Year Show demonstrated. The BBC allowed the event to overrun by more than an hour before a tie was declared, and show jumping became a national enthusiasm. Pat Smythe went on to compete in the 1956 and 1960 Olympics on 'Flanagan' and to win the European Women's Championship four times between 1957 and 1963. In 1969 show jumping was the second most popular sport on TV after soccer but twenty years later it had slipped down the rankings to thirteenth. It lacked appeal to the young, men in particular. But the posh tones of Dorian Williams, the BBC show jumping commentator, were still popular with older viewers, especially women.[7]

For the many women who were indifferent to football, live coverage was happily a rarity until recently. Before the current 'feast of football' there was a famine. Instead of the present massive coverage – addictive to some, tedious for others – there was the occasional mid-week

European game, the Cup final, the England–Scotland game and a few others. Even Scottish and English club sides hardly ever met. Hence the excitement of seeing the likes of Puskas, di Stefano and Gento flitting across monochrome screens in their pure white strips; 135,000 saw Real Madrid retain the European Cup for the fifth successive year in their famous 7–3 victory over Eintracht Frankfurt at Hampden Park in 1960 but millions more saw it on television. European football was becoming a reality north and south of the border with Celtic's famous victory in Lisbon in 1967 followed by Manchester United in 1968 at Wembley. European ties allowed the TV audience to watch Liverpool live as they won their four titles between 1976 and 1985 until the Heysel tragedy shamed English football and temporarily closed the door to Europe.

It was Europe that had made Matt Busby's young Manchester United side into heroes before Munich turned them into martyrs. Seven of the team were killed on 6 February 1958 in a plane crash at Munich while returning from a European fixture, including the young Duncan Edwards, the great hope of English football. The sight of their broken plane lying in the snow was on every television screen. The recuperation of injured players like Bobby Charlton and of Busby himself was followed by the whole nation. Those born in the post-war baby boom were just old enough to know what was happening and to watch the weakened team struggle in the Cup Final a few months later.

However, the key moment in the making of Manchester United into a 'superclub' came later with the new side which won the league just as recorded highlights arrived. From 1964 a vast television audience could watch Denis Law, 'the King' of Old Trafford, with clenched fist and blond hair, scoring nine times in his first eight TV appearances, or the sheer brilliance of George Best and the power of Bobby Charlton, the survivor of Munich and a hero of the World Cup victories of 1966. Winning the European Cup in 1968 was the crowning glory which gave the club its pre-eminent status and allowed it to survive the relatively lean years of the 1970s and 1980s.

Millions more people were watching league football highlights on Saturday night and humming along with the opening tune than standing on the terraces on a Saturday afternoon. London Weekend (LWT) produced *The Big Match* in 1968 offering Sunday afternoon football excerpts. But this was confined to the LWT area and not seen by Granada, Yorkshire or Central viewers. So the BBC kept its national predominance and *Match of the Day* became the way most people kept up with football, often after a few pints in the pub. *Match of the Day* became a key element in Saturday evening scheduling. It cost £80,000 an hour, which was a lot more expensive than other sports broadcasting.

New electronic cameras and action replay machines meant that 'by the late '60s two matches which had finished just a few hours earlier could be shown in colour, sensitively edited, even before the cocoa had cooled'.[8] It was the jewel in the crown, bringing in an audience of 10–12 million, making Jimmy Hill and John Motson national personalities in the process.

Something new was happening. Televised broadcasting of sport was becoming more 'real' than the event itself. For the many viewers who had never been to a live tennis match, Wimbledon *was* a television event. Serious socialites and tennis fans might flock to the All England Club in the lush suburbs of south-west London. But to the British people Wimbledon signalled the start of high summer. Tennis was in difficulties as a participant sport but found a new success as a spectator event. Most of the nation watched some part of Wimbledon fortnight but never followed other tennis events. England hadn't had a champion in the men's singles since Fred Perry in the 1930s. But this hardly seemed to matter. If we didn't have the best players, at least we had the best tournament. British women did fairly well and spotting a new hopeful was part of the fun, along with the breaks for rain and the hypnotic sound of ball on racquet or the umpire announcing the score. Until the 1970s there was little or no argument between players and umpires, ladies didn't 'grunt' and crowds didn't scream. Wimbledon was both English and international, pastoral and suburban, middle class and monarchical.

Interpreting these events to the British public year after year was a man whose name became synonymous with Wimbledon: Dan Maskell. Maskell had a curious pedigree, beginning his career not in prep school but as a ball boy at the Queen's Club. He later turned professional before becoming the coach at the All England Club. He was that particularly English phenomenon: the professional who resembled an amateur. Maskell was one of 'nature's gentlemen', a quietly genial presence, a dignified man respectful of tradition yet enthusiastic about new talent. His maxim was 'economy of words is what the viewers want'. The 'Ooh, I say' which would accompany an exceptional shot passed into the national stock of well-loved phrases. Maskell was the epitome of the BBC's distinctive understated style. His ideals of service to the game, stylishness and fair play encapsulated a certain kind of Englishness which could seem either charming or stuffy, admirable or absurd depending on the viewer's own values. Arthur Ashe said of sports broadcasters 'the standard we seek is Dan Maskell's, and you go from there'. John McEnroe would have been unlikely to agree, especially when Maskell remarked how McEnroe was a 'wonderful player, but killed all that loveliness by his dreadful behaviour'.[9]

Just as Maskell stood for 'our' view of tennis, so Peter O'Sullivan came to speak for the racing gent and the 'sport of kings'. Most striking of all was cricket. Nowhere was 'ideological' authority more seamlessly sewn into BBC broadcast coverage. John Arlott's Hampshire burr came to be identified with the sport on radio whilst Brian Johnston was a kind of cricketing Bertie Wooster. This 'heritage' style strongly influenced television with the addition of a resident Australian in Richie Benaud, whose clipped vowels were a gift to impressionists, and an obligatory northerner like Fred Trueman or Geoff Boycott to provide regional balance and a more populist feel. Johnston's fame spread beyond cricket via his cheerful weekly exploration of the English character in *Down Your Way* on Radio 4. When 'Johnners' died, the Prime Minister, John Major, a genuine cricket enthusiast, said 'summers would never be the same'. Cricket coverage celebrated more than cricket. It made a play of English eccentricity and regional variation, evoking 'warm beer and long shadows over county grounds' as Major famously mused, echoing the received wisdom that cricket is 'peculiarly English, not suitable for export and found only in places where English men have taken it'.[10]

E. W. ('Jim') Swanton was the epitome of this kind of Englishness both as a broadcaster and as a journalist. He was born when W. G. Grace was still playing and wrote his first test match report in 1930, continuing until his death seventy years later, pouring forth millions of words on a game that 'he sincerely believed was a metaphor for life'. He was a regular BBC broadcaster whose close of play summaries, always lubricated by a scotch on the rocks, would often begin 'it has been an absorbing day's play and I shall start by reading the card'. His journalism was direct and simple; a cricket colleague at the *Daily Telegraph* described his style as 'a combination of the ten commandments and Enid Blyton ... Jim was in many ways the sort of man foreigners construct when they caricature the English ... he was High Church and occasionally high handed ... and loathed the vulgarity and gimmickry of modern cricket'. He was given a CBE by John Major.[11]

Other sports, of course, also came to be almost inextricably associated with broadcasters. Henry Longhurst, a Cambridge golfer who slipped into broadcasting via the BBC old boy network, was a familiar voice before Peter Alliss became another jovial presence on and off the course. Coverage of the British Open followed Wimbledon fortnight in what became a long summer of televised sport. Viewers who didn't care much for golf could always linger as the camera panned across the Scottish shoreline or the Lancashire beaches. Each sport had its own 'personality' to speak for it. Their catch phrases and styles became the stock in trade of a generation of impressionists from Mike Yarwood to

Rory Bremner. Their gaffes were affectionately catalogued and endlessly repeated.

David Coleman was especially important, famous not only for the crescendo of his Olympic commentaries but as the anchor man of Saturday *Grandstand* and the host of a sports quiz. *A Question of Sport* has been consistently one of the most popular BBC programmes since its inception in 1970. Ian Botham and Bill Beaumont for several years took on a new public image as genial team captains, mixing factual knowledge and pub banter. Sports personalities queue up to appear on the show for a small fee. In 1990 there was a waiting list of eighteen months just to get a ticket for a Sunday afternoon studio recording and the show has remarkably held its place at peak viewing times under Sue Barker, the former tennis player, enlivened by cheeky 'lads' like snooker player John Parrott and the Glaswegian footballer Ally McCoist.

Commercial Rivalries: BBC, ITV and Satellite

For a good while the BBC had sport to itself. When commercial broadcasting began in 1955 it found the BBC firmly established with three- to five-year deals with most of the major governing bodies. Peter Dimmock, who ran BBC sport, was one of the few senior figures to appreciate fully the potential danger of a new competitor which could snatch exclusive rights and suddenly force up the cost of televising sport. The BBC strategy was to oppose exclusive rights for major events on the grounds of public choice. The Conservative government was surprisingly amenable to restricting the free market. Sport had a special place in the Tory heartlands and an attachment to amateur principles ran deep. The ethos of the All England Club and the MCC on the one hand and the BBC on the other were not so different. As Seymour de Lotbiniere, the head of BBC Outside Broadcasting, chummily known as 'Lobby', admitted, 'I have never attempted to conceal my belief that Wimbledon treated us generously. I assumed it was the deliberate policy of an amateur sport towards a public service.'[12]

How long would the BBC be able to sustain this cosy arrangement? It was not just the refusal of the football authorities to contemplate live broadcasting which undermined commercial sports television. The problem ran deep and bedevilled parliamentary debate over the statutory regulation of commercial television. Should there be a free market in sporting events? Britain had a national broadcasting *service*. A 'service' in this sense went beyond the mere concept of programme making and transmission to include the idea of creating an inclusive national culture, in which sport had a significant place. The BBC stressed their contracts were non-exclusive and simply required that commercial television should play by the same rules. The trouble was they were not playing the same game. The BBC was in effect state funded but independent television had to pay for itself by selling advertising. Advertisers wanted exclusivity to increase ratings.

The government intervened to limit exclusivity by placing some events on a 'national list'. The existence of these reserve powers effectively knocked heads together. The BBC and ITV agreed on a list of ten including the Olympics, the World Cup, the Commonwealth Games, the Cup Final, Wimbledon, Test Match cricket, the Derby, the Grand National and the Boat Race. The commercial television companies were stymied. National culture was a strange beast which defied economic logic. Macmillan's Britain turned out to be a very different place from Eisenhower's America. Conservatives had too much of a cultural investment in Britain's sporting heritage to tolerate a completely free market, even under Mrs Thatcher. The national 'list' has remained but is no longer the effective property of the BBC. Other terrestrial channels have recently made successful bids for key events. The FA Cup is currently on ITV and the rights to televise Test Matches from 1999 to 2002 have gone to Channel 4, who offered £50 million and a more innovative and multicultural approach.

ITV sport on Saturday afternoon for many years consisted of wrestling and horse racing packaged around a results service to which was added a football preview and excerpts of exotic foreign sports. *World of Sport*, presented by the dapper Dickie Davies for over twenty years, was in direct competition with BBC's *Grandstand* which had a wide range of top events in the summer. However, without live football even the BBC had to struggle to fill the winter schedule. Muddy rugby league battles from the far north, wonderfully brought to life by Eddie Waring – that most imitated of northern commentators – filled the gaps in the schedule. Five Nations rugby union, which had its own idiosyncratic voice in the crackling briskness of Bill Maclaren, a border Scot and a school master by profession, enlivened the early months of the year. Through such individuals, who appeared to be more like fans than professional broadcasters, the BBC seemed to tap into the national psyche in a way ITV could not. The 1970s saw dual coverage of some of the listed events including the Cup Final, the Olympics and the World Cup but the BBC kept a broadly 2:1 advantage in viewing numbers.

This was galling and unprofitable for advertisers and commercial TV companies, who hankered after the huge *Match of the Day* audience in particular. In late 1978, ITV broke loose and made a private deal with the Football League for exclusive highlights. A furore ensued with the front pages of the press carrying pictures of the warring executives: BBC's former Welsh rugby union hero Cliff Morgan, whose Radio 4 sports programme was strong on the ethics and national values of sport, against the abrasive young Michael Grade, from a family with a big name in show business. The old dilemma arose once again. Was spectator sport anything more than entertainment? Why should it be specially protected? Grade won the battle but not the war. A compromise was agreed whereby the lucrative Saturday night slot was rotated annually with *Match of the Day* pushed into Sunday afternoons in alternate years.[13]

This arrangement did not bring the rewards and viewers ITV hoped for. Increasingly, commercial television sought live events, especially football, joining with the BBC in 1983 and 1986 in deals with the Football League. Financial inducements along with falling attendance partly caused by hooliganism finally got live league football onto television. The exclusive component in their coverage, however, came from athletics which they snatched from the BBC in 1984 in a £10.5 million deal over five years. This followed the great years of Coe and Ovett. Athletics seemed to offer a new route to the heart of the nation. This was a landmark in sports broadcasting. A key component of BBC sport had been prised away from the Corporation. There had been no complaints from athletics about the quality of BBC coverage. The only issue was money. The future pattern was taking shape. Listed events apart, whoever could pay the most would get the most.

In the late 1970s sports programming occupied around 12 per cent of BBC broadcasting and only slightly less for ITV. The audience for sport was more complex than it appeared at first with a higher proportion of middle-class viewers watching sports events than working-class viewers and a larger number of women than expected, especially for big events. In 1988 the highest proportion of adult men in the television audience was only 53 per cent. Women and children were strongly represented but this does not mean women followed sport avidly on TV. Audience research tended to count heads rather than looking at what was going on inside them. Men took a more serious interest in sports as 'fans' whilst women regarded events as background for other forms of domestic activities. Skating, tennis and show jumping were the only sports with a majority female audience. Amongst men, class differences were striking, too. Apart from football, which increasingly became a mass preoccupation, wrestling, darts and boxing were more popular with manual workers whilst rugby, skiing, tennis and golf were more middle class.[14]

Until the arrival of cable and satellite broadcasting, which rudely ended the duopoly of BBC and ITV, there was a tendency for audience numbers to decline through the 1970s and 1980s. This was not so much because of a lack of interest in sport as a tendency to use television as a 'default' activity when there was nothing else to do. The formation of British Satellite Broadcasting in 1988, however, quickly identified sport as the key to building a mass audience. Exclusivity would force fans to sign up for the entire channel. This led to a battle for exclusive league football. ITV were 'bounced' into a £44 million four-year deal for exclusive live coverage and recorded highlights. This kind of money was simply not available to the BBC, which had to offer a full range of programmes. It also put strains on ITV, which had to make the most of their investment and dropped much of their other sports coverage, losing Dickie Davies and the 1992 Barcelona Olympics in the process.

For a short while ITV seemed to have won the football battle with the BBC. But in the Machiavellian world of television politics, the BBC soon saw its chance to exploit a new player in the market and get back its highlights coverage. In November 1990 British Satellite Broadcasting merged with Rupert Murdoch's Sky to create BSkyB, which was determined to get live football at almost any price. They duly paid £304 million for a five-year deal with the top clubs in 1992, which broke away from the Football League to form the Premiership. The BBC agreed to buy the re-transmission rights and were back in business on Saturday nights.

Television had brought about the biggest change in the game since the FA had agreed to the setting up of the Football League in 1888. Now the FA, fearful of the increased wealth and autonomy of the League, outflanked them by doing a deal directly with the new satellite broadcasters and the club chairmen to create the 'Premiership', as the old First Division was renamed. The future of football – and potentially of all sports broadcasting – was firmly in private hands with the BBC a junior partner. This arrangement was reinforced with the signing of a new four-year deal for live Premiership football until 2001 worth £670 million from Sky plus a further £73 million from the BBC for the highlights. In June 2000 the BBC lost its highlights coverage to ITV as part of a deal worth around two billion pounds. From 2001–4, BSkyB would screen 66 live matches per year and the cable company NTL 40 pay-per-view games annually.

However, there were limits to the power of the Murdoch media empire. These were revealed in their attempt to buy a controlling share in Manchester United for £623 million in 1998. This would have effectively meant the top club would be owned by the same group as the satellite broadcaster with whom the Premier League were in nego-tiations. Moreover, the fate of the club would be in the hands of an international media conglomerate, who could act without reference to the wishes of supporters. This led to a grass-roots revolt organized by the Independent Manchester United Supporters Association, which proved remarkably vociferous and effective. The bid was referred to the Monopolies and Mergers Commission, which declared it against the public interest, and this view was accepted by the government. The decision blocked media companies from outright ownership of sports rights, although there was nothing to stop them buying stock in football clubs providing they did not acquire a controlling interest. Leeds and Newcastle have both seen this type of investment recently and the influence of such big investors will clearly be a factor in future decisions. But it will not be the sole factor.[15]

Sponsorship and Celebrity

All this had a profound effect on football itself. Television and associated sponsorship poured vast sums of money into the game. This was mostly spent on spiralling transfer fees and a staggering rise in wages. There was no subsidy to spectators. Ironically, they had to pay more – much more – to be a part of the live show. Poorer spectators simply couldn't afford a seat. The 'People's game' was becoming too expensive for the people. There had always been a difference in wages and prices between the First and Second Divisions of the Football League but with the Premiership this gap became even greater. The Football League admitted they had been left way behind in the brave new world of satellite sport. Broadcasting and associated sponsorship rights were bringing in an average of around £8 million a year to Premier League clubs in 1996/7 whilst First Division clubs were making only £800,000. Two-thirds of Football League clubs were losing money in 1997.

Relegation from the Premiership was not just a question of losing a share of media revenues. Loss of status was almost instantly translated into falling demand for club merchandise, especially clothing and videos. Manchester United almost doubled its income from merchandising, from £2.7 million to £5.2 million in the first season of the Premiership. Newcastle United fans were spending an average of almost £180 a year each on club goods by 1996–7 with other 'superteams' close behind. Top clubs changed their shirt designs half a dozen times in as many years. In 1997 the accountants Deloitte-Touche estimated Manchester United's global annual turnover at just under £89 million, £30 million more than second-ranked Barcelona and more than double ninth- and tenth-ranked Newcastle and Liverpool, who managed a mere £41 million and £39 million respectively. Manchester United are, of course, a uniquely successful marketing phenomenon – a Gallup survey of May 1999 suggested that 20 per cent of the British population consider themselves to be supporters of Manchester United – but far more modest clubs are moving in the same direction. Hyper-commercialization has even hit clubs like Leicester City, bringing forth dozens of marketing men, new shops, executive boxes and restaurants during the 1990s. Clubs worked at 'branding' themselves, not just with the traditional mascots of the past but with an array of gimmicks such as life-size, Disney-style figures greeting the children of debenture holders in the new dining rooms or saluting the crowd from the touchline. Florida had come to football.

This was not a message that traditional fans necessarily wanted to hear. There was something glossy, vulgar as well as horribly expensive about the whole business – and football, for the first time in its history, was now explicitly a 'business'. Clubs believed in charging what the market would bear not what fans could reasonably afford. For all the television money, the price of seats at the big clubs kept rising as fans clamoured to see the new foreign stars and top teams. Satellite coverage had revitalized football at the top level – at a price. Entry to big games was increasingly restricted to season ticket holders. Clubs wanted to encourage more affluent families to enjoy a 'leisure experience' mixing spectating with eating and drinking and a range of special social events. 'Superclubs' soon had shops, restaurants, even credit cards. Several were floated as public companies on the Stock Exchange. Ken Bates bought a declining and debt-ridden Chelsea for £1 in 1982 and built a glamorous team around expensive imported foreign players, pushing up the total share value towards £200 million. Some directors stood to make a fortune. But what went up could come down. Club share prices fluctuated according to playing success as power switched from the Directors to the City. 'When I stopped playing in 1990 football was still a game,' Alan Hansen observed in 1997, 'now it's an industry.'

An even more profound change was taking place in rugby. Again, the vast potential of television earnings was the motor of change. Rugby, of course, was rooted in class and regional divisions going back to the late nineteenth century. Televised Five Nations matches featuring the great Welsh side of the 1970s helped rugby union to break through to a mass English audience beyond the network of 'old boys' clubs that still made up the heart of the club game. Commercialism was anathema to the 'old farts' of the RFU – as the England captain Will Carling memorably called them – but pressure built up from top players and elite clubs for change. Former bastions of elite metropolitan amateurism like Harlequins or Wasps joined with the best provincial teams like Bath and Leicester to embrace professionalism and sponsorship.

Suddenly teams which attracted a few thousand spectators were paying wages of hundreds of thousands of pounds for star players. Economic logic briefly flew out the window as clubs scrambled to be the big players in the new professional era. This was followed by retrenchment as it became clear that club rugby did not have the mass following of football and could not generate the same income.

Everything was in flux. A European club championship was created bringing in the famous French teams from the Languedoc as well as the best sides from South Wales. The 1999 World Cup, which was based in the new Cardiff Millennium Stadium with matches in England, Ireland, Scotland and France, was sold to ITV with the BBC stalwarts consigned to reporting for radio. At Twickenham the formerly conservative and amateur RFU proposed a new business plan that would increase annual turnover from around £50 million to £300 million over ten years by new catering and conference facilities, merchandising and most importantly through television where technological changes held out the prospect of governing bodies running their own channels on a 'pay per view' basis. There was bitter conflict amongst the Five Nations, which became the Six Nations in 2000 with the inclusion of Italy, about the division of television revenues with the English proving particularly demanding and stubborn.

Even more remarkable things were happening in Rugby League in the mid-1990s. Here the scale and speed of change was quite bewildering. After decades of comfortable northern parochialism and relative poverty, the sport suddenly awoke to the possibilities of playing teams from the suburbs of Sydney after Rupert Murdoch staged a dawn raid on Australian Rugby League in April 1995. Clubs that had rarely been south of the Watford Gap suddenly found the logic of the Murdoch Foxtel empire dictating club fixtures between England and Australia. A new Parisian team was created to give a pseudo-European dimension. Despite fierce opposition from the Australian Rugby League, its English counterpart threw itself headlong into uncharted waters, even switching from winter to summer to secure a three-year deal from Sky worth £84 million. Players jetted across the world between England and Australia playing several games before returning. The switch to summer also meant that league players could sign short-term contracts for rugby union. Former union stars who had defected to the league game, like Jonathan Davies, could return to their first love.

Rugby League itself embraced the new era with a vengeance, abandoning its old 'flat cap and false teeth image' for good. 'Superteams' like Wigan increasingly marketed themselves in the same way as their nearby football rivals like Liverpool and Manchester United. The unanswered question which hung over the two codes was whether some kind of amalgamation was inevitable in the longer term. Perhaps what money had split asunder, money could unite? However, even big media money cannot completely remake a century of sporting traditions and loyalties. Neither sets of fans or clubs wanted a merger and there were limits to the willingness of supporters to accept change imposed over their heads. They would agree to watching their favourite teams play new opposition but they weren't willing to identify with clubs that had no organic link with the past.

The general drift towards the American television model was undeniable as one by one the BBC's leading sporting attractions – Formula One, the Ryder Cup, rugby internationals – came under attack. Cricket, however, was rather different. Declining crowds from the 1960s had pushed the cricket authorities in the opposite direction to the Football League. Instead of blocking live cricket on television, the MCC used its well established links with the BBC to promote the sport in new ways. The problem was that county cricket, which had been at the core of the game for a century, took too long for television. The prestige of the County Championship and the crowds following it declined. What was needed was something that could be shown in a single afternoon; something more akin to the League form of cricket that flourished in the north of England and which the MCC had hitherto considered beyond the pale. Lord's abandoned its long-standing hostility to the one-day game when it abandoned the distinction between Gentlemen and Players. Cricket tentatively embraced a more commercial future. Sponsorship from Gillette, an American company which wanted to make itself more English, came in 1963. The immediate success of the Gillette Cup led the counties to set up the John Player Sunday League in 1967. Once again cricket for all its ingrained traditionalism emerged as more flexible than other sports, dropping the sabbatarian restrictions long before football or rugby. The John Player League showed how keen cigarette manufacturers were to get round a new ban on TV advertising. Benson and Hedges duly joined the fray in 1972 with a third one-day televised competition. ITV beat the BBC for the right to show the Gillette Cup in 1968 but commercial scheduling meant they had to go off air before the end of the final game. The MCC was not amused and reverted to the BBC.

Sponsors liked the BBC because of their large audiences and their lack of other advertising. The one-day game was fine but the real prize, of course, was Test Match cricket. For an ambitious insurance company with a low level of public awareness sponsorship of Test cricket was almost too good to be true. When Cornhill took over as Test Match sponsors in 1977 only 2 per cent of the population knew who they were. By 1981 when Ian Botham led a thrilling England recovery against Australia their public recognition rating was up to 17 per cent. Test cricket for Cornhill has proved a very good deal indeed.[16]

In the same year that Cornhill became sponsors of the England team, a new and quite unexpected challenge to the entire future of the game came from the other side of the world. In a battle with the Australian cricket authorities for exclusive television coverage, the media tycoon Kerry Packer decided to set up his own World Series Cricket and recruited top English and West Indian Test players as well as Australians. Night-time games, white balls, coloured clothes and a host of other innovations followed as Packer spent a fortune to establish the new teams before eventually forcing the governing body in Australia to back down. Packer abandoned World Series Cricket in return for exclusive rights to broadcast Test cricket. English cricket had been caught up in the fallout from a foreign attempt to force the sale of sports rights to private enterprise. Tony Greig, the England captain, who had defected to Packer, was sacked along with several other prominent players. Relationships within the game were soured. Yet the example of what a determined media baron could do was not forgotten. When satellite TV came to Britain, a peculiarly English 'compromise' was reached. Home Test Matches as listed events remained non-exclusive (and the effective cultural property of terrestrial channels). But the Cricket World Cup was sold to Sky in 1992, which also acquired the rights to the England overseas Test programme.

Packer had offered English cricketers five times what they were earning as top professionals in England. Earlier generations of players had earned small payments for promoting products ranging from equipment to drinks and patent remedies. Some got free cigarettes for promoting a particular brand. But there were no fortunes to be made from advertising, not even for the best players. Income came from wages or by using their fame to attract customers to a pub, a newsagent or a sports shop. After the war, advertisers became more serious about sport. The combination of health and attractiveness with competition and success was seductive. This was especially true when it came to products designed for men, who were notoriously hard to reach and sensitive to ridicule from their peers. But if an undisputed sporting hero associated himself with a product, emulation would be a natural response. This, at least, had been the case in the United States, which had a strong influence on British advertising. Hence the logic of the campaign built around Denis Compton, the Middlesex and England batsman, to persuade British men to use Brylcream on their hair. Cricket was so securely English there was no risk of association with dubious foreign styles of masculinity. Compton's wavy hair was part of his debonair image as the 'cavalier' of post-war sport, a thrilling batsman and an Arsenal winger: Compton was 'the first cricketer to be taken up by the advertising industry, to become a brand image, to be deemed to have attained a fame so widespread that entrepreneurs judged, quite rightly, that his face beaming down from the hoardings, from magazines, from backs of buses, would convey its message even to those who knew nothing of cricket'.[17]

Beginning in the 1930s, strongly influenced by the popularity of newsreels and improvements in photographic journalism, sporting heroes became 'faces' that were instantly recognized beyond their own sphere. 'The rule that interests us here is that the further removed the product is from (a performer's) sporting activity, the bigger by definition, the personality rating.'[18] The post-war generation of sports stars were still far from realizing their market value. The great football stars of the fifties made a point of their modesty and team spirit. The brisk handshake after a goal was a far cry from the exuberant, self-glorifying displays that were to come when a goal scorer self-consciously dramatized his abilities to his own crowd and to the television audience. Hence the little gestures, dives, shuffles, flips and shirt waving that multiplied as footballers became aware of themselves as television performers. With the abolition of the maximum wage in 1961, footballers could negotiate their own contracts and had an incentive to promote themselves in new ways.

This kind of individualism was greatly enhanced by changes in the actual filming and cutting of televised sport. Paul Doherty, whose own sporting life had been as a big centre half for Bristol City, moved from working as a journalist and an agent to producing football for Granada in 1974; he had introduced player features and gossip, trying to get the players to show their feelings after almost a century of self-control. The stress on recorded highlights meant that constant action and goals were the diet of television football. This emphasis was heightened by BBC / ITV rivalry, which gradually pushed the BBC to experiment with a wider variety of shots than the camera sweeping the field from an elevated position above the half-way line. Satellite television, however, took this much further with more cameras, new angles and endless agonized or ecstatic close-ups.

Wider advertising opportunities emerged as the media became more expert at dramatizing individual achievement. The combination of changing media presentation with long-term economic growth created exceptional opportunities for the top players to enrich themselves through advertising, endorsements and appearance payments. This first became evident in America. 'There is no precedent for a sports figure becoming the centre of the kind of merchandising empire that now surrounds Arnold Palmer,' wrote the man who had put him in this position – and was to do the same for so many others – in 1967.[19]

This man was an American lawyer, Mark McCormack. A good sportsman himself and possessed of an energy and drive which became legendary in the business community, he quickly spotted the possibility for the global marketing of players and soon extended his US operations to Britain. His protégé, Palmer, who won the US Masters four times between 1958 and 1964, came over to Britain and won the Open in 1961 and 1962. This was televised in full by the BBC. Arnold Palmer was the first of the great American players who came to Britain – from Bobby Jones to Ben Hogan – who the public could see without going to watch him. Palmer was an attractive figure, an attacking player with a nice personality. McCormack exploited this to the full with global clothing and hotel deals, even franchising his name for dry cleaning, lawn mowers and home improvements. McCormack's vast ambitions and special interest in golf and tennis, where American representation in British sport was historically strong, soon led him to take on British clients. When Tony Jacklin won the British Open in 1969, the first British player to do so for a generation, McCormack's company, IMG, had sold the rights to the 'How I Won' story before the final round had begun.

Golf, of course, was especially well suited to this. It was a largely middle-class game where players could often afford sophisticated equipment and were in the market for a range of other consumer items. The same was broadly true of tennis after the amateur/professional distinction collapsed in the 1970s. IMG and its imitators soon spread their activities to embrace sports celebrities of all kinds. The agents understood that television had made top players instantly recognizable and knew the enormous value of this to manufacturers, advertisers and sponsors. Britain's outstanding golfer of recent times is Nick Faldo and an IMG client. He could earn around £100,000 for promoting a new brand of confectionery. Then there were Pringle sweaters, Wilson clubs, Stylo shoes which along with videos, books and appearance money brought in around £1.5 million in 1988 not counting prize money. Faldo's rival, Greg Norman, was making around $5 million a year after winning the British Open. IMG, of course, took their cut, which could be 10 per cent of prize money and up to 25 per cent of sponsorship, endorsements and fees.

Those who played team sports at first found it harder to cash in. But the process took hold in the same way in due course. Shirt sponsorship has become an important part of football with companies like Carlsberg, for example, willing to pay a million pounds a season to have their name on Liverpool shirts. One estimate in 1993 suggested that such exposure was worth about a £100,000 a week in advertising costs. Hence the boom in sponsorship, which had risen dramatically through the 1980s to reach around £256 million in 1994. 'High tech' consumer goods investment from Sharp, JVC and Canon alongside Coca-Cola, Vauxhall and Barclays Bank came onboard with banking and insurance still in cricket. Tobacco companies fought to keep their place in motor-racing and won a temporary reprieve from the ban on cigarette advertising in sport. Of course, members of teams can profit individually as well as collectively from the media-based sponsorship and advertising. Footballers, in particular, now have agents not only to negotiate contracts and transfer fees but to sell pictures and stories to the vastly increased market in glossy sports magazines. Satellite exposure made footballers from famous teams even more highly sought after. Manchester United's Eric Cantona did himself no harm by leaping into the crowd to kick an abusive fan, despite being banned from the game for a while. Young players, of course, had always attracted young women. The explicit presentation of the footballer as sex symbol, which had begun with George Best in the 1960s, had become routine by the 1990s. A few good games and an attractive young man like Manchester United's David Beckham was on the front pages of the tabloids. When he married Victoria Adams, 'Posh Spice' of the Spice Girls, there was a media frenzy. 'Posh and Becks' had their wedding at a castle near Dublin and sold the rights to OK! magazine; the Beckams appeared at celebrity openings and fashion events. Their baby became the most photographed infant of the day. All this was considered important enough for upmarket magazines like *Vanity Fair* to run special features on the 'glitterati' of soccer.

Of course, there had always been gossip. But looking back it is striking how strict the conventions of privacy were. Bill Edrich, a brilliant but philandering post-war batsman with a drinking problem, managed to keep his private life more or less private. Wally Hammond, the supreme English cricketer of the thirties, was similarly able to escape candid public scrutiny of his divorce and 'nights on the town' which he slept off in the changing room. The possibility that he was suffering from syphilis contracted in the West Indies has taken half a century to surface. In the 1980s the boyish, impetuous and rather more innocent Ian Botham has had the press crawling over every aspect of his life, from allegations of smoking marijuana to chatting up barmaids. Botham was a child of his times, both seeking attention and rejecting it, doing publicity stunts for charity one minute, furious about press intrusion the next. What Botham seemed to want – not unreasonably given his England performances – was to become a well loved and well paid national character doing ads and popping up on TV. The boxer Henry Cooper was the first of a clutch of 'celebrity' sportsmen, who seemed to spend their lives playing golf with comedians like Jimmy Tarbuck or appearing on game shows.

Top sportsmen – and sportswomen – increasingly want to be more than top performers. They want to be entertainers. Feeding off itself, television has grasped this new cross-fertilization with comedians like Skinner and Baddiel presenting themselves as football fans and ex-sportsmen like Gary Lineker and David Gower trying to be comedians. A cross between a sports quiz and alternative comedy, does *They think it's all over* take television sport into new more ironic and self-mocking areas? Is it an example of sportsmen not taking themselves seriously? Or is it merely the crude laddish humour of dressing room or public bar with its contempt for the nonconformist? Sportsmen had stopped taking themselves so seriously and were finding a female audience for the first time. But this was still only a postmodern drop in the ocean of televised sport, which remained firmly and conventionally male in tone.

Sensationalism and the Popular Press

Inside stories and breathless hyperbole were hardly a post-war invention. The inter-war years had seen the mass press take up sport, forcing the closure of the old *Athletic News* and devoting several pages to sport each day. The popular Sundays like the *People* and the *News of the World* had four to six pages of sports reporting. In the summer the quality press had cricket to write about and the *Manchester Guardian* had Neville Cardus, whose career spanned the war and gave a new literary respectability to serious sports writing. The sports pages of the popular daily papers were still largely concerned with news-gathering, though with an increasingly gossipy and speculative twist via football columnists like Alan Hoby 'The Man Who Knows'. However, what he and others like him really knew and what their papers were prepared to print remained quite different things.

The Wolfenden Committee took evidence of the effect of the press on top-level performers in 1958.[20] Denis Compton thought no more than 10 per cent of journalists knew much about the sport they were reporting. Judy Grinham, the Olympic swimmer, said 'she was "knocked for six" when she had a bad report in a newspaper and some swimmers, especially young ones, were absolutely broken hearted'. But now she was a reporter herself 'she saw the journalist's point of view': the editors wanted a story more than constructive criticism and factual reporting. Discussing football, Bill Slater, who had played as an amateur for Blackpool and as a professional in the great Wolves team under Stan Cullis, noted the 'tremendous range of reporting ability' and stressed that 'people had to choose their newspaper according to the type of reporting they wanted'. Slater, who worked as a university lecturer in physical education, 'did not think journalists were particularly cruel to young players' and 'on the whole he felt the press did a good job'. Compton agreed and added that good publicity for a top player meant increased earnings outside the game.

The newspapers were anxious to present a respectable image of the country, covering up sexual scandal as avidly as later generations would expose it. Good behaviour was all-important and sportsmanship had to be seen to extend from the individual to the national level. National pride had to stay within the limits of decent partisanship. Patriotism rather than nationalism was the norm. Consider, for example, England's notorious football defeat at the hands of the United States in 1950. The press was very disappointed but their tone was surprisingly measured by contemporary standards. Imagine what a later generation of journalists would have done to an England team manager who was beaten by 500–1 outsiders. Walter Winterbottom did not have to face the wrath of the *Sun* and managed to stay in the job for another twelve years. Press reaction to the 6–3 defeat at home by Hungary in 1953 was mixed. 'There can be no complaints, we were outplayed . . . by a great Hungarian side,' wrote Charles Buchan in the *News Chronicle*.[21] The press debated whether England had been beaten by a new 'collective' football before deciding that the 'Merry Magyars' had learned the game from an Englishman, and so their victory was also ours.

There were, of course, some complaints. John Barrett 'deplored destructive and sensational writing' about tennis, which he put down to editors 'making mountains out of molehills'.[22] Gordon Pirie thought top athletes were caught between their governing body, which wanted to vet everything, and the press looking for exciting stories. 'A top athlete must be most careful with his words at all times, especially just before or after a race.'[23] It was a case of damned if you do and damned if you don't; if you refused to talk you were surly, if you said too much you were a 'big mouth'. All this has an oddly contemporary feel, although the press was not seen as too much of a problem by most sportsmen and women in the 1950s.

Popular sports coverage changed significantly in the sixties and has moved in a more sensational direction ever since. Coverage reached new heights. By 1980 both the *Sun* and the *Star* gave over 20 per cent of their space to sport with the *Mirror* and the *Express* not far behind with 17.36 per cent and 16.45 per cent respectively.[24] Banner headlines, colour photographs, and coverage of every major game produced a paper where the back pages stretched to the centre and sports stories, especially scandal, often got onto the front page. The tone was increasingly strident and chauvinist. When the *Daily Herald* closed in 1964 to be replaced by the *Sun*, the new tabloid announced it would have 'four rows of teeth' and would settle for nothing less than complete success. Victory at home in the 1966 World Cup fuelled vast expectations and nationalist rhetoric, driving a succession of managers out of the job under a torrent of abuse. Bobby Robson was England manager in the Thatcher years when the tide of popular chauvinism reached its height: 'ON YER BIKE ROBSON'; 'BEAT 'EM OR BEAT IT, BOBBY'; 'SENSELESS! SPINELESS! HOPELESS! or just 'PLONKER'. If England won, the rhetoric instantly went the other way with 'BOBBY'S BEAUTIES' or 'BRING ON THE ARGIES' in a self-conscious reference to the victorious Falklands War which set the tone of the decade.[25]

The *Daily Mirror*, the *Star* and the other tabloids adopted the same style and couldn't resist the chance to rake over the past affairs of 'ROMEO ROBBY'. No wonder Robson, after coming so close to the World Cup final in 1990, decided to leave the England job for a managerial career on the continent. His successor, Graham Taylor, who was thought to be 'good with the press', fared far worse. Dubbed 'Turnip' by the *Sun*, he was mercilessly ridiculed and quickly forced out after England failed to qualify for the World Cup in 1994. Glen Hoddle was a different kind of press victim, sacked for a combination of unconventional beliefs, insensitive comments about disability and, it should be said, increasingly erratic results. Hoddle's successor, Kevin Keegan, has all the cheerful populism and national enthusiasm the tabloids expect. But they are unlikely to be any more generous should he fail to produce a winning team.

The growing internationalism of sport, especially football, has proved a blessing for sports journalists in search of a story. The papers increasingly picked up the international angle in the 1990s as European players took advantage of the Bosman ruling on the free movement of players. This was perhaps the most striking change in English football as teams like Chelsea and Arsenal fielded some of the best Italian, Dutch or French stars, all of whom had stories to tell about settling in, British football, rumours of return and so forth. This flood of foreign stars had started as a trickle of British players going abroad. Such was the smug insularity of the British that they scarcely thought of buying foreign players, even after the Hungarians and the Brazilians had shown how much better they could play the game. Scotland, in particular, was inward looking, not even recruiting from England and reluctant to recognize the achievements of the 'Anglos' – those Scots, often star players, who went to play in England. Alternately adored and reviled by the press in his native land, Denis Law was 'The King' at Old Trafford. But amongst a 'tartan' press riding the new wave of Scottish nationalism, his gifts were less fully appreciated.[26] From the 1960s England exported some of its best players, usually to Italy and usually not for long. They missed the beer, the English language, even British food. Now the pattern has been reversed with a vengeance with the press riding a ceaseless wave of speculation about new signings.

Famous foreign sportsmen and women seemed to fascinate and dismay the British press in equal measure. Tennis players, in particular, who were only in Britain for a few weeks a year became temporary celebrities as the appetite for drama and sensationalism grew. Maria Bueno and Margaret Smith had been one thing, Billy Jean demanding equal prize money and Martina Navratilova as a lesbian icon were another. In the men's game it was not so much the robotic consistency of Borg which caught the headlines as the arrogant gamesmanship of McEnroe and his refusal to 'play the game'. John McEnroe took up a lot of space in the tabloids and the quality press in the 1980s. 'A brat' he may have been but a brat that made good copy.

The nineties saw a new development in serious sports writing. Sport and culture would no longer be treated as antithetical. Nick Hornby's *Fever Pitch*, a Cambridge graduate's account of his obsession with Arsenal, proved to be one of the books of the decade. There had always been intellectuals who liked sport but now it became commonplace, even fashionable, to say so. There was a steady expansion in the space given to sport in the broadsheet press, more serious discussion and features – and more tabloid-style gossip as well. Women began to break into the male bastion of sports reporting just as girls and women more generally were drawn to 'the new football'. The quality Sunday papers were always on the lookout for a new angle. The *Observer* packed off Booker Prize-winning novelist, literary critic and self-confessed football virgin, A. S. Byatt, to Euro 96. The *Independent* did the same to Germaine Greer, who, 'bathed in testosterone', was much taken with Gazza's inclination to run after a ball 'with the unflagging enthusiasm of a puppy'.[27]

'Gazza' had been of particular interest to intellectuals for some time. His tears in the 1990 World Cup were analysed by the leading social theorist Anthony Giddens whilst the poet, biographer and football fan Ian Hamilton devoted most of an issue of the literary magazine *Granta* to him.[28] Not much of this was likely to have touched Gazza himself whose Geordie philistinism was part of his fascination. Gazza, in fact, took up a great deal of the press in the 1990s from his injuries to his hair cuts, from drinking to domestic violence. *Hello* magazine paid a fortune for the exclusive rights to photograph his wedding reception, which included a picture of the man himself in a gold morning suit toasting the bride from a gleaming urinal. The tabloids were resentful about being excluded, which made their subsequent denunciations of his wife-beating all the more vehement. Their collective indignation was instructive. Sensationalism had its constructive side. Journalists would no longer cover up for sportsmen, who had to take responsibility for their public and private lives. Those like Tony Adams, who succeeded in changing themselves, were the new media heroes: the prodigal sons and reformed sinners. A lesser player's battle with drugs or gambling made better copy than Alan Shearer painting the garden fence.

The new sensationalism, of course, was not confined to sport. It was part of a much wider shift in popular culture, which finally shrugged off the self-improving legacy of the past. The popular Sunday papers had long pandered to the public's fascination with sex and violence like the Victorian 'penny dreadfuls' before them. But from the 1960s the popular dailies went consciously downmarket and their sports coverage went with them. Sports journalism went in two directions: there was an impressive expansion of lively and serious writing about sport, mostly from the 'quality' press, and a headlong rush into scandal in the 'middle market' papers like the *Mail* and *Express* as well as the tabloids. Like the quality press they were no longer able to rely on match reports to sell papers. Sensing the enormous public interest in the people behind the performances, the mass press threw itself into a frenzy of specu-lation, gossip and sensationalism. Six or eight pages of sport, usually half on football, became the norm and this could expand to fill half the space in the tabloids for big events. A 'good guy' like Gary Lineker could grab the headlines as the nation gathered round to support their striker and his wife when their young son had a serious operation. But it was family break-up rather than family values that the public really wanted – or so the popular press believed. There was nothing like a deserted wife and child pictured alongside her ex-husband frolicking in the surf with a new bikini-clad 'companion' to sell papers.[29]

Sports 'hacks' were a cynical bunch, notably dismissive of anything 'arty' or pretentious, both liberators and destroyers, pushing back the limits of what could and could not be said in public. It was a popular Sunday paper, the *People*, which exposed a gambling and match-fixing scandal in English football in 1965. Of course, there was a vast amount of ordinary reporting, too, especially in the regional and local press. *Match of the Day* only carried the highlights of a few games and even Sky can only cover a fraction of all the football being played. Plenty of fans still like a familiar journalist's account of a game to compare with their own impressions of how the team performed in televised high-lights. The sensational and the mundane sit happily side by side. The

News of the World, the biggest selling newspaper in Britain, cleverly packaged its sports coverage to put big national stories alongside factual regional match reports, often written by former local stars. Jackie Milburn, the hero of post-war Tyneside, wrote a north-east football column for the *News of the World* for twenty years after his retirement. Geordies were less interested in what was said than who was saying it. Press columns, ghosted or not, were a powerful source of myth-making, mixing national stories with local legends.

Current sports coverage ranges from the probing literary article to be found in the weekend sports supplements of the broadsheets – a new feature of good sports writing prompted by the growing middle-class interest in football – to the 'the lad done bad' stories of sex, violence and scandal juxtaposed with ads for sex aids, chat-lines and pornography in the tabloids. The unreconstructed model of aggressive, promiscuous masculinity is alive and well and its most salacious outlet is simply called '*The Daily Sport*'. However, this 'socusoap' with its 'spot the brawl' and unending tales of laddish nights on the town co-exists with a vast amount of serious comment and analysis. The upsurge in new sports magazines, bulging from the shelves, each more glossy than the last, cleverly blends the two angles, appealing to the fan and the man, from complex technical pieces to the picaresque life of a Robbie Fowler who 'fancies any glamorous woman on telly "as long as they've got a fanny and breathe."' Hymns to 'clubbing' and consumption – varieties of Ferrari, BMW or Jaguar are an important part of the story – now play a major part in writing about sport, not so much as a performance, more as a way of life.

Conclusion

We began in 1956 with Jim Laker making his way home from a famous victory against Australia, catching sight of himself on a pub television and slipping off unnoticed. In the years that followed, television transformed the interrelationship of players, the public and the media in complex ways which are still rapidly evolving. Nowadays, only those born to blush unseen in the ranks of small-bore rifle shooting can hope to remain anonymous. Most, of course, want nothing more than to be recognized. Sportsmen and women are queuing up to become celebrities. Technological innovation has created a new kind of visual sporting pleasure, a new stylistic focus on the face of the performer, close-ups, replays and slow motion. This, combined with the arrival of colour in the early 1970s, was a marriage made in heaven, preceded by a long engagement with programmes like *Sports Report* on BBC radio.

Television both transformed sports that were alive and revived ones that were dying, breathing new life into indoor bowls and darts as well as bringing the huge events of world sport like the World Cup or the Olympics into the home with hundreds of hours of coverage and discussion. Snooker was reinvented as a form of mass entertainment by the BBC. Millions of viewers were caught up in the trance-like movement of coloured balls round their screens and the accompanying commentary of 'Whispering' Ted Lowe, finding a huge audience amongst women who had never played the game. Similarly, men surprisingly found themselves caught up in dance as sport with Torvill and Dean's Olympic 'Bolero'. An estimated 20 million Britons watched their unsuccessful attempt to recapture Olympic Gold in 1994 ten years after their triumph in Sarajevo.

The media juggernaught rolls on, picking up momentum all the time, mixing old and new forms, promising more and more channels. Digital broadcasting will even allow viewers to choose their own camera angles. Sport can no longer be confined by time and place. Seasons no longer mean very much. Satellite sport seems to be everywhere and available all the time, in pubs or at home. Whilst sport lovers revel in unimagined freedom of choice, the sports-loathing half of the population are surrounded by what must seem like an incessant, bewildering stream of jargon, tribalism and hype. Like other high-minded radicals of the first half of the century, Orwell would have been appalled at the media-led power of sport in the latter half of the century. Yet the fear that watching would become a substitute for doing turned out to be false. Participation figures have broadly risen alongside viewing figures. Watching football on TV doesn't stop youngsters wanting to go out and kick a ball. But it does influence who they support and how they spend their money. Spectator sport and the media have fused together. The one is inconceivable without the other.

6 Identity

Sporting achievements express the values and aspirations of entire communities. The team is a territorial symbol and a collective metaphor. Supporting a club may unite a whole city or a part of it, drawing upon surrounding areas to create a common fan community. These allegiances run deep and have evolved in complex ways over the last fifty years. Beyond the bedrock of locality, there lies the nation. Unlike most other countries, in Britain the nation and the state are not coterminous. Football and rugby internationals between the component nations of the United Kingdom began before organized club competition. National rivalries run deep and remain tenacious. In football, 'the Home Internationals' were controversially dropped in the 1980s as a response to hooliganism and the increasing congestion of the International fixture list. Yet an England–Scotland tie can still generate intense passions, especially north of the border. Come the rugby or football World Cup 'Anyone but England' is still an instantly unifying Celtic cry.[1] In Britain national affiliation has constantly cut across loyalty to the wider multi-national state. Yet in the Olympic Games, the most important global sporting event, the UK competes as a single nation-state like France. England, Wales, Scotland and Northern Ireland join together, men and women, white and black, under the Union Jack. What the United Kingdom might have done if it had ever been a united force in other sports is a popular source of pub speculation to this day.

The City

Football has been the supreme expression of urban identity in post-war Britain. The structure of club competition still reads like a roll-call of the Industrial Revolution. The textile towns of Lancashire remained a great force in the post-war game. Huge crowds, for example, descended on Burnden Park to support Bolton Wanderers and to see Stanley Matthews play in the FA Cup in 1946, cramming the open embankments in their tens of thousands while more scrambled over makeshift fencing to get in. Thirty-three died and hundreds were injured in the crush. The bleak report that followed – in striking contrast to the Taylor Report into the 1989 Hillsborough disaster – was fatalistic. Huge crowds mostly made up of working men watching their local team were taken for granted as part of popular industrial culture. Twenty-five years later an even worse disaster befell fans at a Rangers and Celtic match at Ibrox, historically the best attended and most fiercely fought club game in Britain. With two minutes left and no score, many of the 80,000 fans began to leave. A late goal, however, caused part of the crowd to surge back. Crush barriers collapsed and sixty-six died. This, at last, produced a major report on ground safety.

The bereaved and injured had accepted the risks with the stoicism of a class who never expected – or demanded – better or safer conditions. They just wanted to be able to pay a small amount at the gate and join the assembled community of supporters, who were there both to be entertained and to affirm their chosen sense of place. During the 1947–8 season when Newcastle United were promoted to the First Division the average home crowd was over 56,000 with fans crammed into rickety wooden stands. Football was cheap to watch and television was only for the affluent minority. Heavy industry still employed men in vast numbers. The huge crowds at St James's Park, for instance, were made up largely of men coming off a Saturday morning shift at shipyards like Swan Hunter, or the great engineering works, Parsons or Armstrong, and from the mines of the Northumberland coalfield. Just as the Durham pitmen, whose coal was exported from the Wear, converged on Roker Park to cheer for Sunderland, so the Northumberland miners were part of a wider Geordie fan community, queuing for the lunchtime buses to 'the toon'. They might even have found themselves standing beside one of the players they were going to see. Very few players had cars and post-war regulations meant that miners still had to do their shift in the pit, even if they were professional footballers.

This was a world where local heroes were still ordinary men. Great players were often seen on the streets or in the pub. Jackie Milburn, star of the Newcastle side, which won the FA Cup three times in the post-war decade, was a miner from Ashington from a big footballing family including Jack and Bobby Charlton, his second cousins. Milburn was a friendly, modest Geordie with a nickname that said it all. Around the Tyne 'Wor Jackie' was 'ours' not just for his goals but for the male virtues and community spirit he symbolized. As the pits and shipyards closed in the 1970s and 1980s, and divorce, crime and hooliganism seemed to spiral out of control, Milburn, a traditional family man, stood for a vanishing way of life. His death in 1988 shook Tyneside with a spasm of grief. There was a large public funeral, tens of thousands filled the streets as the cortège passed. Buses, trains and a new stand were named after him and three statues put up. Here was a different vision of northern man from the Andy Capp world of the feckless male. Kindness, respectability and family stability quietly ruled over the booze and the betting shop.[2]

The modestly prosperous post-war generation, which had grown up in the Depression, fashioned heroes in their own image. Billy Wright, the first player to win a hundred caps for England, was a one-club player and a hero in Wolverhampton. Tom Finney, the 'Preston plumber', and Bolton's Nat Lofthouse, another ex-miner, have a similar iconic standing in their communities. Since the fifties, however, managers rather than players have borne more of the weight of civic expectation. Four men, all born in or around Glasgow, stand out: Bill Shankly at Liverpool, Jock Stein at Celtic, Matt Busby and Alex Ferguson, both knighted for their success with Manchester United. More than politicians or other public figures, more than comedians or musicians, great football managers are the household Gods of contemporary Britain, their every word and deed pondered on the back page of every paper and now on radio and television. It is as if urban communities elect a spokesman – and it is always a man – to lead, inspire and discipline them, to give them a shape and a purpose, to realize their own potential and give them pride. No wonder those who fail have to go. Televising the Premier League in the 1990s has meant relegation banishes a city from the sporting map at home and abroad.

For all the importance of post-war football, attendance at football matches in England declined sharply from around forty million a year in the 1950s to twenty million in the 1970s. Scotland experienced a similar pattern of falling numbers with the smaller clubs harder hit than the big sides. Scottish football was ruled by Celtic and Rangers. Their rivalry expressed sectarian rather than geographical divisions not only within Glasgow but more widely in Scotland. However, with increasing social integration since the 1960s, the old divisions between the descendants of Irish Catholic immigrants and unionist Presbyterian Scots have been greatly eroded. Attachment to the 'Old Firm' is still strong but football no longer represents an objectively divided society.[3] Glasgow Rangers signed their first English players in the 1980s and finally accepted Catholics, presaging a headlong rush to sign foreign stars regardless of faith. This internationalism co-exists with an atavistic attachment to the 'Old Firm' as something tribal and unique to Glasgow. Other rivalries such as between Heart of Midlothian and Hibernian in Edinburgh or the Dundee and Dundee United divide were but pale reflections of this fiercer and peculiarly Scottish reality.

Cardiff and Swansea, of course, had their own followings and their own introverted contest for Welsh dominance. But the context was different. Rugby Union ruled in Wales. Wales had great players like Ivor Allchurch, Trevor Ford and John Charles but they all made their careers outside Wales. Football never had the civic power it enjoyed in England, especially with the rise of regional 'superclubs' like Liverpool and Manchester United. The young and brilliant Busby Babes, on the verge of conquering Europe before half the team were killed in the Munich crash of 1958, sucked support away from smaller clubs with long histories like Bury and Oldham. Manchester United hold the record for the highest average home crowd over an entire season – set in 1968–9, the year after they had become the first English team to win the European Cup. How could lower division sides compete for glamour with a team that had George Best, Denis Law and Bobby Charlton in the forward line?

The overall decline in crowd size was partly a matter of rising affluence and wider choice in leisure activities including television. It was possibly also a response to changes in the structure of family life and the rapid rise in female employment, which placed more pressure on men to help with domestic tasks at weekends. As the old industries declined, so did the settled pattern of life, the familiar weekly itineraries, the routine gender order and division of labour. Football was as popular as ever but it was 'consumed' in different ways. Fewer adult men had the time or the inclination to watch in person.

This had profound and disturbing implications, which went beyond the balance sheet. The pattern of support was changing and with it the controls which older men had exercised over their younger relatives or apprentices. Professional football matches had never been polite occasions. The rough and the respectable were mixed together. Drunken or violent individuals, however, were normally isolated in a sea of relative good humour and restrained partisanship. Derby matches for local or regional dominance were extremely hard fought on the pitch and feelings could run high on the terraces. Football was built around a culture of rivalry in which one team defined itself against another, Arsenal and Spurs, Everton and Liverpool, Newcastle and Sunderland, and so forth. But violent confrontations between groups of fans were quite rare.

All this changed during the 1960s with the rise of a new phenomenon: football hooliganism. This was, in effect, an extreme form of fan identification with a team, based upon a new aggressive youth subculture around football. The visit of a rival club meant the invasion of the home town by gangs of chanting fans, who would then engage in verbal or physical aggression with similar young men, mostly unmarried in their late teens or early twenties, from the home side. Much of the aggression took the form of ritualized violence, obscene synchronized chanting, throwing cans, and scuffles, though more serious incidents occasionally took place when one group of fans tried to invade the other's 'end'. The 'taking of ends' in which one group of hooligans would drive another from their preferred part of the ground, or pin them into a part of it, was mythologized within the hooligan subculture, which had its own hierarchy and divisions of hardness.

Hooliganism peaked in the late 1970s and 1980s. The Thatcher government contemplated introducing compulsory identity cards for spectators in the wake of the Heysel disaster in Brussels in 1985. Surging, aggressive Liverpool fans at the European Cup final caused a panic in which 41 Juventus fans lost their lives. England's reputation was shattered and her teams were banned from European competition. Football had reached a low point. The old working-class culture had gone and a new more middle-class consumerism had yet to emerge. Some young fans – and they were never more than a substantial minority – seemed to have no more than group aggression and a shared loathing of the opposition to hold them together. Football was caught in a downward spiral whereby falling attendances had favoured hooliganism, which in turn pushed down crowd numbers. Watching football was increasingly perceived as a potentially dangerous activity and its young fans as a source of local and national shame.

Sociologists were the unexpected beneficiaries of this new social problem. Government agencies, the football authorities and individual clubs looked around desperately for explanations and solutions. The competing forces of sociological theory joined battle.[4] One school of thought claimed these youths had never been part of the wider 'civilizing process'; they had always enjoyed fighting each other and football had never been free from crowd trouble.[5] Media analysts pointed out how the press sensationalized quite minor incidents, which gave the hooligans a perverse sense of achievement, reinforcing their behaviour and attracting others. Social psychologists like Peter Marsh contended that much of the so-called violence was rhetorical or ritualized.

These views tended to exist in isolation and alongside several class-based 'Marxist' accounts. These ranged from hooliganism as a reaction of the powerless to the capitalist exploitation of football – an argument more suited to the 1990s than the 1960s – to the view that hooligans were expressing in an instinctive, violent and depoliticized form their attachment to the rites of a traditional male working-class culture.[6] Hence the logic of the 'skinhead' subculture where young working-class males would shave their heads to set themselves apart from longer-haired middle-class students and wear traditional workmen's boots. The argument here was that the hooligan was really only an aberrant supporter, who had lost the familiar contours of belonging that football had once provided and was remaking intense community attachments in new and highly antisocial ways, spurred on by the extreme right.

Ethnographic studies in which researchers observed and infiltrated gangs helped to discredit some of the more facile accounts.[7] But a careful social history of hooliganism linking changes in spectating with wider changes in work, consumption and the family remains to be written. Interesting as all this was for academics, it was little use to those with responsibility for football and for public order. The video camera turned out to be the most useful weapon in their armoury, combined with increasingly heavy policing. On the simple principle that hooligans will be much less likely to offend if they run a serious risk of conviction, sophisticated surveillance measures were put in place which dramatically reduced the incidence of violence at grounds, especially in the Premier League. The large football stadium of the 1990s ceased to be an arena where most young fans felt free to indulge themselves in violent group rituals.

Leading clubs have made it clear that racist abuse of players, which was rife in the 1980s, will no longer be tolerated. Even routine verbal abuse of players has been criticized by managers. When Eric Cantona famously leapt into the stand at Crystal Palace to attack an abusive supporter, the furore around his assault and punishment soon gave way to a wider consensus that club stewards had a clear responsibility to curb spectator excesses. As the old working class broke up in the 1970s and 1980s, the established traditions of civic rivalry and decent partisanship also declined, leaving opposing supporters without anything in common but their mutual dislike.

This venom was watered down by the forces of the market, which remade football as a classless commercial entertainment in the 1990s. The 'new football' of the 1990s was not just a matter of old wine in new bottles. The old associations remained deeply entrenched, especially at the lower levels of the Football League, but Sky broadcasting meant that fans could follow the big teams without going to see them. Also the Taylor Report into the Hillsborough disaster of 1989 changed the arrangement of grounds for good. Smaller capacity all-seater stadia replaced the legendary terraces of the North Bank and the Stretford End. Even the Liverpool Kop was transformed in the name of safety and profit. British football at the highest level moved closer to the general European pattern and stopped being a working-class sport. A virtuous cycle took hold in the 1990s as the game was successfully repackaged as fashionable, sexy and classless.

Mass consumption and global marketing co-existed with older loyalties and landscapes. The changing, channel-hopping, style-obsessed electronic culture of the late twentieth century took to footballers as fashion icons. Young fans adopted star players and successful teams ever more promiscuously as clubs marketed their wares nationally and globally. The older territorial link between clubs and supporters seemed to be breaking down, at least at the top level where many of the stars were foreign. Admired and resented in equal measure 'Man U' were the talismanic team of the new football, bringing their reign to a climax in the last year of the twentieth century with the Premier League Championship, the FA Cup and the European Cup.

Yet this kind of designer fandom, epitomized by the marriage of Victoria Adams ('Posh Spice') to David Beckham, co-existed alongside an atavistic sense of place. Manchester United famously have local players like Ryan Giggs and Paul Scholes and there is a huge reserve of regional support. Similarly, in the north-east older forms of allegiance exist alongside the new. The new supporters who fill the Stadium of Light are a mixture of those traditional Sunderland fans from the days of Roker Park who can afford the new prices and a broader cross-section of the provincial middle class. The same is true of the Riverside Stadium in Middlesbrough and of Newcastle. A new pattern is establishing itself throughout football with successful but relatively unfashionable clubs like Leicester making great efforts to capture the family audience. Women are attending football matches in greater numbers. Although they still make up only 10 to 15 per cent of most crowds, territorial identity is crossing the gender divide.

It is also crossing ethnic barriers. The conventional wisdom that Asians don't play football has recently been strongly challenged.[8] There is a striking absence of Asian players at the top level but plenty of participants below, often playing in local leagues. The sociology of football is finally catching up with the changing social structure of modern Britain, although the perception of Asians as physically less robust combined with residual race prejudice is still an obstacle to full integration. 'Why haven't India or Pakistan qualified for the World Cup?', runs the old joke. 'Because every time they get a corner, they open a shop.' This white perception distorts reality. While it is true that Asians often have small businesses, it does not follow that they avoid sport, especially amongst second and third generation males. Gradually, more positive educational, work and leisure experiences may lead Asians to identify more closely with an urban community which is both multicultural and integrated. After a succession of racist rebuffs, especially evident in Yorkshire cricket, a fragile process of identification is starting to take root. Logically, the same should happen in football. England's first indigenous Asian international should prove highly influential.

West Indian men have broken through the race barrier as players but are still underrepresented on the terraces. The fierce competitiveness of top class football meant that merit conquered prejudice. Clubs could not afford to ignore the claims of black players if their rivals were profiting from the new pool of talent. In this way, old rivalries could work in socially progressive ways. Viv Anderson and John Barnes were the first star black players in the 1980s, enduring the taunts of banana throwing bigots and hooligans to become role models for younger players who flocked to the game. Ian Wright became an iconic figure, especially in London's black community. Yet black Britons did not show the same enthusiasm for watching the game. Spiralling ticket costs had some part in this but residual racism on the terraces was probably more important. Black people did not feel quite at home in a world built upon historic territorial antipathy between white communities.

The tension between old and new forms of support was most sharply delineated in what became a cult book, bridging a gap between serious creative writing and feature journalism. Nick Hornby has spawned a whole new genre of creative writing which crosses the barrier of popular and elite culture. *Fever Pitch* is the semi-autobiographical story of a middle-class boy from Maidenhead, clinging to a relationship with his divorced father through football and reinventing himself as a fanatical working-class Arsenal fan. This work struck a chord beyond football. Middle-class women read it as a way of understanding the archaic territorial obsessions of 'new men' and legitimized football amongst the 'chattering classes'. *Fever Pitch* explores identity, not in the sense of growing up with a team in a traditional community but rather the opposite: living on the geographical and social fringes of a sport steeped in older urban loyalties and adopting a new identity through football.

The English

The Cup Final provides a bridge between club and national loyalties. As Jeff Hill has shown, a public ritual grew up around this event, giving it a significance which went far beyond the actual outcome of the match. Most striking was the programme of military music and pre-match community singing, which began between the wars, and included 'Abide With Me'. A hymn about death at a festive sporting occasion was a peculiarly English innovation. But one which made sense in the aftermath of the First World War. What is more surprising is that it was still being sung fifty years later. The original logic had been long forgotten but it became a cherished English ritual along with the trip to Wembley itself, the pre-match build-up which provided a rare opportunity for extensive televised football, and the presentation and parading of the Cup in the presence of royalty. England enjoyed this game as a nation and enjoyed the fact it was so widely followed around the world. By the 1950s even *The Times* acknowledged that football was too important to be left to the masses. It was part of the fabric of English national life.[9]

Professional football involved such intense club loyalty that international rivalries were pushed into second place. The England national team was revered and supported, of course, but it was not followed with such intense passion in the post-war decade as it was later. There were constant complaints that the FA selection committee was too southern and amateurish, biased against the north despite the preponderance of northern stars: the slightly built, blond-haired Wilf Mannion who grew up in the shadow of Middlesbrough's ground; Raich Carter, a publican's son from Sunderland; Stan Mortensen from South Shields; Tommy Lawton and Tom Finney from Lancashire; and Matthews himself from Stoke. There was pride in the national team, which was expected to beat all other teams. Passionate support, however, was still a club phenomenon. The English football public seemed more concerned that Stanley Matthews would finally get a Cup-winner's medal in the 1953 Cup Final against Bolton than with the Magyar destruction of the myth of English invincibility later in the year. Similarly, it was the Busby Babes who caught the public imagination rather than England's attempts to qualify for the World Cup in Sweden in 1958. Historically, English and British nationalism – the two were often inextricable in the English mind – had other global and imperial priorities. International success at football was satisfying but not central to the national psyche. English self-confidence meant that football did not have to bear the weight of national expectation it aroused in Scotland.

However, this historic superiority, which had allowed the English to take a relatively relaxed attitude to success in world football, was coming to an end. The loss of Suez and rapid African decolonization came as a shock to the English. Combined with the marginalizing of Britain in the cold war and de Gaulle's veto of British membership of the new European Economic Community, England's world prestige was suddenly and sharply diminished. The English could no longer afford to view the efforts of its national teams with such apparent detachment. Winning became more important. The popular press, sharpened by the increasingly chauvinist tone of the new tabloids, saw England's victory of 1966 as a restoration of the natural order of things.

The press and public had built up the event for months before, although north of the border a mood of resentful silence prevailed. Scotland hadn't qualified for an event on their doorstep for which

England, as hosts, were not required to qualify. A total of 1.6 million tickets were sold. After the drama of the theft of the Cup and its recovery in a bush in South London by a dog called 'Pickles', which was given a medal and a year's supply of treats 'for outstanding service to world football', the tournament began for England with a dreary goalless draw with Uruguay. But with Brazil falling by the wayside and a bad-tempered 1–0 victory over Argentina, England were in the semi-final. A goal in each half by Bobby Charlton took them past a strong Portuguese team and into the final. England had played at Wembley throughout, which foreigners including the Scots thought was unfair. English luck continued when a Russian linesman ruled that the ball had crossed the goal line in extra time to put England 3–2 ahead, to which Hurst, completing his hat-trick, added a fourth in the dying minutes. Kenneth Wolstenholme saw some spectators encroaching on the pitch, 'they think it's all over . . . it is now', he said as Hurst's shot went high into the net.

For a few years England had a team to challenge the best in the world. This was the sixties when Britain briefly led the world in other areas of popular culture like music and fashion. But national resurgence was short-lived. A narrow defeat in the quarter final in Mexico in 1970 against Germany – Alf Ramsay famously took Bobby Charlton off during the match and Gordon Banks, the goalkeeper, was sick – could be explained as a heroic defeat. But failing to get to the finals in either 1974 or 1978 could not, especially as Scotland qualified on both occasions. Reaching the quarter finals in 1982 and 1986, where England were robbed by 'the hand of God', was not enough for a nation where expectation continued to outstrip performance. Success in 1990 where England lost a famous semi-final penalty shoot-out against Germany was soon forgotten as England again failed to qualify in 1994 and went out against Argentina in 1998. The intensity of national support was almost in inverse proportion to the success of the national team.

The contemporary cultural dominance of football has been such that it is easy to forget cricket commanded more interest in post-war England. Test matches, especially against Australia, were the most important English sporting events. Great batsmen, in particular, had an iconic status, and a surprisingly large number of female admirers. At least this was true of Denis Compton, that son of a north London lorry driver who left school at fourteen, and looked like a public school gent. This 'Happy Warrior' played in a dashing style and in the summer of 1947 broke the record for the number of runs and the number of centuries scored in a season.[10] England was restored to itself and, after the sufferings of war and post-war austerity, temporarily brightened. The sun shone after a terrible winter, Compton and Edrich destroyed

South Africa and the following year Bradman led Australia for the last time in England, failing by a duck and a decimal point to achieve a career average of one hundred in Test Matches. England respected Bradman, the son of a Suffolk artisan, and his knighthood in 1948 was both a form of personal recognition and an acknowledgement of the cultural importance of the Ashes.

To be made captain of the England cricket team was still the highest honour in English sport. The opening up of this position to a professional with the appointment of Len Hutton in 1952 was a class breakthrough and a breath of fresh air in the stuffy world of the MCC. As we have seen Hutton came from a working-class Yorkshire family but had distanced himself from his northern roots, softened his vowels and sent his sons to public school. The public required their heroes to embody a certain kind of Englishness. Len Hutton fulfilled this role until his retirement in 1955. He was happily married to the sister of another Yorkshire player, successful in business and a straightforward character whose main fault was a rumoured reluctance to buy a round.[11] Wally Hammond, the greatest all-rounder since Grace, was a sublime player but a poor post-war captain. Worse still, he had treated his first wife badly, divorcing her for a South African beauty queen he had met during the war. He was haughty with the press and he was quietly dropped from public life, slipping off to South Africa and relative obscurity.[12] Jack Hobbs, however, Hammond's predecessor as England's greatest batsman – and a thoroughly nice man – was rewarded for his services to English cricket with a knighthood in 1953.

Hammond had transgressed the rules of English society both on and off the pitch, offending against good fellowship as well as respectability. Compton liked a drink and married several times as did his Middlesex and England batting partner, Bill Edrich. But in their case the press and public turned a blind eye because they were friendly and accessible individuals. There was no question of sensational public exposés of what went on during the tours of Australia. Compton got away with being a bit of a 'lad', always arriving late and occasionally dishevelled after a night on the town. The English had a soft spot for Compton's swashbuckling style. Ted Dexter was the last of the great amateur batsmen. 'Lord Ted's' aggressive stroke-play and penchant for motorbikes and sports cars appealed to what was left of the romantic ethos of elite English sport. In the 1980s David Gower took over the role of the aristocratic 'natural', who somehow found himself in the wrong century – and has played up to the image on television ever since.

Cricket failed to mobilize the enthusiasm of immigrants from the West Indies and the Indian subcontinent for the game, which was still rooted in a 'village green' dream of England. The best-known personalities in the game ceased to be the leading players. Instead radio and television commentators like John Arlott and Brian Johnston ('Johnners') were seen as English symbols on account of their love for cricket. Cricket slipped gently into self-parody and an increasingly second-rank status in terms of the rest of the world. Lord MacLaurin, the business brain behind the Tesco supermarket chain, was brought in to revitalize the game from the grass roots in the 1990s. But by then the unthinkable had happened. England was a second-rank cricket power and the national team had become almost a national joke.

It would be quite wrong to think that the English had ceased to care about winning cricket matches. The public was increasingly volatile, losing interest quickly when things went wrong but suddenly finding new reserves of enthusiasm when there was a chance of success. From the 1980s a core of fans, 'The Barmy Army', followed the England cricket team in a new kind of festive tourism. When the cricket World Cup was held in England in 1999 it was widely seen as a perfect opportunity to relaunch the game. But England were eliminated half-way through and interest collapsed. National fervour came mainly from ethnic minorities, especially Indians and Pakistanis, supporting their former homelands. The refusal of West Indian immigrants to support England had infuriated the Right in the 1980s, and the leading Thatcherite, Norman Tebbit, in particular. His nationalist doctrine held that all who lived in England had a patriotic duty to the England team. By implication those who failed the 'Tebbit Test' should 'go home'. The possibility of multinational sporting loyalties was denied along with the wider notion of multiculturalism itself. The debate rumbled on with a highly controversial article in *Wisden Cricket Monthly* in 1995 entitled 'IS IT IN THE BLOOD?' which claimed that black players lacked commitment to the England team, whilst defending the loyalty of white Africans like Hick and Lamb.[13]

As cricket lost its aura of national prestige and amateur virtue, rugby union increasingly took over the mantle of pure English sport. English rugby union was a predominantly southern public school phenomenon. There was no national competitive structure. Clubs played their own fixtures and were run for their middle-class members as players and spectators. London Welsh or London Scottish were clubs based around expatriate allegiances whilst Harlequins or Saracens had a social rather than a territorial base in the west of London. In the 1950s and 1960s the Rugby Football Union picked a national team, which attracted large crowds to Twickenham. But it was not until the televising of the Five Nations championship that rugby became accessible as a popular sport for the spectator. Bill Macleren and his fellow commentators explained the rules and the traditions just as colour television conveyed the speed and excitement of the game.

Rugby began to get a wider audience in England. When football abandoned the Home Internationals in the 1980s, rugby was there to provide an exciting alternative. Unlike football, the famous names of early English rugby like Stoop, Poulton-Palmer and Wavell-Wakefield had never meant much to the wider English public. But rugby's new role as a vehicle for a more popular English nationalism changed this, making the England captain into a national celebrity. First there was Bill Beaumont, bulky and brave with an easy geniality in front of the camera; then came Will Carling, the most successful England captain of modern times and the first to experience the full force of public indignation when his private life was revealed in the press. A lucrative series of farewell games and speaking engagements had to be called off as the tabloid press, having already exposed an alleged relationship with Princess Diana, turned on him for leaving his partner, who happened to be the sister-in-law of the wholesome footballer Gary Lineker. When Carling's successor as England captain was temporarily dropped over drug allegations in 1999, rugby was at last forced into the same camp as football. The purity of the amateur game so prized by the English elite had gone.

Scotland

Rugby in Scotland also had a middle-class image to which was added a rural populist element in the shape of Border farmers and artisans. For all the passion for Rugby in Kelso, Hawick and Jedburgh, however, it was the 'former pupils' of Edinburgh's private schools who dominated the game. The national stadium was appropriately located in an exclusive Victorian suburb of Edinburgh. Scottish rugby was quite different in its ethos from Welsh rugby. As in England, Scottish rugby has become more popular and professional in the 1990s. But this has been a painful and unfinished process. For most of the post-war period it remained a privileged enclave of middle-class patriotism. The Scots, of course, relished beating England for the Calcutta Cup but the tone was more subdued and gentlemanly than football. At first, rugby was relatively untouched by the emergent forces of Scottish nationalism. The rule of Scotland from the Home Counties by a female Conservative gave rugby internationals a rather more nationalist tone with the singing of 'Flower of Scotland' and the waving of the Scottish flag. Genteel Murrayfield had to be asked not to boo the English.

Of course, for most of the second half of the century it was football, which inspired popular nationalism in Scotland. Crowds of 100,000 and more – some of the largest in the world at that time – watched England–Scotland games at Hampden Park. Despite Scotland's having only a tenth of the population of England, honours were even between the two countries in football. This was a source of immense satisfaction to a historic nation which felt itself under the economic and political heel of the English. Beating England, especially at Wembley, was the best way to deal with the condescension or indifference, real or imagined, of the English.

Hence the enormous success of the 'Wembley clubs'.[14] Men would save at work or through the local pub for the biennial trip to London. There were ecstatic scenes in 1967 when a team that included Denis Law and Jim Baxter beat the World Champions on the very pitch where they had won the previous year. Ten years later with Kenny Dalglish in the side, Scotland won again at Wembley, prompting a pitch invasion and the digging up of pieces of the turf. England was appalled but the Scots were unrepentant. Scotland began to think she could win the 1978 World Cup in Argentina, for which England again had failed to qualify. Nemesis was swift. 'Ally's Army' came back from Argentina having lost to Peru and drawn with Iran. Despite victory over Holland, the losing finalists, Scottish self-confidence had taken a battering which some thought had a bearing on the failure of the Devolution referendum to get a clear mandate in 1979.

Beneath the increasingly festive style of the 'tartan army', which tried to distance itself from the crude aggression of a section of the England fans, there was a divided sense of cultural identity.[15] On the one hand, there was the tough Presbyterian tradition of hard teamwork instilled into players at Rangers. Big defenders like George Young, who captained Scotland in the 1950s, and John Greig were one kind of Scot. On the other, there was the ball-playing, creative 'Celt' like Celtic's Jimmy Johnstone. The best Scottish teams combined a 'Big Man' and a 'Jinky'. Dour efficient Rangers had a supremely creative midfielder in Jim Baxter whilst Jock Stein's Celtic, who in 1967 became the first British side to win the European Cup, had strength at the back as well as flair in attack. Combining the two was never easy and in Scotland's case was complicated by a marked prejudice against the 'Anglos', who had forsaken the Scottish league to play in England.

Denis Law, Scotland's most successful post-war goal scorer, is a case in point. Law was born in Aberdeen in 1940 but played all his club football in England. Despite his success south of the border with Manchester United, Law was a typically anti-English Scot, who famously played a round of golf while England won the World Cup.

The Scots themselves oscillated between adulation and denigration of their great striker. When the team won, the brilliance of the 'Anglos' like Law was acknowledged. But when the side lost – and there were some spectacular defeats such as the 9–3 by England in 1961 – the wrath of the Scots was turned on the overpaid, individualistic 'Anglos'. An 'all tartan' option of a national team composed of only Scottish league players would then be tried. When this failed to deliver, the 'Anglos' would be recalled.[16]

And so it went on until Scottish football itself began to change profoundly in the 1980s and 1990s. Celtic and Rangers increasingly scoured the English and then the continental markets for talent. Great forwards were especially thin on the ground in a country which had always been able to produce them. No one could really say why. Was it the deindustrialization of Scotland? The mines and shipyards that had for so long been the heart and soul of Scottish football had gone. Schools no longer seemed to care so much about football and traffic had killed off street games. Just when the rewards for playing had become so great, Scotland was bereft of great players. When England faced Scotland for a play-off position in the European Nations Cup in November 1999, even Scotland accepted that England had almost all the best players. England duly sailed through the first leg in Glasgow 2–0. Not even the Scots gave themselves much chance in the second leg at Wembley. And yet they went to London, won 1–0 and almost forced England out. This was a heroic failure in the purest Scottish tradition. Better to win the last match at Wembley and the last of the century than qualify by a series of dull, efficient results.

Some thought the new Scottish parliament would mean football would become less important in the national psyche. Clearly this was not so. For weeks the nation was obsessed with the fixture. The 'auld enemy' rhetoric was duly revived but this time there was a backlash against extreme chauvinism. Anti-Englishness became an issue in its own right and the media split over whether anglophobia was racist. 'Give us an Assembly, we'll give you back your Wembley', the fans had chanted after digging up the turf in 1977. Twenty years later they had their own parliament. Beating England, of course, was still sweet. Football was still a national symbol but it was no longer a substitute for the sovereign rights of a historic nation.

Wales

Rugby in Wales was an even greater cultural force than football in Scotland. Scottish football was a class sport where Welsh rugby was classless, binding the nation together in a way which was unique in the British Isles and could only really be compared with New Zealand. There was, of course, support for the Welsh football team, especially in North Wales, in Wrexham and in parts of Cardiff and Swansea. But this was small beer beside the collective passion for rugby. Rugby belonged to all of Wales: to the elite schools that founded the early teams and the liberal professions that still loved it; to the miners of the South Wales valleys who took up the game and made it their own; to the policemen and the steelworkers who were so often at the heart of the team; and to those who became teachers instead of following their fathers to the pit. Those who initially took the teaching route included Barry John, Gareth Edwards and Gerald Davies – the incomparable backs of the great Welsh team of the early 1970s.

Wales, of course, had a long history of David and Goliath victories over England beginning in the 1890s with the first hero of Welsh rugby, Arthur Gould, running through disappointing years in the Depression where the best players 'went north' to play Rugby League, to the glory days of the early fifties. Wales carried all before them in 1949–50 and again in 1951–2 winning the Five Nations and the Triple Crown (beating all three other home nations in a single season) to take the Grand Slam. The star players of this team became national heroes: Ken Jones, who had reached the semi-final of the 1948 Olympic 100 metres, tearing down the wing for the line; Bleddyn Williams, the stylish centre and the son of a coal trimmer whose eight sons all played for Cardiff; and, of course, Cliff Morgan of 'Trebanog, a precipitous offshoot of the Rhondda . . . from a non-conformist home where Mam ruled and Sunday was for chapel', the stocky fly half brought up in the Urdd (the League of Welsh Youth) who could sing snatches from Handel's 'Messiah' with the same gusto as he would shrug off a tackle. Refusing the lure of Rugby League, he joined the BBC and became an influential radio presenter, celebrating the myth-making and moral qualities of sport.[17]

The Welsh triumphs of the 1970s were even more spectacular than the early fifties, winning the Five Nations Championship six times between 1968–9 and 1979–80. The media-led cult of celebrity, which had begun in football around George Best, began to invade Welsh rugby – still an amateur sport – and seems to have led to the early retirement of Barry John, whose place was ably taken by Llanelli's Phil Bennett. Wales went from strength to strength. However, the success of the national team temporarily obscured the changing patterns of work and education, which would combine to bring the game into crisis from the late 1980s onwards.

National expectation was so great and the playing base so small that

Wales had to have its schools, pits and factories all pulling together and fully committed to stay at the top. This delicate balance was disturbed by a collapse of traditional industry and a transformation of the secondary educational system. In a fine essay, which brings up-to-date their classic history of Welsh rugby, Dai Smith and Gareth Williams note the parallels between the 1980s and the 1930s as bleak decades for Welsh industry and Welsh rugby.[18] But with a difference. For in the 1980s it was not a matter of trade recession but of the permanent closure. There were 27,000 miners in 36 pits in 1981. This was few enough by the standards of earlier times when there had been 50,000 miners in the Rhondda alone. But in 1990 there was just one working pit, Tower Colliery, which became a workers cooperative in 1995. There were no miners and precious few steelworkers to maintain the host of small teams that had fed the big clubs. Worse still, the privileged position of rugby in the state grammar schools was eroded by the creation of larger comprehensives running fewer teams. Teachers were increasingly resentful of government neglect and the demands of the national curriculum. The likes of 'Ned' Gribble, who had nurtured Cliff Morgan at Tonyfrail Grammar School, had gone and new physical education teachers were urged to consider a wider variety of sporting activity. 'By the early 1990s fewer than thirty state schools in the whole of south Wales were playing any meaningful rugby on Saturday mornings.'[19]

Small wonder that Wales failed to win a single game in the Five Nations championship in 1990 and 1991. England triumphed at Cardiff Arms Park for the first time since 1963. The rot set in and Ireland, historically the weakest of the home nations, beat Wales on four successive occasions between 1995 and 1997. Welsh rugby was in danger of going under whilst Will Carling's England enjoyed its most sustained period of success for many years. It was the fervour and constancy of Welsh support combined with a gifted New Zealand coach, Graham Henry, that turned Wales around. Henry admitted he had not realized that 'the crowd would regard itself as part of the team' in a way that even surpassed New Zealand's level of devotion and identification. Wales duly beat France in a brilliant match in Paris in March 1999 and then beat England at Wembley in April in the dying seconds of the game. Wembley had been a temporary home during the building of the new Millennium Stadium on the site of the old Cardiff Arms Park. Wales inaugurated the new national stadium by staging the Rugby World Cup and singing 'Land of My Fathers' – or 'grandfathers' in the case of several Englishmen and New Zealanders in the side.

The Welsh were adjusting to new realities, taking advantage of the rugby diaspora to help compensate for demographic size and endowing the new 'foreign' internationals with honorary Welshness. The Scots did the same. The legalizing of professionalism in 1995 meant that a new clutch of talented players could play club rugby in Britain and possibly be available for UK national teams. The world had moved on. As older sources of talent dried up, new ones emerged to carry the banner of nations with which they had little previous connection. The public no longer seemed to care. What would have been heresy in the 1970s was orthodoxy in the late 1990s. What mattered to the Welsh was that they kept winning or, at least, avoided humiliation. Who did it for them was a secondary consideration.

Northern Ireland

In sport, as in so many other respects, Northern Ireland was unique. In no other part of the United Kingdom was sport so bitterly divided and politicized. Two different communities inhabited the same territory and aligned themselves with two opposed national traditions. For the Protestants, whose ancestors had colonized Ulster and who made up around 60 per cent of the population, union with Great Britain was the cornerstone upon which their lives were built. The Catholic republicans of west Belfast, the Bogside of 'Derry' (even the city's name was disputed), and border areas like South Armagh, denied the very legitimacy of the Northern Ireland state itself. A devolved government with a built-in unionist majority and a system of residential and occupational segregation was policed by the Royal Ulster Constabulary (RUC). An uneasy truce held until the late 1960s when a Catholic civil rights movement provoked a violent unionist backlash. This in turn led to the formation of the Provisional IRA, a bombing and asssasination campaign and the deployment of large numbers of British troops for almost thirty years.

Sport was profoundly affected by this climate of sectarian hatred and violence. Instead of representing a national consensus, sport in Northern Ireland both reflected and exacerbated existing national divisions. Many within the Catholic community refused to play 'British' sports at all and formed a particularly militant element within the Gaelic Athletic Associaton (GAA), which had been formed in the late nineteenth century to challenge what was perceived as British sporting imperialism. The GAA proved exceptionally successful in Ireland before and after independence. GAA clubs were to be found in all the Catholic enclaves of Ulster. Until the early 1970s GAA members were officially forbidden to play other sports and under Article 21 no member of the British army or the RUC could join a GAA club. GAA clubs in 'the north of Ireland', as republicans like to call it, have insisted on retaining this ban and in conducting their meetings in the Irish language. GAA clubs were always a bastion of militant Irish nationalism and became an obvious target for the RUC and the Protestant paramilitaries during the 'Troubles'. The three thousandth victim of the Troubles was killed outside a Belfast GAA club and in 1988 Aiden McAnespie was shot dead by the British army at a checkpoint while on his way to play a GAA game. This, of course, made the GAA into an even better recruiting ground for the IRA. The cycle of retribution was remorseless and sport was trapped within it.[20]

Soccer was a shared enthusiasm across the sectarian divide. But far from healing communal hatreds, it exacerbated them. Since independence there had been two Irish Leagues: the original Irish Football Association now ruled only in the north whilst the Football Association of Ireland ran the south. In the north the usual civic tribalism of football was overlaid with a deeper menace. Between the wars Linfield and Belfast Celtic had emerged as the leading Protestant and Catholic teams. Their games were frequently marked by crowd violence. On Boxing Day 1948 the Linfield crowd invaded the pitch at the end of the match and attacked the Belfast Celtic team, causing serious injuries, including breaking the legs of a Belfast Celtic forward. He never played again. Belfast Celtic withdrew from senior football in Ulster and never came back. This was a different and darker world where nationalism was neither festive nor ritualized.

Football became impossible on the inter-communal level once the Troubles began. Derry City, the leading Catholic club, had difficulty getting Protestant teams to play at Brandywell in the heart of the Bogside and allowed their ground to be used for civil rights and nationalist political rallies. On 11 September 1971 local youths set fire to the bus belonging to the visiting Ballymena team and there was serious rioting and gunfire outside the ground. Derry were forbidden to use their home pitch by the RUC and the staunchly Protestant Irish Football Association. Derry City withdrew from the Ulster League in 1973 and spent twelve years in the wilderness before gaining admission to play professionally in the Republic.

Sporting nationalism was a strange beast in the island of Ireland, varying greatly from sport to sport. Rugby, predominantly the sport of the privately educated urban middle classes, was an all-Ireland structure in which the social solidarity of professional men kept nationalist antagonism at bay. Jackie Kyle, the star of the immediate post-war years, was a Protestant graduate of Queen's University, Belfast. So was the greatest of all the post-war players, Mike Gibson, a Belfast solicitor, who along with another northerner, Willie John McBride, dominated

Irish international rugby through the 1960s and 1970s. These men played at Lansdowne Road in Dublin under the Irish flag, wore green and yet remained British. This required a supple and detached view of sport, which was beyond most of the public, especially in the north.

Like rugby, boxing had only one governing body, the Irish Amateur Boxing Association. The IABA was recognized on both sides of the border and by the International Olympic Association. This meant Ulster boxers had to fight in the Olympic Games for the Republic of Ireland. At seventeen Wayne McCullough was the youngest competitor in the Irish team and was given the honour of carrying the Irish flag into the Olympic arena in 1988. The only problem was that he was a Protestant from the Shankhill Road. Four years later McCullough again represented Ireland in the Barcelona Olympics where he won a silver medal, and a young Dubliner, Michael Carruth, boxing in another division, won a gold. There was a great civic reception for them both in Dublin and warm words from the Taoiseach, Albert Reynolds. This stood in sharp contrast to the lukewarm reception that awaited McCullough in Belfast, to which Carruth was not even invited. Rank and file unionists could not bring themselves to celebrate anything Irish and their man's success for the Republic was an embarrassment.[21] For all his sentimental Irishness and pre-match renditions of 'Danny Boy', it was easier to accept Barry McGuigan, a Catholic from just across the border, who married a Protestant and chose to box in Britain, than a Protestant who fought for Ireland. In Northern Ireland, individual or collective sporting excellence was always seen through the lens of sectarianism. Rugby apart, sport could never rise above the brutal reality of political nationalism.

Great Britain

The imperial British state had a greater resonance within England than in Wales or Scotland or even Ulster. Englishness and Britishness were constantly confused, especially in the Home Counties. The global patterns of British sport reflected the imperial role of a great trading power, and the introverted nature of a group of peoples who had always seen themselves as set apart from Europe. Hence British representation in world sport was really quite limited. Association football, the most popular of all sports, had no representative British dimension at all. No one seriously thought of combining the might of the United Kingdom into a single team as all other states did with their component 'regions'. The power of British football was expressed through English club sides: George Best of Belfast, Bobby Charlton, a Geordie, and

Denis Law from Aberdeen in Matt Busby's Manchester United attack in the 1960s, and the 1986 Liverpool Cup-winning team was Welsh, Scottish and Irish. The British preferred to keep their old national loyalties instead of pooling their talents to win.

Rugby was different. In 1924 a British touring team was created to take on the might of South Africa and New Zealand. This proved popular with rugby fans, although the fact the British Lions did not play in Britain meant they never acquired a wider British following. However, outstanding service against the All Blacks or the Springboks came to be seen as the real test of rugby greatness. Cliff Morgan was voted 'player of the series' in the 1955 Lions tour of South Africa whilst Gareth Edwards went on three tours including the famous British victory over the All Blacks in 1971 – the only British touring team ever to win a series there – and the even more remarkable unbeaten South African tour of 1974, both under the captaincy of Ireland's Willie John McBride. The British Lions came from the whole of the British Isles. England had no special place and Bill Beaumont was the first Englishman to lead the Lions for fifty years.

The public schoolboys, who made up so much of the crowd at Twickenham and Murrayfield, had been keener on mixed touring teams like the Barbarians. The 'Babas' were defiantly British and amateur, priding themselves on taking only the most entertaining players of the home nations and playing for the fun of it. They have faded almost into insignificance now, a kind of bourgeois anachronism, victims of the demands of the professional game. The singing of 'Flower of Scotland' and England's incongruous 'Swing Low Sweet Chariot' are part of a wider sense of belonging to a national rather than a British rugby culture.

Television has not succeeded in creating a great spectator demand for more all-British teams. The formerly British Ryder Cup team, which included Ireland, is now European. To abandon a regularly defeated British team for a more powerful European one which includes Spaniards, Germans, Italians and Swedes has proved very successful in terms of results, marketing and support. Anti-americanism triumphed over Euro-scepticism. The success of the European Tour in golf and of the Ryder Cup team has given large numbers of television fans a sense of European identity, cheering Swedes and Spaniards as well as the British.

The Davis Cup involves a British team but it has been too English and too middle class to catch the public mood. Tim Henman is an appropriately Home Counties hero. Wimbledon is both the glory and the weakness of British tennis, tying the sport culturally to suburban England. Too much of the national effort was focused around London for a few weeks a year. Tennis has been caught in a downward spiral.

Lack of success breeds lack of interest, which in turn restricts support. An English winner at Wimbledon would change all this and make a British hero of the champion. But would this make the Davis Cup matter to the British people?

The Olympic Games has been a crucial arena for Britain to compete as a nation-state. Historically, the British had never been completely comfortable with an event created by a Frenchman, even if he was inspired by Victorian public school sport. The British tended to doubt the genuine amateurism of foreigners. The British Olympic Association was expected to raise its own money. Sport was still held to be a private affair, belonging to civil society, into which the government ought not to interfere. The crowning glory of post-war British athletics was not an Olympic gold medal but a domestic affair, run by undergraduates at Oxford in 1954. Roger Bannister, the first man to break the four-minute mile, had come fourth in the 1500 metres in Helsinki. By the next Olympics at Melbourne, he had retired.

As the Soviet Union and the United States fought out the cold war through Olympic track and field events, the British not only failed to fund Olympic competitors seriously but divided their attention between the Olympics and the Commonwealth Games, which became increasingly important as the old Empire turned into an association of self-governing states partly held together by the legacy of athletic sports. Unlike the Olympics, British athletes in the Commonwealth Games reverted to the domestic pattern of competition in four national teams.

Television clearly gave a new national significance to Britain's role in the Olympics. Technology and Olympic ceremony combined to give a new impetus to the United Kingdom as a unitary state. The sight of athletes and swimmers receiving their medals, watching the hoisting of the Union Jack and hearing the national anthem was an intense patriotic and public moment. As Britain's world power diminished, so the ability to produce world-class athletes came to be more highly prized. Fortunately for a Britain ardent for Olympic glory, women's sport came to the rescue with new track stars like Mary Rand, Anne Packer and Lillian Board. Formerly, the role of British sporting hero had been the preserve of men. Now it was women who were staking Britain's claim to world recognition. Olympic success in the decades which followed switched between the sexes but was the property of neither. Mary Peters won a pentathlon gold at 33. This was the great British achievement of the 1972 Games just as Coe, Ovett and Cram dominated in 1980 and 1984 – the same year that Tessa Sanderson, who competed in a record five Olympics from 1976, won a javelin gold.

Increasingly, in the 1980s and 1990s it was black athletes from the inner city not white middle England who led Britain's Olympic revival: Daley Thompson, Linford Christie, Colin Jackson and other outstanding black sprinters of the 1990s along with Tessa Sanderson, Fatima Whitbread and more recently Denise Lewis. Here was a new British athletic identity forged through multiracial sport symbolic of a changing multicultural Britain. Stuart Hall, an influential contemporary intellectual, has remarked that 'I used to be an Afro-Caribbean. And now I would regard myself as black British . . . I am you know one of the new cosmopolitans. There are millions of us.' He added that his son, a student in Edinburgh, 'calls himself English in Scotland and black or Asian British in England'.[22]

Britishness, according to Hall, 'has a future especially among the ethnic minorities'. To be a minority in a mixed federal Britain is perhaps more comfortable than in a devolved Scotland or Wales built around the idea of ethnic and historic difference. It remains to be seen whether black sportsmen and women can wear leeks or tartan and will be able to represent the nations of Britain as effectively as they now represent Great Britain. Race, of course, can still saturate the language of the British media. Tabloid editors, for example, were quick to exploit the white obsession about black genitals. They clearly thought Linford Christie lacked a sense of humour for getting so upset about press fascination with his 'lunchbox'. Even in the late 1990s there was still some way to go before black athletes would be treated with the same consideration as whites, though the new media were no respecters of the privacy of white celebrities either.[23]

Shrouded in the Union Jack, Olympic athletes, white and black, embraced professionalism, plunging into fashion and pop culture alongside new bands, videos and football in the New Labour rebranding of Britain as 'Cool Britannia'. The festive waving of the national flag became commonplace. Just as the United Kingdom was profoundly restructured through devolution, the Union Jack and the English Cross of St George were more popular than ever, printed on hats and shirts, painted on bodies and faces, and draped around the shoulders. The two flags were still confused and mixed by the English at Wembley or Wimbledon in an unintentionally accurate expression of the problematic identity of Britain.

Of all the sporting figures who have come to stand for Britain, the fighter has been the most enduring as a national symbol. The founder of boxing, the eighteenth-century pugilist Jack Broughton, was probably Britain's first sporting hero. Britain liked to think of itself as strong and resilient, an embattled island race, symbolized by John Bull, who was both English and British in his associations. In the course of the twentieth century the boxer came to stand for Britain's heroic resistance to the overwhelming might of the United States: from Tommy Farr, the Rhondda heavyweight, taking Joe Louis the distance in the 1930s, through to Henry Cooper's 'hammer' blow to Cassius Clay in 1963. This was played and replayed on British television. Though he lost the bout – and the rematch with the renamed Muhammad Ali – Cooper became an instantly recognizable figure throughout Britain, appearing in pantomime and in numerous adverts.

His successor as the kind-hearted heavyweight was Frank Bruno, who appeared driven by the same patriotic simplicity as Cooper. Bruno was another 'panto' star and celebrity panelist but with a difference: he was black. No one was more British or patriotic than Frank Bruno, who was very popular as a consequence. But this popularity attracted criticism from radicals for 'selling out' to the stereotypical white image of a big, simple, black immigrant. Bruno was considered too grateful and deferential, and his image was manipulated in a condescending way, which kept black people in their place. A different way of looking at his career, however, might stress his successful use of racial stereo-types for his own benefit and the way his love of Britain made it harder for racists to label blacks as unpatriotic. Heroic resistance against the toughest American opponents, notably his five rounds with Mike Tyson at his prime, earned Bruno a *Sun* headline that read: 'Arise Sir Frank'.

Lennox Lewis has been a much more successful boxer but has found it hard to succeed in the same way as a British hero. A black Londoner, who emigrated to Canada at the age of twelve and won an Olympic gold as a Canadian, it was harder for Lewis to play the patriotic card when he resumed British citizenship as a professional boxer. His accent was mid-Atlantic and his style less obviously populist. But his career went from strength to strength, culminating in winning the world title in 1999 for which he was voted the BBC Sports Personality of the Year. Naseem Hamed, the leading flyweight in the world, who came from a Yemeni family in Sheffield, was even further removed from conventional images of Britishness and appeared to care little about his popularity. He was arrogant and unsentimental about Britain but pointed out that he was a national hero in the Yemen. Accordingly Prince Naseem did not receive the kind of public adulation his achievements merited. He didn't play the game.

Different sports had different structures and myths celebrating the unity and diversity of the United Kingdom and its component parts. Representative sport works at several levels, both asserting identities and transcending them. The club gives way to the nation, the nation sometimes bows to the state but more often does not. The role of different sports in carrying the weight of public expectation has fluctuated according to cycles of sporting success – winning teams are far more potent as symbols of identity than losing ones – and is increasingly influenced by media and marketing. Yet, this apart, there is no simple pattern. Individual fans make their own cultural arrangements and compromises. The tribalism and 'plasticity' of sport probably expresses the complexity of identity better than any other phenomenon in contemporary Britain.

7 Government

During the twentieth century the state was transformed from a very limited system of force and regulation to a provider of a much more extensive network of services.[1] Since the end of the Second World War we have come to expect governments to manage the economy and supply a range of social policies and services popularly known as the welfare state. Government intervened much more in individual lives, and although not all the interventions were welcome many people got into the habit of thinking that the provision of state welfare was an important part of the democratic process and some government attempts to shape behaviour a reasonable price to pay for it. Of course, hostility to state intervention persisted and it was particularly active in the fields of the arts and leisure.[2] The Attlee government's top priority was to promote economic recovery and to provide that financial security for ordinary people which had been so lacking in pre-war Britain. But the government also wanted the people to enjoy their leisure to the full. In February 1947, Michael Young produced a paper entitled 'The Enjoyment of Leisure', leisure widely interpreted to include physical recreation, in which, while recognizing enjoyable leisure as a good in itself, he also emphasized the practical benefits to society. All work and no play not only made Jack and Jill dull but in the long run would lead to reduced productivity. The ability of Britain to solve its economic problems would depend in part on the government's continuing commitment to the extension of leisure. When Stafford Cripps halved the Entertainment Tax on the theatre in 1948 to make it more accessible to working people he was reflecting this commitment.[3]

As we saw in chapter 2 the post-war Labour government did not have a sports policy. Sport was almost the quintessential voluntary activity, part of that long tradition of British voluntarism in which people pursued a wide variety of cultural, intellectual and social activities not because the state wanted them to but because they freely chose to. All British sports were anxious to retain their autonomy. Yet in the special circumstances of wartime, the British Olympic Association and influential figures from the world of sport such as Stanley Rous had looked to the state to provide aid for sport after the war. The 1944

Education Act reminded Local Education Authorities (LEAs) of their responsibility to provide facilities for sport and physical education in secondary schools. The new Ministry of Education gave some money for the employment of a small number of coaches in several sports. It channelled funds to the CCPR, some of which helped to establish Britain's first indoor sport and recreation centre at Bisham Abbey in 1946. Without government aid the 1948 Olympics could not have been held in London. Some local authorities also had a tradition of spending on facilities for recreation. But given the wider issues of reconstruction, central government was unlikely to offer sport more aid. And given sport's strong sense of independence and its muscular voluntarist ethos it might not be seeking it. In 1953, the National Playing Fields Association, whose President was the Duke of Edinburgh, launched an appeal for funds under the slogan, 'The battle for recovery will be won on the playing fields of Britain', a reference to old myths about an explanation for the victory at Waterloo in 1815 allegedly offered by the Duke of Wellington.[4]

The government could intervene in sport when it seemed in the national interest to do so. During the fuel shortages of 1947, for example, it banned not only greyhound racing but all mid-week football, amateur and professional. The outcry this latter action provoked led to the ban being lifted after two days.[5] None of this could be remotely called a sports policy. What forced a shift of direction were changes both within sport itself and, perhaps more importantly, in British society.

Influential members of the sports lobby such as the National Playing Fields Association had often pointed out the relative lack of sports facilities and how their provision was always outstripped by demand. In the mid-fifties and early sixties physical educators at the University of Birmingham produced research which showed how much better off in terms of sports funding and facilities other European countries were. Their key reforming proposal was the establishment of a representative advisory or general council capable of speaking for sport as a whole. They also raised a handful of questions which they felt it was 'a patriotic duty to answer' including whether the interests of British sport would be best served by continued participation in, or withdrawal from, international competition![6]

This was one reaction to the growing feeling, fanned by an increasingly irritated and outspoken press, that Britain, the inventor of modern sports, could no longer hold its own; not just with the major sporting powers of a free market United States and a state socialist Soviet Union, but also with smaller European nations. It reflected not only British failures at the Olympic Games but also the disappointment provoked by too many days like 29 June 1950. On that Tuesday, the West Indies won their first cricket test in England, by 326 runs, at Lord's; the England football team, in its first World Cup, lost 1–0 to the spectacularly unfancied United States; and on the second day of the lawn tennis championships at Wimbledon, the last British player in the men's singles had been eliminated. Days like this contributed to strong feelings that all was not well with British sport and led to the Central Council of Physical Recreation commissioning its own inquiry into the subject in 1957. The chairman was Sir John Wolfenden, a former public school headmaster who had won a hockey blue at Oxford. He was to produce an influential document which would be debated in Parliament and did much to persuade both politicians and sportsmen and women that there ought to be an enhanced role in sport for the public sector.[7] But even more crucial than these internal debates within the world of sport itself was the changing world outside the gymnasium, race track and sports ground.

By the end of the fifties the British people were making their great leap forward into affluence. Most of them had more money to spend and more goods on which to spend it than ever before, particularly the young. There was more leisure time than ever before, again most notably for adolescent youth. But alongside material progress had grown an apparently less disciplined society. Affluence was accompanied by a decline of deference and a rise in juvenile delinquency. Moreover one of the perceived training grounds of male youth, national service, was ended in 1959. The importation of American popular culture caused many anxious palpitations and not just among the members of the Carlton Club. But the Conservative Party did set up its own Arts and Amenities Committee at the end of the fifties to consider the whole issue of leisure and what was to be done with it. The chairman was Keith Joseph who thought that since the war the emancipation of the adolescent had taken everyone by surprise.

> Young people nowadays have more spare time, more money and more surplus energy than they have ever had before. What all too many of them lack, however, is a corresponding sense of purpose and of personal responsibility. We expect the end of 'call-up' and the 'bulge' emerging from the schools to make this a compelling issue in the early sixties. The time is therefore ripe for the Conservatives to formulate a comprehensive policy embracing sport, recreation and the arts . . . for leisure, wrongly used, constitutes a real threat to society.[8]

This emphasis on the importance to the community of sport and leisure was underlined by the Albermarle Committee on the Youth Service in England and Wales which also reported in 1960. There had to be more facilities and therefore opportunities for physical recreation.

Sports and physical activities generally were a major leisure time interest in the lives of the adolescent, an interest unrelated to academic ability or manual skill. It was an interest which cut across class lines. There was evidence that 'work and their present leisure' failed to satisfy the increased physical energies of many young people. Team games were fine but there were other activities that provided more opportunities for social mixing and which appealed especially to girls; the report then suggested badminton, camping, canoeing, dancing, fencing, golf, judo, motor racing, mountaineering, pot-holing, rambling, riding, rowing, sailing, skating, skiing, swimming, tennis and waterskiing. These could and should be available to many wage earners. The report went on to stress the need for more facilities, the wider and more intensive use of existing facilities particularly those in schools and sports clubs, and the expansion of coaching and cooperation within localities between the representatives of the youth service and those of sport.[9]

The Wolfenden Committee both contributed to and benefitted from the changing context in which these general debates about the place and future of leisure and recreation in society were conducted. Established by the Central Council of Physical Recreation, Wolfenden was a very significant moment in the history and development of British sport. It was the first time that a body of responsible men and women had sat down to examine the relationship between sport and the welfare of society.[10] The Committee recognized that British sport and recreation was in need of a new deal and to that extent Wolfenden looked bravely into the future. But the Committee was also hamstrung by history and therefore had more than one eye on the past. The need for more playing facilities could easily be agreed. Wolfenden was at one with Albermarle there. The Committee was in favour of the wider use of existing facilities, those managed by local education authorities and employers, and the construction of multi-purpose sports centres providing indoor as well as outdoor opportunities. They agreed that a most important group was the fifteen- to twenty-year-olds who fell into that painful category of being neither in school nor easily able to join adult clubs. They pointed out that the facilities provided for women's games were less adequate than those for men's. But they could not agree about what to do with 'amateurism'. Their attitudes towards international sporting competition, the coverage of sport by the press, and spectator sport on Sundays had an old-fashioned feel. And although the members of the Committee recognized the need to improve the administration and organization of British sport, they were cautious in their recommendations for structural change. Yes, there should be improved coordination of the relations between the national governing bodies of sport, and between them and the multi-sport institutions such as the British

Olympic Association and the Central Council of Physical Recreation. But the Committee decided that there was 'no public desire for one single large organisation charged with the duty of co-ordinating all sport in this country'.[11] What Wolfenden did recommend was a small Sports Development Council which would distribute government funding and be either responsible to the Lord President of the Council or directly appointed by the Chancellor of the Exchequer. During the 1960s, the case for a Sports Council which would control and spend money on sport for the benefit of the community as a whole was gradually accepted by the Conservative and Labour Parties. In 1966 a modernizing Labour government led by Harold Wilson created an advisory Sports Council to which the Conservatives added executive powers in 1970 and a Royal Charter and extra staff in 1972, both suggestive of some independence from the state source of funding. These were important changes and implied a relationship with government which was to be quite unlike anything which had gone before.

In 1972, then, the Sports Council became the intermediary between government and sport, selecting the destinations for the first money ever specifically allocated by government for the development of British sport. The new body was handed four main tasks. The first was to promote a general understanding of the importance of sport and physical recreation throughout society as a whole; the second was to increase the level of sports facilities; the third was to encourage wider participation in sport. Finally the international performance of Britain's sportsmen and sportswomen was to be improved. As it turned out, the last two were to prove rather more difficult than the first two.

The project was given an impressive start by the use of the Council of Europe's memorable slogan 'Sport For All'. It was based on the idea that access to sport and physical recreation was a right of every citizen, its provision an essential social service. The 1975 White Paper on Sport and Recreation underlined the notion, emphasizing the contribution which physical activity could make to a full life and to mental and physical health. 'Moreover by reducing boredom and urban frustration participation in active recreation contributes to the reduction of hooliganism and delinquency among young people.'[12]

In its first decade the Sports Council was mainly concerned with the provision of new facilities. The results were impressive: multi-purpose sports centres and swimming pools were built: where there had been 27 sports centres in 1972, for example, there were 770 by 1981. All-weather sports pitches, many fitted with floodlights and running tracks, were also part of this extensive building programme. This was supplemented by the efforts of local government, which was stimulated by the activities of the Sports Council and to some extent in competition with it. The 1970s was the decade when the municipal leisure centre became a common feature of many British towns and cities. Local authorities built a thousand new sports centres between 1971 and 1989 as well as 700 new swimming pools.[13]

But raising the levels of participation proved more difficult; persuading those groups whose participation rates were traditionally low proved even beyond the positive thinkers in Southampton Row. Most people in the sports world knew that who played what or whether they played at all was governed by social factors and inequalities. As early as 1973 the House of Lords Select Committee on Sport had recommended that inner cities should be recreational priority areas and the 1975 White Paper required the Sports Council to bring its grant-awarding strategies in line with the government's urban areas of special need. But participation is a slippery concept: what counts as participation? There seems little doubt that the expansion of both private and public facilities together with technological changes which allowed physical recreation on an exercise bike or in front of a video at home did boost the number of adults involved. One measure suggests that the 9.8 million adults who took part in some form of physical activity in 1979 increased to 12.4 million in 1984 and 13.2 million in 1989.[14]

But if participation improved it was mainly among the already active, the affluent meritocrats from the male, skilled, managerial and professional groups. The same groups who made the best use of education and the health services also made the most of what sports facilities were being provided. Several scholars have pointed out that the persistence of the 'Wolfenden Gap', the 15–18 year olds out of school but not in sports clubs, after two decades of campaigning and building new facilities, was a mark of the failure of 'Sport For All'.[15] Peter McIntosh and Valerie Charlton, for example, noted that the increase in participation was very uneven both between sections of the population and between sports. They even claimed that outdoor sports were in decline and that the increase in numbers walking, jogging and playing snooker did not owe much to Sport For All. Their conclusions were pessimistic: ' "Sport For All" . . . is not a reality and our findings suggest it may never be . . . its basic premise, that it fulfils social functions, ought to be questioned. Some of the social functions which Sport For All was intended to fulfil might be as effectively fulfilled by other "Leisure Activities For All".' They proposed a policy for fitness and health and harked back to an earlier age: appealing for sport to be promoted for its own sake! The goal would be the attainment of skills and the development of individual personalities and, a word you don't come across very much in the literature, fun! McIntosh and Charlton, though members of the sports lobby, were actually recognizing what some of the more gung-ho bureaucrats in the sports business refused to face, that sport was very limited as a social instrument. Sport had to be more honest and therefore more modest in its claims. It could not solve political problems, like that in Northern Ireland, for example, nor prevent the urban riots of 1981 in England. Indeed as society became more polarized along class and ethnic lines through the 1980s sport not only reflected this but contributed to it.[16]

Even in the more prosperous 1990s, when more people played sport than ever before, and the sporting lifestyle with its component of physical recreation became a prominent media feature, most people in Britain were not much interested in active, regular and more or less organized participation in sport. A study of teenage schoolchildren by St Luke's College, Exeter, found that most were uninterested in sport or physical exercise and a large proportion were already overweight. A National Association of Head Teachers survey of facilities in schools in 1999 found that 94 per cent of primary schools had no swimming pool, gymnasium or tennis court and 172 schools had no playground.[17]

Moreover, interest in watching others play sport did not look particularly substantial when compared with a whole range of other leisure activities such as entertainment in all its many forms, media consumption, tourism and sex. Active participation in sport remains a minority activity. It may be prominent in less physically active forms, such as watching it on television or gambling; this relatively limited interest may be growing in these more affluent times, especially for those in good jobs or in households with several incomes, but it doesn't appear to have much to do with national policies on sport.

The fourth priority of the Sports Council was to improve the international performance of British sportsmen and sportswomen. In 1976 the Sports Aid Foundation was set up by the Council to attract money from both public and private sources to help fund athletes in training for major events. Five years later, in 1981, trust funds were established in which earnings such as appearance money could be retained until retirement and from which payments of expenses could be made. Even when the Sports Council was proclaiming in its annual report of 1982–3 'If the work of the Sports Council can be summed up in one word, that word is participation,' a growing proportion of funds were already being diverted towards the governing bodies of the individual sports with the clear understanding that most of it would go to the best performers. Critics have pointed out the contradiction. But the assumption at the heart of the Council's policy was that the strength of popular participation and that of the sporting elite were closely related. You discovered your best sportsmen and sportswomen by building up the broadest possible base of sporting participation. That was how the

Soviet Union and East Germany and their allies had attained their strong position in sport. We now know that the base of the east European sports pyramid was neither broad nor healthy; that their sports policy was largely based on talent spotting at an early age, special schools and the ruthless application of sports science, together with a concentration on a particular group of Olympic sports. In other words the Soviet system was designed to seek out sporting excellence and develop it so that its victories would enhance the image of the regime as a whole.

Interestingly this concentration on finding sporting excellence, supporting it and developing it was taken up in a very different society, Australia. The Australian Institute of Sport (AIS) was established in Canberra in 1981. It had been proposed by the Federal Government after Australian athletes had failed to win any gold medals at the 1976 Olympic Games, and followed the controversy over whether to participate in Moscow in 1980. The AIS was to recruit and prepare the best athletes in the country using the most up-to-date facilities and sports science. This gold medal factory concentrated on seven sports: athletics, baseball, gymnastics, netball, swimming, tennis and weight-lifting, to which rowing and water polo were later added. State sports institutes were later established with Perth focusing on hockey, Adelaide specializing in cricket and cycling, Brisbane in squash and diving, and Sydney on Rugby. The results were spectacular in the nineties, beginning with the plethora of gold and other medals won at the 1990 Commonwealth Games.[18]

Moreover in 1985 the Federal Government set up the Australian Sports Commission to coordinate approaches to sports development overall, both for the elites and for popular participation. A primary aim was to maximize funding for sport from the private sector. In 1989 the Commission established its own Women and Sport unit. By 1994 this long-term planning was showing results in terms of medal hauls at major athletic events and international victories in a range of team sports. In their annual report of that year the Australian Sports Council (ASC) identified a direct causal relationship between the level of funding for a sport and its competitive success. It was important to have a solid participatory sporting base but what had achieved significant results was focused concerted action at the elite levels. Furthermore the success of the AIS and the ASC provided a national focus and inspiration for both potential elite athletes and the top performers themselves. The message from Australia was clear and it was beginning to penetrate some members of the British sporting establishment.

Perhaps even more importantly, from the time John Major became Prime Minister in 1990, government began to focus seriously on sport

in a way it had never done before. In some ways this was a result of the
new prime minister's own enthusiasms. He was a genuine fan of the
national summer and winter team games of cricket and football. He
was a member of the Surrey County Cricket Club and a regular
supporter of Chelsea football club. He was a believer both in the value
of sport to the individual and in the leading role which it could play in
developing a sense of national well-being.[19] Sport was part of what he
called the national heritage and it was foremost among those cultural
concerns of the new Department of National Heritage which the Major
government established after the Conservative Party's general election
victory in 1992.

Government determination to invest in British sport had also been
encouraged by recent reminders of its cultural and emotional power.
Millions had watched the unsteady but exciting progress of the England
football team to the semi-finals of the World Cup in July 1990, had
shared the tearful realization of Paul Gascoigne that his yellow card
would cost him a place in the final, and then saw victory snatched away
by the unkindest kick of all: a penalty shoot-out. The summer of 1992
had brought spectacular medal success at the Barcelona Olympics on
both the athletic and cycle tracks and the river. The makers of Government sports policy were impressed by Barcelona, by the economic and
social renaissance that investment in the Olympics had apparently
brought to the city and by the benefits which a modernized infrastruc-
ture, and the prestige and tourism, would continue to bring.[20] The
British Government's support for Birmingham's Olympic bid had
matched the lack of public belief that it could possibly succeed: in 1993
John Major launched Manchester's bid to host the Olympics in 2000
not only with essential rhetoric: 'the Manchester bid is the British bid.
It is a national undertaking strongly supported by the British Government,' but with the commitment of almost £2 billion of taxpayers'
money.[21]

Such a commitment to sport by government could hardly fail to be
accompanied by some determination to reshape it, to shift the balance
and emphasis of its priorities. Although no government could say it was
not interested in the grass-roots levels of sporting participation it was
the sporting elite that really mattered. Of course the government and
the Sports Councils would continue to encourage the appropriate
provision of facilities; but it also wanted to see individuals striving to
improve their own performance so that champions could develop.
International sporting success was good for the people who achieved it
and good for the country. The Sports Council was restructured in 1994.
A United Kingdom Sports Council was to bear overall responsibility for
policy and planning. The national Sports Councils, and especially the

English, withdrew from the laudable but secondary aims of promoting increased participation, health through sport and informal leisure activities to pursue the goal of higher standards of sporting achievement.[22]

This shift of policy emphasis was spelt out even more clearly in *Sport. Raising the Game*, the oddly titled paper published by the Department of National Heritage in 1995. John Major wrote a three-page preface in which he stated the aim of government sport policy: 'to rebuild the strength of every level of British sport'. Although all sports would be helped, the then Prime Minister was 'determined to see that our great traditional sports – cricket, hockey, swimming, athletics, football, netball, rugby, tennis – are put firmly at the centre of the stage'.[23] There would also be a British Academy of Sport for the best and to go with it an improvement in both the spotting of talent and the provision to support it.

As for the grass roots, there were the usual pieties about bringing every child in school within reach of adequate sporting facilities by the year 2000. There was the nostalgic notion about returning sport to its place at the heart of weekly life in every school. Indeed helping to improve school sport ought to have the 'highest priority'. Mr Major actually accepted what many had claimed: that there had been a decline of sport in schools since the teachers' dispute of 1984–5 and the educational reforms which had followed it.[24] Some of this laid the government open to more criticism as it had been the Conservatives who had promoted the sale of 5000 school playing fields between 1987 and 1995. Moreover research suggested that many young men had previously chosen teaching as an occupation because it was one of the few jobs which allowed them to combine a love of sport with their daily work. Perhaps the decline of sport in schools that John Major had identified was also a factor in the fall in the numbers of young men entering teaching in the decade after 1985: and the fall in male recruits may also have played a part in the decline of sport in schools.

It was the fact of Conservative responsibility for the condition of sport in schools which was the target of New Labour in its own sporting policy document, *Labour's Sporting Nation* (1997). School sport was an indispensable pillar of education alongside the vocational, moral and academic, and as such it must be promoted by the state. The selling off of school playing fields would be stopped if New Labour won the election. The 'Wolfenden Gap' would be bridged by a Youth Sports Unit which would develop sporting opportunities for the young and help tackle the problems of youth crime.

In general *Labour's Sporting Nation* was a more balanced, thoughtful and sophisticated document than *Raising the Game*. It was dedicated to Denis Howell, Lord Howell of Aston, twice minister responsible for sport in the Labour governments of 1964–70 and 1974–9. It was based on previous policy papers on angling, football, and the proposed British Academy of Sport, all this designed to emphasize that a traditional rather than a fashionable concern was at work. It stressed the democratic aim of increasing sporting opportunities. Like John Major, Labour accepted that competitive team games should 'continue to be the mainstay of school sports provision' and it was careful to point out that there should also be sporting activities to suit the needs of every child, such as aerobics, movement, dance and outdoor pursuits.[25] But it echoed *Raising the Game* in urging the need to improve national sporting performance. Everyone had a right to strive for sporting excellence and must also strive to 'put Britain back on the sporting map'. This meant not only performing with distinction on the sportsfields of the world but keeping the headquarters of international sports governing bodies in London and increasing British efforts to host major international events. Even before the general election of May 1997 New Labour had campaigned vigorously for England to stage the World Cup of 2006 – hardly one of the country's greatest needs.

It seems doubtful that football was much of a vote winner but New Labour certainly appears to have tapped into the soccer chic of the 1990s. Even before the excitements of Euro 96 Tony Blair gave an interview to the *Independent on Sunday*, spread over 7½ columns about football, in which he emphasized that New Labour was developing a strategy for football, in essence more money for the Football Trust and the setting up of a football task force to explore the grievances of the fans.[26] After the election victory New Labour leaders were keen to show their support for particular clubs and the first two ministers responsible for sport in the newly created Department of Culture, Media and Sport, Tony Banks and Kate Hoey, were well publicized supporters of Chelsea and Arsenal respectively. It was all very different from the Conservatives, even under the sport-loving John Major, and perhaps provided another illustration of how New Labour was in touch with modern sensibilities in ways that Conservatives were not.[27]

It is obviously much too early to make any significant assessment of the sporting policies of New Labour in government. But it is interesting to see what has been started since the general election of May 1997. The proposal for a United Kingdom Sports Institute (UKSI) for the preparation and training of elite sportsmen and women was put out to competitive tender. Sheffield won, leading to claims that it was Britain's first city of sport. The new Institute was to be the home for five sports – athletics, judo, road cycling, swimming and triathlon – and three English sporting organizations would have their national headquarters there (netball, squash and table tennis). But neither the athletes themselves nor many of the governing bodies were happy with the chosen location of the UKSI and in the spring of 1999 the government announced that an eleven-centre network would make up the Institute. The progress of this project will be carefully monitored by analysts.[28]

The Football Task Force was set up under the chairmanship of David Mellor and its away days and meetings provided opportunities to explore some of the conflicts between what was increasingly being seen as the two sides of the football industry: the owners, managers and workers on one side, and the supporters who refuse to become consumers on the other. A constructive compromise between these two sets of interests will be difficult to achieve, although it may be that some form of independent auditing of football could result.

The government has also established yet another monitoring body which will act as a gadfly on the flanks of the arts and sport. QUEST, quality, efficiency and standards, will report directly to the Secretary of State for Culture, Media and Sport and its reports will doubtless become a crucial source for commentators and even historians.[29]

Finally the government has proposed a £50 million levy on the next television agreement negotiated by the Premier League in an attempt to redistribute some of the bounty to football's grass roots: the recreational game, where basic facilities such as pitches and dressing rooms will be improved, the poorer professional clubs, even free tickets to top matches for the less well off. A further recent announcement of the spending of £2 billion on the more underprivileged sections of the sports world, most of it to be allocated to community projects, seems to illustrate New Labour's commitment to its more traditional social concerns.[30]

As for sport in schools, the new government claims to have stopped the sales of school playing fields but it is not clear how many schools or local authorities have actually had applications to sell refused. Six specialist sports colleges were set up at comprehensive schools in 1997. Additional facilities allowed them to place extra emphasis on physical education and sport. By April 2000, the original six had grown to 37 with a planned increase to 110 by 2003. The Prime Minister has promised £60 million of Lottery money to revive competitive school sports and to encourage the will-to-win in the next generation of sportsmen and sportswomen. This is partly to be achieved by employing 600 sports coordinators whose job it would be to organize inter-school fixtures outside the normal school hours. As there are 5000 secondary schools they are clearly going to be kept busy. Without the nostalgic regard for school sport as a central part of the school week to which the previous government appeared to subscribe, New Labour wants to increase the influence and prestige of sport in schools, especially in the secondary sector. Yet Physical Education remains a core, rather than a foundation subject in the National Curriculum. In the primary sector, the government has announced a similar scheme with a spending of £150 million in the next two years to provide 300 primary schools with multi-purpose sports and arts facilities. Again, although welcomed by the sports lobby, educationalists have reminded us that there are 18,000 primary schools in England. The government also refused to appoint a Parliamentary Select Committee to investigate the alleged decline of school sport. In any event, it will be some time before the impact of these policies can be assessed.[31]

Of course, there are other ways for politics and politicians to become embroiled in sport apart from the matter of sports policy. Football hooliganism became an increasing concern of successive governments from the 1960s, a concern reflected in the Harrington and Lang Reports of 1968 and 1969.[32] But a crisis point was reached in 1985 between 11 and 29 May: fifty-five spectators died in a fire in the main stand at Bradford City. The same afternoon, during an outbreak of fighting between some supporters of Birmingham City and Leeds United, a teenage boy was killed when part of a wall fell on him. Finally on 29 May at the Heysel Stadium in Brussels, before the European Cup Final between Juventus and Liverpool, 41 mainly Italian supporters of Juventus died after being crushed against a wall following a charge by Liverpool supporters. The Bradford fire was not caused by crowd disorder although there was media speculation that a smoke bomb had precipitated it. In fact, the real cause was the build-up of combustible material which the club had failed to remove. Yet the main recommendations of the Popplewell Report were greater powers for the police to search crowds outside football grounds and for smoke bombs on grounds to be made illegal.

The Birmingham incident was obviously hooliganism and a range of crowd disciplinary measures were recommended to deal with it. A membership scheme together with the exclusion of away supporters and the casual spectator were probably the most controversial. Modern technology was to be applied to controlling the football hooligan with the use of closed circuit television and perimeter fencing.

Luton Town actually implemented a membership scheme and banned all away fans from the 1986–7 season following a serious disturbance during a cup replay with Millwall in March 1985. The Football League and most supporters' groups were vigorously opposed to the scheme, the League excluding Luton from the 1986 League Cup competition. But Prime Minister Mrs Thatcher defended Luton and tried to persuade the Football League to change their attitude and their policies. This was the first time any prime minister had interfered in the affairs of the

League. The events of 1985 provided the impetus for Mrs Thatcher's determination to make every football supporter carry an identity card. Convicted hooligans would have their cards taken away and would therefore be kept out of the grounds.

Mrs Thatcher was not impressed by the condition of professional football. The behaviour of a violent minority of English supporters, especially, both at home and abroad, harmed Britain's reputation. She believed that the state should enforce discipline by tougher policing inside and outside stadiums, combined with a national identity card scheme. The Football Spectators Bill was designed to achieve this even though it was opposed not only by many football interests but also by the police who said that such a scheme would increase tension and therefore the opportunity for violent confrontations by delaying entry into the grounds. And the Bill would almost certainly have become law if it had not been for the Hillsborough disaster and the Report of the Lord Justice Taylor which followed it.

On 15 April 1989 the FA Cup semi-final between Liverpool and Nottingham Forest at Hillsborough, Sheffield, was abandoned shortly after the start. Overcrowding on the terraces behind the Leppings Lane end goal led to spectators being crushed against the perimeter fencing. Ninety-six people died and many more were injured. The tragedy was the result of a failure of command among senior police officers on duty at the ground 'which led to a safety problem being wrongly identified as a security problem'.[33] There were several major accidents involving serious loss of life in the 1980s but Hillsborough had a particular impact partly because you do not expect such a catastrophe at a site whose object is enjoyment.

The Government commissioned Lord Justice Taylor to investigate how and why the accident had occurred and make remedial recommendations.[34] The interim report was published in August 1989 and concentrated on what had happened and why. In the short term it suggested further cuts in the capacity of standing terraces and set out basic security procedures. The final report was published in January 1990 and took a broader view of the problems of safety at sports grounds. In particular it examined the wider context of football. Seventy-six recommendations were made in all; most of them were implemented. The major public effects were the removal of all perimeter fencing; the elimination of standing accommodation by August 1994 from the grounds of all clubs in the top two divisions in England and Wales and the top division in Scotland; the establishing of a football licensing authority with statutory powers, which would inspect grounds and give out safety licences; the appointment at all clubs of a safety officer together with the training and appointment of more stewards for duty inside the grounds. Taylor also came out against Mrs Thatcher's national identity card scheme.

The result has been a transformation in the way top football is watched in this country: the traditional standing terraces have gone and been replaced by all-seater stadia. Moreover the new ethos for football which Taylor also wanted to see, of more welcoming attitudes and more consultation with supporters has also in part, at least, been achieved. But all this came at a price. Installing seats instead of standing places has cut capacities and led to dramatic increases in ticket prices. The social composition of the crowd has changed and many commentators have suggested that fans are in the process of becoming consumers. Implementing the Taylor Report was expensive and seems to have provided the final push to the top English clubs to break away from the Football League and, under the auspices of the FA, establish the Premier League in 1992. This enabled the biggest and richest clubs to construct a much more lucrative bargain with television with no redistribution of earnings to the less well off.[35]

With the growth of international sporting competition in the twentieth century it was inevitable that sport would become a medium of diplomacy. At international contests and festivals like the Olympics and the World Cup national prestige was at stake. Hence in May 1938, on the eve of the football match between Germany and England in Berlin, the Foreign Office was anxious that the England team should give a good account of themselves and made sure their views were made known to the FA Secretary. As appeasement remained government policy it was also thought prudent to insist that the English team performed the Nazi salute during the preliminaries to the game. A wish to remain on good terms with Japan also led the Foreign Office to exert pressure on the British Olympic Association to withdraw London's bid to stage the 1940 Olympics in favour of Tokyo.[36]

After the war, the government was eager to capitalize on a brief Oxbridge-based flowering of middle-distance running in the 1950s to improve relations with both the Soviet Union and the United States. After Roger Bannister became the first man to run a mile in under four minutes, he was sent on a goodwill tour of America. The government, and the British sporting public, supported the athletics matches at the White City between London and Moscow in 1954 and between Great Britain and the Soviet Union in 1957. Together with return fixtures in Moscow, these events were both a sign of a thaw in the cold war and also a small contribution to the improvement of relations between the two countries.[37]

It would be mistaken to give the impression that British sport would always do the government's bidding. This was never better illustrated than by the confrontation which Mrs Thatcher engineered in 1980 with the British Olympic Association (BOA). Two years before, the Soviet Union had invaded Afghanistan. The Olympic Games were due to be held in Moscow in the summer of 1980 and early in the year Jimmy Carter, President of the United States, warned the Soviets that if they did not withdraw from Afghanistan then the United States would boycott the Moscow Games. Interestingly Carter sent Muhammad Ali to five African countries including Kenya, Nigeria and Tanzania to seek support for his policy. He also put pressure on the United States Olympic Committee who voted for a boycott. The British government fully supported the boycott and apparently without consulting any British sports organizations, called on the BOA to join in. There were full-day debates in both Houses of Parliament, the first time a sporting issue had received such attention, and both the Lords and the Commons produced resolutions calling for withdrawal. Mrs Thatcher wrote three times to the British Olympic Association (BOA), and threatened to stop the leave of competing civil servants. The Foreign Office, the Home Office and the Department of the Environment all tried to force the BOA to comply. But they refused to be bullied. The BOA left the decision with the governing bodies of the individual sports and with only a few exceptions, all chose to send athletes to Moscow. Moreover, the Sports Council, a client body of the Department of the Environment, also refused to support the boycott. Nor did Mrs Thatcher have much success in unifying the country behind her cause. The best she could get was a symbolic condemnation of the Soviet invasion by the team, which marched under the Olympic flag rather than the Union Jack. The BOA did not like being told that it could not send a team to Moscow when Anglo-Russian diplomatic and trading relations continued. All the sports bodies saw it as a moment to exert their independence in a democratic state.[38]

British governments also found themselves having to intervene in sporting relations with South Africa. Apartheid, or the idea of separate and unequal development, had been the policy of the South African government since 1948 and by the mid-1950s racially integrated sport was effectively banned. During the 1960s, as racial attitudes appeared to soften in both Europe and the United States, they were hardening in South Africa. Moreover a large group of Afro-Asian countries had achieved political independence from their former European rulers. Many of them had joined the Commonwealth, from which South Africa had withdrawn in 1961.

Trevor Huddleston, in his critical account of South Africa, *Naught For Your Comfort*, published in 1956, had been one of the first to suggest that sporting isolation would damage the self-assurance of white

South Africans. What seems to have persuaded some western opinion was the decision of the South African government, taken in 1962, to ban racially mixed teams from taking part in sport either inside or outside South Africa.[39] Trying to dictate the racial composition of sporting opponents was a violation of widely accepted sporting practices. The IOC excluded South Africa from the 1964 Olympic Games.

Basil D'Oliveira was a cricketer prevented from playing with the best in South Africa because he was a 'Cape Coloured'. He was helped to settle in England where he played effectively first for Middleton in the Central Lancashire League and then, from 1965, for Worcestershire in the County Championship. He first played for England in the following year and was a regular all-rounder until 1972 making three major overseas tours. But in 1968 he was controversially omitted from the MCC team to tour South Africa. Had the English cricket establishment capitulated to pressure from Pretoria?

Early in 1967, the South African Interior Minister had stressed that mixed teams would not be allowed to play in South Africa and that D'Oliveira, if chosen, would not be permitted to enter the country. This not only drew criticism from opponents of the regime but the following Foreign Office instruction to the British Embassy in Pretoria:

> While generalised attacks on apartheid do no good in South Africa (however well they may go down at the UN), we should not hesitate to attack for all we are worth when we catch the South Africans on grounds which the better among them feel to be indefensible.

The Minister for Sport, Denis Howell, sought and received an assurance from the MCC that the team for South Africa would be chosen on merit. He also said in the Commons that the government was 'confident that if any chosen player is rejected by the host country the tour would be abandoned'. It seems that Prime Minister Vorster was looking for 'flexibility' in the policy of apartheid in sport and might accept racially mixed teams from countries, like Britain or New Zealand, with which South Africa had traditional sporting ties. Meantime the British government did not condone apartheid, but 'did not want to pursue an active policy of ostracism'.

D'Oliveira made 158 against Australia in the last Test of the summer of 1968. But he was not selected, a decision which the Secretary of the MCC announced was entirely a cricketing one. Not too many people believed him and it has recently been suggested that the MCC may have been misled by the advice of Sir Alec Douglas-Home.[40] The *News of the World* then reported that they had offered D'Oliveira a contract to cover the tour as a cricket correspondent. The MCC was under pressure when it was announced that owing to an injury to the originally selected Tom Cartwright, a place would be found for D'Oliveira after all. In cricketing terms this could be interpreted as a straightforward substitution of one all-rounder for another: except that Cartwright was really a bowler who could bat a bit while D'Oliveira was a batsman who could bowl.[41] The South African Prime Minister, doubtless with problems of his own, declared that 'the team as it now stands is not the team of the MCC selection committee. It is the team of the Anti-Apartheid Movement, of Sanroc, of Bishop Reeves and of the political opponents of South Africa.'[42] With the chosen team not acceptable to South Africa, the tour was cancelled.

The British political context of all this needs to be remembered. Race relations and immigration policy remained difficult problems for successive governments. Enoch Powell made his notorious 'rivers of blood' speech in April 1968. The European minority in Rhodesia had unilaterally declared their independence. Apartheid was an important issue for the new nations of the Commonwealth.

The D'Oliveira affair did not settle the issue. A South African rugby team toured in 1969. A cricket tour was due to follow in 1970. Demonstrators organized by the Anti-Apartheid Movement and the Young Liberals followed the rugby tourists around. At Swansea, locally recruited stewards from Welsh rugby clubs knocked the protesters about with some relish.[43] Cricket grounds would be even harder to protect. The 'Stop the Seventy Tour Campaign' would insist on their peaceful protests, which could easily produce a serious problem of law and order in an election year. Nor would such a tour do much for Commonwealth relations, and on a practical level the Commonwealth Games were due in Edinburgh in the summer of 1970. A boycott by the African states was likely if the cricket tour by South Africa went ahead. Even Anglo-American relations might be placed in jeopardy if a welcome was extended to the sportsmen of apartheid. In the event, Home Secretary James Callaghan asked the Cricket Council to cancel the tour on grounds of broad public policy. They did it but they did not like it, hence the plethora of private and 'rebel' tours through the seventies and eighties.[44]

International sport provided a point of contact between South Africa and other countries where the difference in sporting practice produced conflict. This conflict was not undermined by the continued importance of the trading and other economic interests tying Britain and other western countries to South Africa. This was emphasized in 1977 when representatives of Commonwealth governments produced the Gleneagles Declaration in which it was agreed 'to withhold any form of support for and . . . [to take] every practical step to discourage contact or competition by our nationals with sporting organisations, teams, or sportsmen from South Africa'. Most commentators agree that the sports boycott played a symbolic role in the eventual downfall of apartheid, though the extent to which it influenced political decision-making in South Africa is debatable.

Post-war governments have increasingly accepted that sport was an important voluntary activity that mattered to a lot of people, mainly men but including growing numbers of women. Governments have sought to encourage sport and physical recreation in schools and to promote it as part of the leisure lives of citizens after school and college. Physical recreation has become more and more accepted as part of a healthy lifestyle though in the 1990s a growing body of professional opinion has begun to stress the importance of individual as opposed to team sports and non-competitive over competitive activities. Walking, jogging, swimming and recreational badminton and tennis, these are the kinds of things many people choose to do in their leisure hours.[45]

Both government and the sports lobby have continued to demonstrate their strong belief in the social benefits of sport. As we noted earlier, the Wolfenden Committee thought that sport played an important part in promoting team spirit, self-discipline, commitment and dedication as well as fun, friendship and health. In 1981, after the inner city riots in Bristol, Liverpool and London, Michael Heseltine, Secretary of State for the Environment, emphasized the provision of sport as a necessary ingredient in any attempt to raise the quality of life in depressed areas. And as recently as 1997 the English Sports Council, in its Policy Briefing, stressed the value of sport in reducing the propensity among active participants to take part in crime. More cautiously it pointed out that for some of them, active sport had proved a turning point in their lives. All this suggests that although 'sport for all' may no longer be the favoured slogan, pushing up levels of participation is important. The present government has recently promised £2 billion of Lottery funding to the grass-roots underprivileged of English sport. No one wants to be top of the European Obesity League.[46]

If governments have always been interested in the role of sport and physical recreation in contributing to the health of the nation they have also come to grasp the importance of the elite, spectacular end of the sporting spectrum. After the war there was a gradual recognition of professional sporting achievement through the honours list. An Australian, Don Bradman, was the first playing cricketer to be knighted, in 1948, followed by the jockey Gordon Richards and the cricketers Jack Hobbs in 1953 and Len Hutton in 1956. The first knighthood to be given to a playing footballer was to Stanley Matthews in 1965. Sporting honours are now a regular part of every list.[47]

We saw earlier how the Labour government supported the 1948 Olympics in London in the difficult circumstances of post-war austerity. Already the national prestige involved with such an international event together with a hoped-for expansion of dollar-earning tourists were good enough reasons for government interest. We also noted how the creation of the Sports Council to channel taxpayers' money directly to sport was partly as a result of British failures in international competitions. As with the British economy, some commentators felt that Britain was not doing as well as it ought to have done. There was also a growing awareness that success in international sport cut across class boundaries and contributed, however briefly, to what would later be clumsily called 'the feel good factor'.

Harold Wilson was shrewd enough to see the importance of sport – as he noted in 1965, 'one of the subjects essential to Britain's economic and social development which had not been given adequate priority in the past'. The Wilson government gave £500,000 to the Football Association to help with the expenses incurred in hosting the 1966 World Cup. He also saw the value of association with the winning team, flying back from Washington where he had been negotiating an important IMF loan to be present at the final and join the celebrations afterwards. The Thatcher government waived normal naturalization and registration procedures in order to ensure that the South African athlete Zola Budd, otherwise banned from international competition and whose grandfather was British, could run for Britain in the 1984 Olympics in Los Angeles.

So government attitudes and policies towards sport were changing and so was the context and structure of competitive sport. From the 1960s there was a rapid increase in the number of competing nations as the old western empires lost their imperial grip: two decades later the collapse of the Soviet bloc was to provide another bunch of 'new' nations. New nations joined international organizations, the UN, of course, but also the IOC and FIFA. Sport could give a young nation visibility, modernity and identity more quickly and less expensively than just about anything else. Sport also started to attract more commercial sponsorship, especially as colour television began its march across the globe in the seventies. Sponsorship helped sport to grow away from 'games' with a more or less small commercial sector into a real business. By the beginning of the nineties over 1000 companies in Britain were injecting £200 million a year into a variety of sports, especially motor racing and football. In 1990–1 sport may not have been getting much direct from central government: £43.7 million directly from the Sports Council, £670,000 from the new Football Licensing Authority. Local government, however, was spending £389 million in current expenditure on sport and £243 million in capital expenditure. Moreover, from the point of view of central government, sport was paying, in revenues and taxes, £2.5 billion.[48]

These processes were both reflected and enhanced in Britain by the National Lottery. It began on St Valentine's Day 1994 when Camelot was awarded a seven-year contract to run it. For each pound spent, 28 pence was to be allocated to 'Good Causes', to be divided equally between charities, the Millennium projects, arts, heritage and sport. Table 7.1 below shows the very large sums which have gone to British sport since 1995. There can be no doubt that the National Lottery and the growing amount of money paid to sport by television have accelerated the process of sporting industrialization which we have sketched out.

No government can ignore an industry the size of sport and leisure, which not only accounts for about £10 billion annually of consumer expenditure but employs 750,000 workers and currently pays £3.5 billion per year in tax revenues.[49] Sport is Britain's eleventh largest industry and expanding fast. Perhaps it is not surprising that the attitudes of the Major and Blair governments have been a mixture of the hard-nosed accountant and the fan (rather than the consumer). The government claims to play a facilitating rather than a directing role. But there can be no doubt of their ever closer involvement. In 1996, after the British Olympic team in Atlanta had finished 36th in the medal table and won only one gold, the team manager was summoned to Downing Street to explain the poor show. Will there be a repeat after Sydney 2000 or 2004, for which Sport England has already predicted eight gold medals and a top ten place in the medals table?[50]

Table 7.1   Sports and the Lottery

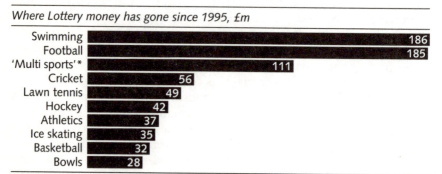

Where Lottery money has gone since 1995, £m

Sport	£m
Swimming	186
Football	185
'Multi sports'*	111
Cricket	56
Lawn tennis	49
Hockey	42
Athletics	37
Ice skating	35
Basketball	32
Bowls	28

Note: * Centres offering common facilities for a range of sports such as basketball and hockey.
Source: The Guardian, 24 August 1999.

The sports lobby is more powerful than it has ever been, though it is still somewhat fragmented, which perhaps prevents it punching its weight. There were recent complaints that government had not done enough to help the hosting of the Rugby World Cup. The CCPR would like to see government recognition of sport's power and importance in the twenty-first century by the appointment of a Minister of Sport who was not tied to the Department of Culture, Media and Sport and had a seat in the Cabinet. Perhaps government will be tempted to a more proactive coordinating role. The sports minister at the time of writing (April 2000), Kate Hoey, says she believes in sport for all. She wants to change the ethos of school sport, and make sport a 'central tenet of government policy' not just the sideshow that some critics claim it still is.[51] Sport a 'central tenet of government policy'? Such ideas are a measure of the change which has taken place in the relationship between sport and government since 1945.

Conclusion

Affluence brought choice, and choice has meant diversity. This has been the most striking feature of sport for the ordinary participant over the last half-century. Dozens of new sports have been added to the large number of existing ones, from 'soft adventures' like mountain biking for 'empty-nesters' – to use the jargon of the tourist boards – to the new enthusiasms of the young like skateboarding on the streets and snowboarding down the slopes. Indoor sport developed even faster than outdoor pursuits. Old established sports like snooker were reinvented by television and became exceptionally popular with both men and women, especially in pub-related forms like the American game of 'pool'. Darts was another old pub sport, which had a new lease of life thanks to television coverage of a new professional darts circuit with its catch-phrases and characters.

Diversity, of course, did not mean everyone could do everything. There were more than physical barriers to wider participation. Occupation was still the most important determinant of who could play what and where. There were strong social continuities amidst the rapid changes in styles and varieties of sport. The class character of particular sports remained important, although access became easier over time. Private golf clubs, for example, continued to expect new members to be proposed by existing ones. But sheer ability to pay counted for more than it had done before. Britain was moving towards a more commercial and meritocratic model where income was more important than family, education or refinement in defining status. This American social model was less apparent in the field sports of the upper classes themselves, which continued relatively unchanged with a mixture of county families and city money, than elsewhere. But it spread through middle-class sport from skiing to sailing. The modestly affluent middle classes even bought shares in racehorses.

This 'democratizing' of the elite, which was so closely identified with the inexorable rise of the grocer's daughter from Grantham, was reinforced by the changing social structure itself. There were far more people in 'middle-class' jobs in the second half of the twentieth century than there had been in the first. There had been a transformation of higher education, beginning in the 1960s with large numbers of new graduates – male and female – gaining access to the growing state and service sectors. Increasing social mobility was reflected, for instance, in the rise of golf as a popular participant sport. The boom in media jobs, computing and the new 'knowledge-based' economy in the 1980s gave a boost to aerobic sports like running and squash, which could be fitted into the busy timetable of the young executive. There was a clear correlation between career success and sporting activity. Competitive exercise was a preparation for the competitive life and an extension of it; it allowed the individual both to escape from work and to forget it for a while whilst disciplining the mind and body for the next day at the office.

As the young executive got older there was golf, or 'trekking' activities, often combined with holidays, or water sports or hill walking, to occupy his or her time actively. Combined with this there was a wealth of new opportunities for spectator sport on television or the chance to watch live games in greater comfort than before. Interestingly, the loss of spectators for live football, which had been such a feature of the 1950s and 1960s with the decline in the traditional heavy industries and textiles, was arrested in the 1990s. The expanding middle classes took a new interest in the game after the hooligan problem had been reduced to manageable proportions by higher prices and better surveillance.

Growth in female participation was a striking feature of post-war sport, especially in the 1980s. There were famous examples of working-class girls making good in sport, like Dorothy Hyman, a miner's daughter born near Barnsley; or Mary Bignall who won a sports scholarship to Millfield and became Mary Rand, the 'golden girl' of the 1964 Olympics. But they were exceptions. Most of the big names were middle class like most of the participants. Tennis was the preserve of the suburban woman. Its stars were women like Ann Jones (for some years 'Haydon-Jones') from the affluent suburbs of Birmingham; Christine Truman who married a company director; Virginia Wade, who had a B.Sc. from Sussex University. The 1950s was the highpoint of tennis as a club-based game. It declined thereafter but it was still widely played in middle-class areas.

More casual forms of recreation like cycling and swimming, which appealed to around 15 per cent of adult women in the 1990s, have been a key area of growth. Even more successful – and one of the most remarkable features of recent years – is the rise of aerobics, 'keep fit' and yoga, which were the most popular of all organized female activities. Research showed that weight control was a factor in the decision of seven out of ten women to exercise. Women, also, were far better informed about their health than before. This was not just a matter of maintaining fitness. Women's magazines had undergone a complete transformation since the 1950s with frank discussion of sex alongside endless articles about how exercise could make you feel better and more attractive. Knitting patterns and recipes were relegated to remote corners – unless of course they were quick, low-fat meals for the woman on the move. This redefining of sport away from the competitive to the cosmetic was a feature of the nineties and concentrated amongst women in sedentary office jobs, who were a key element in the expanding female workforce. Working-class participation rates were about half that of middle-class women. In this sense, not so much had changed.

Although there was far more female sport it was still very different from male sport. Apart from netball and hockey, neither of which took off as post-school spectator sports, women had been effectively excluded from competitive team games. There were, however, signs of a fundamental change. Women's football began to grow dramatically in the 1990s – a trend that looked set to continue with the promise of a higher-profile professional league. The question was whether female football would attract women that other sports had failed to reach. Football was the only major sport in which the skilled male worker remained dominant. With the massive television coverage of Premier League football in the 1990s combined with the mid-week Champions League – effectively a European 'superleague' by the back door – there was a feast of football. Too much, no doubt, for many women. But girls now had much easier access to the game as spectators and there was extensive coverage of the 'new football' on pop music radio stations, in magazines and on a wider range of TV programmes. The sporting barrier between men and women was coming down. Football was no longer a purely male form of popular culture.

The tension between change and continuity was especially evident in football. At one level there was relatively little difference between the post-war years and the present. With the exception of a few striking successes like Wimbledon and some equally dramatic failures such as Wolves and Burnley, the composition of the First Division and then the Premier League remained fairly stable with sides like Arsenal, Spurs, Chelsea and West Ham maintaining a powerful London presence, which fitted into the wider socio-economic and political dominance of the Home Counties in the second half of the twentieth century. In the north there was a marked shift from local teams to regional 'super-clubs'. This began with the 'Busby Babes' in the 1950s drawing support away from the likes of Stockport and Bury, and was apparent on Merseyside with the exceptional success of Liverpool in the 1970s. In the 1990s support for Manchester United was both national and international. The televising of football around the world, especially the English Premier League, had created new fans in the Far East and India. A Buddhist temple in Thailand had a statue of David Beckham on display.

Intense regionalism coexisted with globalization. On one level local support was as strident as ever. Tyneside in the 1990s was as obsessed with the fortunes of Newcastle United as it had been in the glory days of the 1950s. Local rivalries and resentments were still strong – arguably fiercer than before – and yet top clubs now had a player- and a fan-base that was increasingly international. What had begun as identity and entertainment for northern industrial towns had become part of a European structure with a world market. Just as we exported our teams, so they sold us theirs in what became an endless exchange of sporting entertainment and images. Some sports largely dispensed with the national framework. Tennis was played on a world circuit and top golfers similarly jetted between the 'European Tour', which included Australia and the Middle East', and the United States. For Britain the key issue was to maintain commercial sponsorship and television income for the British component in the world tour. Here the British did well, successfully marketing their heritage and keeping Wimbledon and the Open at the top of world sport.

Globalization did not weaken national loyalties, although the 'Home Internationals' were ended in 1984 to avoid hooliganism and the congestion of international fixtures. The hugely popular England–Scotland game was controversially scrapped in 1989. England's defeat on penalties in the 1990 World Cup was taken far more seriously than the defeats of the 1950s. The image of Paul Gascoigne weeping became a metaphor of national disappointment. The 'tartan army' went from strength to strength despite the modest fortunes of the Scotland side, whom they accompanied round the world in kilts and tammies, proudly advertising the difference between the supposedly violent nationalism of the English and the cheerful, boozy patriotism of the Scots.

Football replaced cricket as a national symbol in England in the 1960s. This was not just a matter of England winning the World Cup in 1966, though it was a famous victory. Somewhere between the late 1940s and the mid-1960s Test cricket stopped being so important to the English. When England mourned its sporting heroes, it was foot-ballers like Bobby Moore and Stanley Matthews who were the chief focus of public grief and nostalgia. Denis Compton's death came nearest to producing the wave of emotion that Moore and Matthews evoked. But the greatest batsman of the 1950s and one of the most successful England captains of all time, Peter May, seemed to pass away with little ceremony. His kind of dignified self-restraint and public school English-ness had lost its appeal.

Cricket lost its cultural centrality. The game had been so deeply identified with the Empire and the idea of the English gentleman that it suffered particularly from decolonization and the gradual change in national mood after Suez. The 'gentlemen–players' distinction became embarrassing and the sport as a whole reeked of privilege and stuffiness. 'Plum' Warner and his generation died or lost influence in the sixties and cricket itself changed, but it could never recover its former glory. It could no longer capture the imagination of a youthful post-imperial generation for whom South Africa was anathema and the Common-wealth an irrelevance. There were moments when cricket enjoyed a revival as a symbol of English national pride, such as the summer of 1981 when Ian Botham took on Australia. But this proved a false dawn. If anything, cricket became a convenient metaphor for England's diminishing place in the scheme of things, failing even to make our mark on home ground in the World Cup of 1999. Rugby, on the other hand, benefitting from television coverage, became more important as a national symbol than before. The relative success of the England rugby team in the 1990s was sometimes presented as a triumph of the tough competitive spirit of 'Thatcher's children' in a sport which embraced the market with a vengeance in 1995.

This was all a far cry from 1945 when the amateur elite returned from active service to run sport. The 'blazerati' were back – in truth they had never gone away – and took over the running of the 1948 Olympic Games, promoting an ideal of amateurism which equated competing for money with a loss of moral fibre. Remarkably, most athletes agreed that being paid to play would be wrong, though they wanted a more realistic system of expenses – a looser kind of amateur-ism. Professionals in football, cricket and rugby remained socially subordinate and legally restricted in different ways. Footballers had a maximum wage and a transfer system that tied them to their club whether they liked it or not. Rugby League players often had to do another job to make ends meet. Professional cricketers were subject to additional humiliation at the hands of amateurs in their own team who insisted on making it crystal clear who was the gent and who was not.

The old world of rigid class distinction began to break up in the 1960s. Professional footballers threatened to strike if they were not able to negotiate freely, and won their battle. Class divisions in cricket started to work against the public school cricketer, who could no longer afford to play as an amateur, and the distinction between 'gentlemen' and 'players' was scrapped in 1963. The press and television were a new factor here, less docile than before and more critical of the snobberies and hypocrisy of the old order. Wimbledon went open in 1968, but athletics and rugby remained nominally amateur sports into the 1990s. It was the market power of performers whose television appearances attracted the interest of advertisers and sponsors that eroded the amateur ethic. Amateur bodies could charge large sums for television coverage, which they used for the general good of the sport. But the performers who earned these fees were increasingly unwilling to play the role of Robin Hood, robbing the rich to help the poor participant.

The incessant growth of media interest in sport created a celebrity cult around top players and made many of them very rich. The difference between the 1990s and the 1950s is instantly apparent. It was not a question of fame itself. Denis Compton's head, suitably plastered with Brylcream, had been ever present on post-war hoardings and in popular magazines. Men like Stanley Matthews or Len Hutton were widely recognized. However, the press respected their privacy. This allowed a man like Wally Hammond to be a sporting hero despite being a distinctly unpleasant individual in private. By the end of the century it sometimes seemed as if private life was more important than sporting achievement. Tabloid competition with television had created a sensationalist sporting press. By the 1990s top players were in the full glare of publicity, damned if they were wild or, like Alan Shearer, damned if they weren't. Like members of the royal family, some sports stars became almost paranoid about the media, refusing interviews to journalists, who could bestow fame one minute and dole out shame the next. For most, of course, the lure of publicity was too strong. It was a case of any publicity being better than no publicity and top sportsmen and women increasingly employed 'press agents' to deal with the media for them.

'Media First', a public relations firm backed by a credit card company, recently announced that they were putting a hundred top athletes through a special course to make them 'comfortable and confident' in front of the press and television. Image management became almost an obsession with politicians and business people as well as sportsmen and women. It was easy to see why. The England manager, Kevin Keegan, comparing his own time as a player under Bill Shankly and his experience as a manager of Newcastle United in the 1990s, underlined the transformation that had taken place in less than thirty years. Bill Shankly often only had a few local journalists to deal with. But by the 1990s after any game there were television interviews, often with foreign as well as British channels, hosts of journalists – the tabloids had teams of reporters – along with local press and radio. And then there were the magazines. Not just the specialist football magazines but the 'lifestyle', celebrity ones like *Hello* or *OK!* for whom sports stars were just another part of the global celebrity circus. Increasingly, as the BBC's John Humphrys observed, 'the world of sport is now a creation of the public relations industry. Image is reality, just as it is in so many other spheres. If you wish to prosper in a big way, then you sign up to that reality.'[1]

It was not only the press that took a new interest in sport. Governments in the 1950s had also regarded sport as an area of private life in which they had little part. This liberal tradition, which had its origins in the Victorian 'small state', remained strong after the war. There had been a few sensitive moments in the 1930s when the government had used sport to placate Germany and Japan for diplomatic reasons. But this was rare. Sport was still seen as a part of civil society and was only gradually incorporated into the idea of the 'welfare state'. The state took the view it had a duty to promote sport through the Sports Council and other bodies for the good of the citizen. This was a gradual process which began with influential inquiries like the Wolfenden Report in the late 1950s and went on to 'Sport for All' in the 1970s and 1980s. There were major improvements in the provision of facilities on the municipal level. But school sport, which had been a distinctively British tradition coming from the Victorian public school into the state sector, went in the opposite direction. Industrial disputes led to teachers refusing to organize extra-curricular sports and budgetary tightening meant playing fields were sold off. At the end of the twentieth century, school sport was generally in a weaker state than it had been in the 1950s, although the influx of funds from the National Lottery did hold out a realistic hope of longer-term improvement.

The government had switched its sporting priorities from the base to the apex of the pyramid. This was apparent when the Prime Minister himself took a leading role in formulating elite sports policy as part of his wider 'Back to Basics' agenda. John Major's *Raising the Game* began with the fact that 'we invented the majority of the world's great sports' and reflected the extent to which sport had become an essential component of national prestige. This steady politicizing of international sport was partly a consequence of the cold war. The arrival of the Soviet Union and its satellites in world sports, especially the Olympics, had upset the British but it did not produce an immediate response. The British left it to the United States to vindicate the free world by winning medals. However, this relative detachment, which for so long had been the accustomed position of the British state towards international sport, could not survive the transition from Empire to Commonwealth. Sport had a special role within the new structure as a shared cultural bond and as a force for racial equality. Under the Gleneagles Agreement successive governments urged a ban on sporting contacts with South Africa in order to maintain the solidarity of the Commonwealth. Mrs Thatcher applied the same logic to the Soviet invasion of Afghanistan and tried to stop the British Olympic team from going to Moscow in 1980. But interfering in the Olympic movement for ideological reasons turned out to be far harder than isolating South Africa. The decision of the British Olympic team to go to Moscow in 1980 against government wishes was a striking instance of the continued independence of sporting bodies from the state.

However, the general trend was clear. The autonomy of sporting bodies was under threat. Sport was too important to be left to the sporting. Failure at the international level whether in the World Cup or the Olympic Games was seen as an intolerable humiliation and a sign of national weakness. In the 1990s money from the National Lottery was used as a new source of funding for high performance sport. Britain was determined to hang on to its sporting heritage and the demise of the Soviet bloc certainly eased the pressure in Olympic terms. However, a rash of positive drug tests – the results of which were hotly contested by athletes – showed how far the world had come from the days of the under-funded amateurs who had gone to the Melbourne, Rome and Tokyo Olympics and had come back with gold medals.

High performance sport became increasingly cosmopolitan at the end of the century. Sport in the 1950s had been predominantly male and strongly ethnocentric. Very few foreigners played football in Britain. British players began to go abroad, a few stars like Law and Greaves to Italy in the 1960s and more to the United States in the 1970s. But European players did not come back here in large numbers until the 1990s when the European Commission's directives on free movement of labour made it impossible to maintain quotas on non-nationals. Chelsea famously fielded teams without a single British player. More remarkably, Rangers did the same. Until the 1980s both Celtic and Rangers had refused to sign English players let alone east Europeans or South Americans. Rugby Union's shift to professionalism in 1995 was accompanied by a frantic search for southern hemisphere stars with Welsh or Scottish grandparents. The new money available produced several important recruits whose Welshness turned out to be fictional while Scotland capped a Bristol player 41 times on the basis of an Edinburgh grandfather, who turned out to have been born in England. In the past the smaller playing base of the 'Celtic nations' had been less important. But the advent of professionalism aggravated the imbalance in population, leaving the way open for England to recruit from a broader social range than before, and sustain a higher level of club rugby than was possible in much smaller countries with fewer resources.

Monoculturalism was challenged from within as well as without. Non-white immigrants to Britain had been few and far between in the post-war decade despite athletic stars like Arthur Wint. However, immigration was to have a profound impact on British sport in the final quarter of the century. Afro-Caribbeans transformed British athletics and boxing in the 1980s and 1990s. Football, too, benefited from an influx of black players, who survived ugly racial abuse and occasional violence to establish their place prominently in the national sport. Racism, of course, still existed in sport but majority white opinion had shifted decisively from the racial stereotypes of post-war imperialism, which had regarded interracial relationships with revulsion, towards a more general acceptance of a multicultural society.

Perhaps the greatest change of all was in attitudes to sport itself. The virtues of amateurism were taken as read by all but a small number of professional players after the Second World War. The new orthodoxy: that the sporting 'entertainer' should be paid whatever the market can bear, was unknown. There was a widespread post-war belief that sport was something to which a financial value should not be attached. Even an athlete like Gordon Pirie, who was bitterly critical and outspoken in his condemnation of the Oxbridge governing elite, did not think athletes should race for prize money. This would not only open the door to gambling and corruption but would somehow tarnish the sense of glory that came from doing something for its own sake. This aristocratic disdain for commerce, which had marked British sport so strongly since the Victorians, melted under the onslaught of new media-driven market forces. Britain had become more like America. The amateur ideal of the athlete as undergraduate was replaced by the athlete as entrepreneur. For a moment Sebastian Coe seemed to combine both possibilities. But not for long. He became a dogmatic free market ideologue and a Thatcherite MP. Amateurism increasingly belonged in the past along with the rest of the sentimental baggage of the Tory 'wets'. Professional sport reflected the values of the new and less paternalistic Britain: more competitive, more meritocratic, more culturally diverse and more materialistic.

In the 1950s sport 'occupied a niche – a massive one perhaps, but still a niche – whereas now it is flowing into every nook and cranny of society, refusing to be compartmentalised in the traditional way'.[2] Although specific sports retained a distinct social profile, satellite television democratized spectating and linked it to a globalizing of consumption. Branded sports clothes and shoes like Nike were increasingly universal, every designer label had a sports range. Wearing football shirts became common dress. It was as if the youth of the 1950s had all put on cricket flannels and sweaters. By the end of the century, it was commonplace to refer to sport as an 'industry' – a term that would have sounded strange to post-war ears when industry still meant activities like coal mining and shipbuilding. Manchester United, for example, was a major employer in the north-west of England. The differences between those few who succeeded at the highest level and the rest was enormous and growing, earnings were beyond the imagining of most fans though they knew the figures. Differentials had grown in business, too, as the 'winner take all' philosophy became more pronounced. Sport had to be promoted as if the product, like jam or jeans, tea or toothpaste, was always at the same level of consistency and quality: fiercely hyped, always thrilling and forever young.

Notes

1 Playing and Watching

1   Walter Winterbottom, 'The Pattern of Sport in the United Kingdom', 9 July 1966, Proceedings of the Conference 'Sport in Education and Recreation', 1966, pp. 19–31; Lucy Clifford of the Sport England Information Centre kindly provided this important unpublished paper.
2   B. Butler, *The Official History of The Football Association* (Queen Anne Macdonald, London, 1991), p. 94.
3   Winterbottom, 'The Pattern of Sport', p. 19.
4   Ibid, pp. 21–2.
5   R. Brown et al., 'Leisure in work: the occupational culture of shipyard workers', in M. Smith, S. Parker and C. Smith (eds), *Leisure in Britain* (Penguin, London, 1973), p. 100.
6   Winterbottom, 'The Pattern of Sport', pp. 21–2.
7   M. Marqusee, *Anyone But England: Cricket, Race and Class*, p. 138.
8   We are grateful to Peter Lewis of the British Golf Museum, St Andrews, for attendance figures for the Open Championship; see also R. Laidlaw, 'Golf is Big Business', in G. Menzies (ed.), *The World of Golf* (BBC Publications, London, 1982), p. 179.
9   *New Society*, 3 September 1981, p. 394.
10   J. Williams, 'Churches, sport and identities in the North', in J. Hill and J. Williams (eds), *Sport and Identity in the North of England*, p. 115.
11   Winterbottom, 'The Pattern of Sport', Appendix A.
12   J. Child and B. Macmillan, 'Managers and their leisure', in M. Smith et al., *Leisure in Britain*, p. 115.
13   P. Wilmott and M. Young, *The Symmetrical Family* (Penguin, London, 1973), p. 257.
14   *Digest of Sports Statistics for the UK*, p. 73.
15   Winterbottom, 'The Pattern of Sport', Appendix B.
16   C. Gratton and A. Tice, 'Trends in sports participation in Britain, 1977–1987', *Leisure Studies* 13 (1994), p. 49.
17   *General Household Survey, Trends in Adult Participation in Sport in Great Britian, 1987–1996*, p. 3.
18   S. Glyn and A. Booth, *Modern Britain* (Routledge, London, 1996), p. 182.
19   *Digest of Sports Statistics*, p. 5.
20   M. Price, 'The Kings Cross Steelers', MA dissertation, Dept. of Politics, Warwick University, 1999 (unpublished).
21   F. Kew, *Sport: Social Problems and Issues* (1997), pp. 87–8; for a good

overview see M. Polley, *Moving the Goalposts: A History of Sport and Society since 1945*, chap. 6.

22 *General Household Survey*, 1996, p. 7.

23 B. Holland, L. Jackson, G. Jarvie and M. Smith, 'Sport and racism in Yorkshire: a case study', in J. Hill and J. Williams, *Sport and Identity in the North of England*, pp. 165–86.

24 T. Harrison, *Tanni* (Collins Willow, London, 1996), p. 174.

25 We are grateful to Julie Anderson, who is completing a doctorate on the history of disabled sport at De Montfort University, for her generous help.

26 *A Digest of Sports Statistics for the UK*, p. 7.

27 *The Guardian* (Education section), 29 February 2000, p. 4.

28 *Trends in Adult Participation, 1987–1997*, p. 9.

2 Reconstruction

1 Entitled *Agenda* it ran from 1942 to 1944.

2 On the history of what became, in 1944, the Central Council of Physical Recreation, see Evans, *Service to Sport*, and McIntosh, *Physical Education in England since 1800*.

3 Sir William Beveridge, Social Insurance and Allied Services (1942) Cmd 6404. Their headline was 'Has Sir William Beveridge Forgotten Sport?' (It seems unlikely that sport played any part in the life of the twentieth-century's people's William.) *World Sports* 10 (1), November–December 1942.

4 *World Sports* 10 (2), February–March 1943.

5 TUC, *The Problem of Leisure* (1943), p. 7. This anxiety about the 'looker-on' was widely shared by radicals. Watching sport was 'sport by proxy' not active citizenship. In particular watching football was condemned as escapist and compensatory with the spectators not attracted purely by interest in the game but by famous names, the virtuoso standard of play and the love of a winning team. The satisfaction and comradeship of actual participation in physical exercise was absent. As for the football pools, it was anti-social to think that it was possible or desirable to get something for nothing. Norman Crosby, *Full Enjoyment* (Nicholson & Watson, 1948), p. 23.

6 TUC, *The Problem of Leisure*, p. 12. *World Sports* 10 (2), February–March 1943.

7 Royal Commission on Betting, Lotteries and Gaming, 1949–51, Report, Cmd 8190, Minutes of Evidence, (41) VIII.

8 PRO HO 45/20250/12 June 1941. Youth Advisory Council, *The Youth Service After the War* (1943).

9 McIntosh, *Physical Education in England since 1800*, pp. 251–2.

10 Evans, *Service to Sport*, p. 73.

11 It was later renamed *Sport and Recreation* and lasted until 1972.

12 One contemporary commentator confidently predicted the death of the bookmaker with bigger and better racecourses dominated by the totalisa-tor. 'Newmarket Heath', 'The Turf To-Day and To-Morrow', *National*

Review, Jan. 1945, pp. 60–8. On the Report of the Racing Reorganisation Committee (Ilchester Committee) more generally the authority is Vamplew, *The Turf*.

13   Inglis, *League Football*, pp. 169–70. See also Alan Hardaker, *Hardaker of the League* (Pelham Books, 1977).

14   Inglis, *League Football*, p. 180.

15   Most of what follows is based on FA Minutes, 'Post-war Development'. Memorandum prepared by the War Emergency Committee for the consideration of the Council, May 1943, and 'Post-war Development – An Interim Report', October 1944. See also some comments by Rous in his autobiography, *Football Worlds. A Life time in Sport* (Faber, 1978), p. 212.

16   Though someone at the MCC had not entirely agreed and had set up the Findlay Commission in 1936 to report on the first-class counties. Its 23-page report stressed the need for attacking play, reducing the number of counties in the championship to fifteen and more representative matches in order to strengthen the England team. But as Warner said, there was no need for brighter cricket as it was a 'leisurely, intricate game of skill'. *Wisden's Cricketers' Almanack* (1943), p. 65.

17   *Wisden's Cricketers' Almanack* (1944), pp. 83–4.

18   'The case for relieving Cricket, and other similarly placed games and pastimes, from Entertainments' Duty, submitted by the MCC for the consideration of the Chancellor of the Exchequer' (typescript, 1944), p. 3. The tax on cricket was reduced.

19   *Wisden's Cricketers' Almanack* (1952) pp. 97–8. See also the *Almanack* for 1950, which included an article by John D. Eggar on 'Coaching the Schoolboy', pp. 103–5. *Report* of the Cricket Inquiry Committee (1950), 44 pp., also reproduced a detailed report of the work done by the Nottinghamshire Youth Cricket Advisory Committee set up in 1949, and an article by John Arlott entitled, 'The case for teaching Cricket', which included the following encomium to cricket in schools. 'The good games-master will produce in his cricket pupils a degree of physical fitness, dexterity, bodily control, strategic reasoning, discipline, self-reliance, comparable with those developed by woodwork, eurythmics, geometry and military training. More, his charges will develop some knowledge of practical psychology, a respect for patient application and a standard of manners which will make them acceptable in any reasonable company. His chances of success in so wide a field are good because cricket, sympathetically taught, compels a greater degree of enthusiasm in a larger proportion of boys than any other school activity.'

20   It was apparently in response to a written question. HC Deb. 419 (1945–6) col. 85.

21   *World Sports* 11 (2), October–November 1944. 'Let us have the next Olympic Games in London' was the headline in red, on the front.

22   *World Sports* 11 (3), December 1944–January 1945; 11 (4), April–May 1945. He buttered up the Americans by telling them that Los Angeles had been the 'best games ever, partly because it had been conducted in the

English language which, of course, ought to be the official language of the games rather than French'.

23 The authority on the background is Norman Baker, 'The Games that almost weren't: London 1948', *Critical Reflections on Olympic Ideology* (Centre for Olympic Studies, University of Western Ontario, London, 1994), pp. 107–15.

24 PRO FO 371–54785.

25 Alan Bullock, *The Life and Times of Ernest Bevin*, vol. 3, *Foreign Secretary 1945–51* (Heinemann, 1983), pp. 229–30, 287.

26 *Evening Standard*, 2 September 1947.

27 PRO CAB 128/9, 27 March 1947.

28 Quoted by M. R. Polley, 'The Foreign Office and international sport 1918–1948', unpublished PhD, University of Wales (1991), pp. 303–4.

29 2,300 could be housed comfortably at Uxbridge and 700 at West Drayton.

30 *Manchester Guardian*, 23 August 1948.

31 British Olympic Committee, Minutes Executive Committee of the Organising Committee 16 January 1947. *The Times*, 18 April 1949.

32 See Cecil Bear (ed.), *Official Report of the London Olympic Games* (BOA, 1948).

33 *World Sports* 14 (5), May 1948.

34 Ibid.

35 *Daily Express*, 20 July 1948.

36 A purchase meant a suit, a dress length, a pair of shoes or six handkerchiefs. *World Sports* 14 (7), July 1948.

37 *The Times*, 26 August 1948. On the tourist effort see also *Cavalcade*, 24 July, 1948.

38 HC Deb. 466 (1948–9) col. 52.

39 Even the *Boston Herald* suggested that sending the strongest American team ever to war-scarred Europe and one which had been eating well and had the best and uninterrupted training facilities was shameless as well as unsporting. *Boston Herald*, 9 July 1948.

40 The Osbert Lancaster cartoon was in the *Daily Express*, 23 January 1948. On ticket sales see BOA Minutes, General Purposes Committee, 15 June, 27 July 1948; and on the estimated net surplus, 15 February 1949. *Daily Herald*, 3 August 1948.

41 *Observer*, 1 August 1948.

42 *Daily Express*, 29 July 1948; *Evening Standard*, 2 September 1948.

43 *The Listener*, 2 September 1948. Harold Nicolson also watched the Games on television and was much impressed by it rather than them. *The Spectator*, 13 August 1948.

44 The MP was Mr Mack who represented Newcastle-under-Lyme. HC Deb. 466 (1948–9) col. 123.

45 *The Economist*, 21 August 1948. For a less hard-nosed view see *Daily Herald*, 3 August 1948.

46 Evans, *Service to Sport*, pp. 66–7.

47 T. Leski, 'Sports centre for London', *Architects' Journal*, 6 January 1949, pp. 13–14. Crosby, *Full Enjoyment*, pp. 114–117.

3 Amateurism

1   N. Duncanson and P. Collins, *Tales of Gold*, p. 41.
2   N. Baker, 'The amateur ideal in a society of equality: change and continuity in post-Second World War British sport', *International Journal of the History of Sport* 12 (1), April 1995, p. 104.
3   *New Society*, 9 August 1985, p. 90.
4   D. Compton, *End of an Innings*, p. 105.
5   M. Marshall, *Gentlemen and Players: Conversations with Cricketers*, pp. 136–7; an absorbing oral history of social relationships.
6   D. Mosey, *Laker: Portrait of a Legend*, p. 65.
7   Ibid., p. 66.
8   Marshall, *Gentlemen and Players*, p. 257.
9   Gordon Pirie, *Running Wild*, p. 31.
10 Ibid., p. 33.
11 D. Hyman, *Sprint to Fame*, p. 118.
12 Minutes of oral evidence presented to the Wolfenden Committee, 12 May 1959.
13 *Daily Express*, 10 May 1960.
14 J. Crump in Tony Mason (ed.), *Sport in Britain: A Social History*, p. 57.
15 N. Duncanson and P. Collins, *Tales of Gold*, p. 97.
16 G. Whannel, *Fields in Vision: Television, Sport and Cultural Transformation, pp. 140–7.
17 *Independent on Sunday*, 9 January 1984, p. 8.
18 Ibid.
19 A. Smith, 'The Clubs, the RFU and the impact of professionalism on Rugby Union, 1995–1999', in D. Porter and A. Smith (eds), 'Amateurs and professionals in post-war British sport', *Journal of Contemporary British History* 14 (2), Summer 2000, gives a good overview.
20 *The Times*, 24 November 1997.
21 *Digest of Sports Statistics for the UK*, p. 7.
22 Birmingham City Parks Department, appendix to W. Winterbottom, 'The Pattern of Sport in the UK', Appendix A.
23 *The Observer*, 20 June 1993, p. 43.
24 Wolfenden Committee (see note 12).
25 Ibid.
26 H. Walker, 'Lawn Tennis', in T. Mason, *Sport in Britain*, p. 269.
27 *The Observer*, 26 June 1983, p. 9.
28 Richard Evans, *John McEnroe: A Rage for Perfection* (Sidgwick and Jackson, London, 1982).
29 E. Halladay, *Rowing in England: A Social History* (Manchester University Press, Manchester, 1990); also N. Wigglesworth, *A Social History of English Rowing* (Frank Cass, London, 1992).
30 C. Dodd, 'Rowing', in Mason, *Sport in Britain*, p. 283.
31 Wolfenden Committee (see note 12).
32 Duncanson and Collins, *Tales of Gold*, p. 123.
33 Jennifer Hargreaves, *Sporting Females* (Routledge, London, 1994), p. 251.

4 The Professionals

1   The estimate was by Geoffrey Nicholson in his excellent book *The Professionals*.
2   On the panel bowlers see Nicholson, *The Professionals*, pp. 53–63.
3   Evidence given to the Wolfenden Committee by the British Boxing Board of Control, WSC/57.
4   1951 Census Occupation Table for England and Wales.
5   Geoffrey Nicholson suggested 20,000 in 1964, which may have been an overestimate.
6   Ted Farmer, *The Heartbreak Game* (Hillburgh Publishers, 1987), pp. 11–12.
7   On horse racing see Wray Vamplew, 'Still crazy after all these years: continuity in a changing labour market for professional jockeys', in Porter and Smith (eds), *For the Love of the Game*.
8   Nicholson, *The Professionals*, p. 108.
9   Harris, *Two Wheels to the Top*, pp. 4–5.
10 Farmer, *The Heartbreak Game*, p. 13; Bowler, *Danny Blanchflower*, p. 60. It was a commonplace among British football management that if you denied players the ball during training they would want it more on matchdays.
11 Harris, *Two Wheels to the Top*, pp. 20–1, 45, 49. Though he claimed that when he first turned professional he had to sell his new Mark IV Jaguar he had bought as an amateur and replace it with an old Vauxhall. Ibid., p. 80.
12 See Vamplew, 'Still crazy', pp. 5–8.
13 See Hull City A.F.C., *Bye-Laws and Training Rules for Players 1939–40 Season*.
14 Richard Holt, *Stanmore Golf Club 1893–1993. A Social History* (Stanmore Golf Club, 1993), pp. 1–4.
15 Nicholson, *The Professionals*, pp. 21–3.
16 Harris, *Two Wheels to the Top*, pp. 130–1, 139.
17 Vamplew, 'Still crazy', p. 9.
18 Farmer, *The Heartbreak Game*, pp. 54–5, 70–3, 86–99. No Wolves official visited Farmer while he was in hospital for treatment. Derek Dooley scored 63 goals in as many games for Sheffield Wednesday but on 14 February 1953 broke a leg in a collision with the Preston goalkeeper. The leg had to be amputated so ending another potential champion career at the age of 23.
19 Chalke, *Runs in the Memory*, pp. 107–8.
20 Quoted by Nicholson, *The Professionals*, p. 113.
21 Nicholson, *The Professionals*, pp. 86–7.
22 Harris, *Two Wheels to the Top*, p. 90.
23 Nicholson, *The Professionals*, p. 113.
24 Geoffrey Moorhouse, *Lord's* (Hodder and Stoughton, 1983), p. 152.
25 Chalke, *Runs in the Memory*, p. 111.
26 For more details on the average earnings of professional footballers in the

fifties and sixties see the Department of Education and Science Report of the Committee on Football (HMSO 1968, The Chester Report), pp. 35–6; Tony Mason, 'Football', in Mason (ed.), *Sport in Britain*, pp. 161–2; and Russell, *Football and the English*, pp. 175–6. There was no minimum wage in Scotland where Celtic and Rangers, the two biggest clubs, with their sense of representing wider communities than football, may have thought that there were more important things than cash. See H. F. Moorhouse, 'Shooting stars', pp. 179–97.

27 Eddie Firmani, *Football among the Millionaires* (Sports Book Club, 1960) John Charles, *King of Soccer*, p. 146, and Farmer, *The Heartbreak Game*; pp. 12, 29, 35, 45.

28 Bowler, *Danny Blanchflower*, pp. 165–85.

29 Matches on Christmas Day were last played in 1958.

30 Chalke, *Runs in the Memory*, p. 107.

31 Firmani, *Football among the Millionaires*, pp. 42, 68; and Shelley Webb, *Footballers' Wives*, p. 91. It was not clear whether not having TV was a lifestyle choice. Although one of their sons went on to play football professionally, David insisted that academic achievement came first.

32 See his obituaries in the *Guardian* and *The Times*, 7 November 1996.

33 *The Times*, 22 July 1957.

34 *Wisden* (1963), p. 138. The rest of this section is based on M. Marshall, *Gentlemen and Players*; Jack Williams, 'Cricket', in Mason (ed.), *Sport in Britain*; and Chalke, *Runs in the Memory*.

35 The European circuit had already been merged with the British in 1971. This section is based on Ray Physick and Richard Holt, ' "Big money": the tournament players and the PGA 1945–75', in Porter and Smith, *For the Love of the Game*.

36 See Kate Brasher, 'Traditional versus commercial values in sport. The case of tennis', in Allison (ed.), *Politics of Sport*, pp. 198–215.

37 Wolfenden Committee Minutes, 5 August 1959.

38 Quoted in John Harding, *For the Good of the Game*, p. 270.

39 John Charles, *King of Soccer*, p. 149.

40 Between May and June 1961 three English and one Scottish forward went to Italy: Jimmy Greaves from Chelsea to AC Milan, Joe Baker and Denis Law from Hibernian and Manchester City respectively to Torino and Gerry Hitchens from Aston Villa to Inter Milan. The first three soon returned being unable to settle in another culture. Greaves scored 9 goals in only 10 matches. Hitchens had a supportive wife, did not drink nor behave as boorishly as the young male British were wont to abroad, and stayed for seven years going on to play for Torino, Atalanta and Cagliari.

41 This provided grounds for an appeal which, in 1962, overturned the verdicts of the commission. The players received awards which covered their loss of wages and damages. For more detail see Harding, *For the Good of the Game*, pp. 266–75; and Inglis, *Soccer in the Dock*, ch. 8, pp. 116–139.

42 See table 4, *1991 Census, Economic Activity Volume, Great Britain*.

43 See Sport England, Lottery Fund, Revenue Awards to date, www.english.sports.gov.uk. I would like to thank Peter Smith and Kate Neal of the UK Sports Council, for providing information.

44 *Independent on Sunday*, 13 February 2000.

45 Phil Pilley (ed.), *The Story of Bowls*, Guardian, 9 March 1988, 9 August 1999. A conversation with Gary Smith, 13 March 2000.

46 Coe, Teasdale and Wickham, *More Than A Game*, p. 24.

47 *Guardian*, 13 March 2000. At least football managers would have directed the apology to the supporters!

48 *Guardian* 18 December 1997.

49 But in the stables female workers were much sought after. See Vamplew, pp. 3–4.

50 *Guardian*, 5 July 1996.

51 See Dave Hill, *Out of his Skin*, and his article in *New Society*, 11 December 1987. Ernest Cashmore, *Black Sportsmen* (1982).

52 *Independent on Sunday*, 16 April 2000.

53 John Williams, *Is it all over? Can Football Survive the Premier League?* (South Street Press, Reading, 1999), pp. 48–50.

54 *Independent*, 9 February 2000. The PFA and some clubs have been trying to persuade young players not to sign up with agents but to use the resources of the PFA to negotiate their salaries and conditions of employment. *Guardian*, 3 March–19 April 2000.

55 *Guardian*, 13 January 2000. Not all the players were British of course. The prize money for the British Open in 2000 was just over £2 million.

56 Vamplew, 'Still crazy', pp. 14–15.

57 Hughes, *A Lot of Hard Yakka*, pp. 246, 277.

58 Pete Nichols (ed.), *BBC Radio 5 Live Sports Yearbook* (2000); *Guardian*, 7 March 2000; and *OK!*, 16 July 1999. Victoria Adams is a member of the Spice Girls and top of a list of the 100 richest people under 30 years old.

59 Reported by the *Guardian*, 12 March 1997. Seventy per cent disagreed with the proposition that Alan Shearer was worth every penny of his £15 million transfer from Blackburn Rovers to Newcastle United.

60 Williams, *Is it all over?*, pp. 40–1; and Pierre Lanfranchi, *On Y Va! European Footballers on the Move* (European Movement, n.d.).

61 Quoted by Christopher Dodd in 'Rowing', Mason, *Sport in Britain*, p. 283.

62 Hughes, *A Lot of Hard Yakka*, pp. 245–6. Edward Tenner, 'The Technological Imperative', in *Wilson Quarterley*, Winter 1995, pp. 26–34.

63 *Sunday Times*, 29 October 1989.

64 *Guardian*, 30 July 1994.

65 *Guardian*, 20 March 2000.

66 *Careers in Sport Compendium* (Sports Council, 1996), pp. 24–5.

5 Media

1 D. Mosey, *Laker: Portrait of a Legend* (Queen Anne, London, 1989), p. 30.

2   For an overview of international research, see Lawrence A. Wenner (ed.), *Mediasport*; on Britain see Asa Briggs, *The History of Broadcasting in Britain*, vol. 4; Garry Whannel, *Fields in Vision: Television Sport and Cultural Transformation*, is a key text; see also S. Barnett, *Games and Sets: The Changing Face of Sport on Television*.

3   Christopher Martin Jenkins, *Ball by Ball: The Story of Cricket Broadcasting*, p. 169; see also D. A. Allen, *Cricket on the Air: A Selection from Fifty Years of Radio Broadcasts*.

4   A. Adams (ed.), *50 Years of Sports Report*, pp. 11, 217–18.

5   Gordon T. Stewart, 'Tenzing's two wrist watches: the conquest of Everest and late imperial culture in Britain, 1921–1953', *Past and Present* 154 (1995).

6   Ray Physick and Richard Holt, ' "Big Money": the tournament player and the PGA', *Journal of Contemporary British History* 14 (2), Summer 2000.

7   Barnett, *Games and Sets*, pp.47–8.

8   John Motson, *Match of the Day: The Complete Record since 1964*, p. 7.

9   *The Guardian*, 11 December 1992.

10 'Political and economic planning report' (1956), cited in J. M. Chandler, *Television and National Sport: The United States and Britain*, p. 112.

11 *Sunday Telegraph*, 23 January 2000, p. 11 (news) and p. 6 (sport).

12 A. Briggs, *History of Broadcasting*, vol. 4, p. 859.

13 The BBC/ITV battle is well covered in Whannel, *Fields in Vision*, pp. 55–8.

14 G. Whannel, 'Reading the sports media audience', in L. Wenner (ed.), *Mediasport*, pp. 223–4.

15 Adam Brown, 'Tilting at windmills: Manchester United and the defeat of the BSkyB bid', *Soundings: a Journal of Politics and Culture* 13 (Autumn 1999), pp. 118–28.

16 Barnett, *Games and Sets*, p. 177.

17 Denis Compton, *End of an Innings*, p. ix.

18 S. Hawes, 'Making faces: when "Socusoap" was young', *Soundings: a Journal of Politics and Culture* 13 (Autumn 1999), p. 156.

19 Stephen Aris, *Sportsbiz: Inside the Sports Business*, p. 16.

20 Minute of Oral Evidence to the Wolfenden Committee, 12 May 1959.

21 Cited in Stephen K. Kelly, *Back Page Football: A Century of Newspaper Coverage* (Queen Anne, London, 1988), p. 107; we are grateful to Jeff Hill for his insights into England–Hungary in 1953–4.

22 Wolfenden Committee, 12 May 1959.

23 G. Pirie, *Running Wild*, p. 10.

24 Cited in J. Hargreaves, *Sport, Power and Culture*, p. 139.

25 S. Wagg, 'Playing the past: the media and the England football team', in J. Williams and S. Wagg, *British Football and Social Change: Getting into Europe*, pp. 230–2.

26 R. Holt, 'King across the border: Dennis Law and Scottish football', in Grant Jarvie and Graham Walker (eds), *Scottish Sport in the Making of the Nation*, pp. 62–3.

27 *The Observer*, 30 June 1996; *The Independent*, 28 June 1996.

28 Ian Hamilton, 'Gazza Agonistes', in *Granta* 45 (Penguin, London, 1993).

29 Stuart Cosgrove, *Hampden Babylon: Sex and Scandal in Scottish Football*, is a joyous parody of football and the tabloids, which influenced D. Campbell, P. May and A. Shields, *The Lad Done Bad: Sex, Sleaze and Scandal in English Football* (Penguin, London, 1996).

6 Identity

1   The phrase comes from Mike Marqusee, *Anyone But England: Cricket, Race and Class.*

2   R. Holt, 'Heroes of the North', in J. Hill and J. Williams, *Sport and Identity in the North of England*, p. 151.

3   H. F. Moorhouse, 'From Zines like these? Fanzines, tradition and identity in Scottish football', in G. Jarvie and G. Walker (eds), *Scottish Sport and the Making of the Nation*, pp. 173–94.

4   The literature on hooliganism is extensive. For a useful survey of the 1980s material, see J. Williams, 'Having an Away Day: English football spectators and the hooligan debate', in J. Williams and S. Wagg, *British Football and Social Change*, pp. 160–84.

5   E. Dunning, P. Murphy and J. Williams, *The Roots of Football Hooliganism.*

6   For example, P. Cohen, 'Subcultural conflict and working class community', in S. Hall, D. Hobson, A. Lowe and P. Willis (eds), *Culture, Media and Language* (Routledge, London, 1980).

7   Gary Armstrong, *Football Hooligans: Knowing the Score*, provides the most detailed field work to date.

8   J. Bains and S. Johals, *Corner Flags and Corner Shops: The Asian Football Experience* (Gollanz, London, 1998).

9   J. Hill, 'Cocks, cats, caps and cups: a semiotic approach to sport and national identity', *Culture, Sport and Society* 2 (2), Summer 1999, pp. 1–21.

10 J. Hill, 'The legend of Denis Compton', *The Sports Historian* 18 (2), November 1998.

11 D. Trelford, *Len Hutton Remembered* (Witherby, London, 1992).

12 D. Foot, *Wally Hammond: The Reasons Why.*

13 M. Marqusee, *Anyone But England*, esp. ch. 8.

14 H. F. Moorhouse, 'We're Off to Wembley!', in D. McCrone, D. Kendrick and F. Straw (eds), *The Making of Modern Scotland: Nation, Culture and Social Change* (Edinburgh University Press, 1989).

15 See S. Cosgrove, *Hampden Babylon: Sex and Scandal in Scottish Football.*

16 R. Holt, 'King over the Border: Denis Law and Scottish football', in G. Jarvie and G. Walker (eds), *Scottish Sport in the Making of the Nation*, pp. 58–74.

17 Dai Smith and Gareth Williams, *Fields of Praise: The Official History of the Welsh Rugby Union*, p. 340; an outstanding example of how an official history can also be a major work of social history.

18 Dai Smith and Gareth Williams, 'Beyond the fields of praise: Welsh rugby 1980–1999', in H. Richards, P. Stead and G. Williams, *More Heart and Soul: The Character of Welsh Rugby*, pp. 205–32.

19 Ibid.
20 M. Cronin, *Sport and Nationalism in Ireland: Gaelic Games, Soccer and Identity since 1884*, ch. 6; see also J. Sugden and Alan Bairner, *Sport, Sectarianism and Society in a Divided Ireland*.
21 M. Cronin, 'Which nation, Which flag?: boxing and national identities in Ireland', *International Review for the Sociology of Sport* 32 (2), June 1997, pp. 131–46; we are most grateful to Mike Cronin for his expert analysis of Irish national identity and sport.
22 From a transcript of *Analysis*, broadcast on Radio 4, 2 December 1999.
23 For a useful summary of race and sport see E. Cashmore, *Making Sense of Sports*, pp. 97–116.

7 Government

1 The serious and complex issues produced by this process are extensively analysed in S. J. D. Green and R. C. Whiting (eds), *The Boundaries of the State in Modern Britain* (Cambridge University Press, 1996).
2 On the attempt by the wartime coalition and early post-war British governments to build a robust national culture see Richard Weight, 'Pale stood Albion: the promotion of national culture in Britain 1939–56' (University of London PhD, 1995).
3 Quoted in Weight, 'Pale stood Albion', p. 83. For a fascinating debate in 1952 on the impact of the entertainment tax on sport, see HC Deb. 500 (6 May 1952) cols. 201–32.
4 That it had been won on the playing fields of Eton. As Weight points out, the slogan also emphasized the superiority of the philanthropist over the civil servant and in sport, the amateur gentleman over the professional player. At least some people saw voluntarism as the noblest form of welfare. See Weight, 'Pale stod Albion', p. 168, and chapter 3 above.
5 See Norman Baker, 'Going to the dogs – hostility to greyhound racing in Britain: puritanism, socialism and pragmatism', in *Journal of Sport History* 23 (2), 1996, pp. 97–119, and Nicholas Fishwick, *From Clegg to Clegg House. The Official Centenary History of the Sheffield and Hallamshire County Football Association 1886–1986* (Sheffield and Hallamshire CFA, Sheffield, 1986), p. 65.
6 See *Britain in the World of Sport* (Physical Education Association of Great Britain, Birmingham, 1956), p. 68. Other important contributors to these debates included Philip Noel-Baker, 'A state subsidy', in H. A. Meyer (ed.), *Modern Athletics* (Nelson, 1958), pp. 30–40, and D. D. Molyneux, *Central Government Aid to Sport and Physical Recreation in Countries of Western Europe* (Birmingham, 1962).
7 On Wolfenden see Evans, *Service to Sport*, especially ch. 9. The Report was debated in the House of Lords on 15 February 1961 and in the Commons on 28 April 1961.
8 Quoted by Weight, 'Pale stood Albion', p. 229. See also *The Challenge of*

Leisure (Conservative Party, 1959) and *Leisure for Living* (Labour Party, 1959).

9   See the Albermarle Report on the Youth Service (1959–60), ch. 5.

10 It is interesting to recall the Committee's membership. Apart from the chairman it included Mrs Betty Clark, Headmistress of Benenden; the Bishop of Chester who had a rowing 'blue'; Sir Godfrey Ince, Chairman of Cable and Wireless, a cricket and football enthusiast; Jack Longland, Director of Education for Derbyshire, former Cambridge athletics 'blue' and mountaineer; David Munrow, Director of the Physical Education Department at the University of Birmingham; Tony Pawson, industrial welfare officer, sports journalist, Oxford 'blue' at cricket and football; and Sir Arthur Porritt, Oxford and Olympic sprinter and member of the International Olympic Committee. These were leading figures in the world of physical education and recreational sport, and popular participation and its social effects interested them more than the preparation of sporting elites.

11 See the Wolfenden Report, *Sport and the Community*, ch. 3. On some of the general questions raised see the interesting essay by Maurice Roche, 'Sport and community: rhetoric and reality in the development of British sport policy', in J. C. Binfield and John Stevenson (eds), *Sport, Culture and Politics* (Sheffield University, Sheffield, 1993), pp. 72–112.

12 Department of the Environment, *Sport and Recreation* 3, para. 13.

13 Most of the money spent on sport and recreation in Britain is spent by local government.

Expenditure on Sport 1985

	£ million
Direct Government Spending	
Sports Council	32
Sports Minister	32
Local Authorities (England)	800
Voluntary Sector (England)	1500
Consumer Spending on Sport	2
Gambling	1–2

The Sports Council, *Into the 90s: A Strategy for Sport 1988–1993* (Sports Council, 1988). Quoted by Roche, 'Sport and community', p. 82.

14 Cited in Richard Holt and Alan Tomlinson, 'Sport and leisure', in Dennis Kavanagh and Anthony Seldon (eds), *The Major Effect* (Macmillan, London, 1994), p. 447.

15 See McIntosh and Charlton, *The Impact of Sport For All Policy*, and Roche, 'Sport and Community', on which much of what follows is based.

16 Belfast was allowed the resources to build fourteen new leisure centres in the 1970s when the optimum number for a city of its size should have been eight. The money was made available in the hope that the provision of leisure and sporting opportunity might 'offset the tendency towards civil disorder'. But promoting a sporting solution to a political problem was unrealistic and it could not work. See Sugden and Bairner, *Sport, Sectarianism and Society*, chs 5 and 6.

17 *Guardian*, 5 March 1999.
18 On the Australian Institute of Sport see *The Oxford Companion to Australian Sport* (Oxford University Press, Australia, 1992), p. 31.
19 See, for example, the interview he gave to Michael Parkinson in the *Daily Telegraph*, 23 August 1993.
20 Spanish sporting success at Barcelona was also influential, showing what could be done with the planning and application of management, material and scientific resources.
21 *Guardian*, 18 February 1993. The necessary facilities were to be provided jointly by the private sector and the government.
22 It was the English Sports Council, now Sport England, which was to have the responsibility of distributing annually over £200 million of National Lottery money.
23 Department of National Heritage, *Sport. Raising the Game* (1995), pp. 1 and 3. Nobody would have believed a politician if it had been entitled 'Playing the Game'.
24 The Secondary School Headmasters' Association claimed that research showed a decline of over 70 per cent in the number of school sports fixtures on weekday evenings and Saturday mornings between 1987 and 1994. *Guardian*, 21 June 1999.
25 See *Labour's Sporting Nation* (1997), p. 8.
26 *Independent on Sunday*, 22 January 1995, in which he predicted a championship win for Newcastle United in the next four years. See also *Financial Times'* Sport Section, 8 August 1997. He also spoke at the 80th birthday tribute to Sir Stanley Matthews organized by the Football Writers' Association.
27 See *Guardian*, 17 December 1997, 2 March 1999; *Independent on Sunday*, 21 December 1997, 6 June 1999; *The Times*, 9 November 1998.
28 The eleven centres are Bath, Bedford, Bisham Abbey, Crystal Palace, Gateshead, Holme, Pierrepoint (Nottingham), Lilleshall, Manchester, Sheffield, Southampton. The National Lottery Sports Fund will provide the money to modernize existing facilities and support expert assistance in sports medicine and sports science.
29 *Guardian*, 23 December 1999; *Independent on Sunday*, 31 January 1999, 14 March 1999.
30 *Guardian*, 21 October 1999; *Independent on Sunday*, 26 December 1999.
31 *Independent on Sunday*, 6 June 1999; *Guardian*, 19 May, 8 June, 21 June 1999; *The Times*, 6 April 2000.
32 What follows is mainly based on David Conn, *The Football Business* (Mainstream, Edinburgh, 1997), Anthony King, *The End of the Terraces* (Leicester University Press, London, 1998), Russell, *Football and the English*, and Williams and Wagg (eds), *British Football and Social Change*. See also chapter 6.
33 David Lacey in *Guardian*, 15 April 1999.
34 The Hillsborough Stadium Disaster, 15 April 1989. Inquiry by Rt Hon. Lord Justice Taylor. Final report, Cm 962 (HMSO 1990). He also recommended a Stadia Advisory Design Council, which was set up but

abandoned in 1993 when the FA and the Football League withdrew funding. It is interesting that perimeter fencing remains a feature of most football grounds in Europe.

35 The best account of these changes in the structure of and support for football is probably Anthony King, 'The Premier League and the New Consumption of Football', unpublished PhD thesis, University of Salford (1995). King also argues that the financial burdens of the Taylor Report provided the opportunity for a new business class of entrepreneurs to become involved in football, which has become favourable to financial investment and profit making on a scale unknown until now. It should be stressed that the recommendations of Taylor also applied to other spectator sports, notably cricket and rugby. Someone from the world of cricket told Taylor that his report had cost Surrey County Cricket Club one million pounds to improve their Oval ground. *Guardian*, 8 April 1994. See also Conn, *The Football Business* (Edinburgh, 1998, edn), esp. ch. 7.

36 Martin Polley, 'Olympic diplomacy: the British government and the projected 1940 Olympic Games', *International Journal of the History of Sport* 9 (2), August 1992, pp. 169–87; Peter Beck, *Scoring for Britain. International Football and International Politics, 1900–1939* (Frank Cass, London, 1999).

37 The 1954 meeting under floodlights included the 5000 metres between Vladimir Kuts, the European Champion, and Christopher Chattaway, which Chattaway won narrowly in world record time. The 1956 match was cancelled after the British authorities insisted that the courts could not be compelled to drop charges of shoplifting against a Russian woman discus-thrower. She had allegedly stolen five hats.

38 Christopher Hill, *Olympic Politics* (Manchester University Press, Manchester, 1992), pp. 120–55. Mrs Thatcher later claimed in her memoirs that unlike the Russians 'our athletes were free to make up their own minds'!

39 This section is based on Polley, *Moving the Goalposts*, pp. 30–2, *Guardian*, 8 February, 15 November 1999 and Marqusee, *Anyone But England*, ch. 6.

40 See the report of a paper given by Professor Bruce Murray of the Witwatersrand University, South Africa, to Sporting Traditions XII, New Zealand, February 1999, *BSSH Newsletter* 10 (Autumn 1999), pp. 13–14.

41 The point is clearer if their first-class careers are compared. Cartwright played for 25 years scoring nearly 14,000 runs, average 21 but taking 1536 wickets at 19 runs per wicket. D'Oliveira played for 19 years, scored almost 19,000 runs, average 40 per innings and took 548 wickets at 27. Cartwright only played in five Test Matches, whereas D'Oliveira represented England 44 times.

42 Quoted by *Guardian*, 8 February 1999.

43 See the account of an eye-witness, *Guardian*, 15 November 1999.

44 The Conservative MP John Carlisle tried to persuade the MCC to send a team to South Africa in 1983. The members supported their committees' refusal by 6604 votes to 4344. In 1986, 32 out of 58 Commonwealth

nations boycotted the Edinburgh Games over the refusal of the British government to implement a programme of economic sanctions against South Africa.

45 For example, see the comments of the first Professor of Youth Sport at Loughborough University, *Guardian*, 27 August 1999.

46 *Guardian*, 27 August 1999.

47 For example, Sir Stirling Moss and Sir Henry Cooper were in the 2000 New Year list as were the six previously 'unhonoured' members of the England team which won the World Cup in 1966.

48 These figures are taken from Tony Cook, 'Sponsorship in sport', in Sir Roy Shaw, *The Spread of Sponsorship* (Bloodaxe Books, Newcastle-upon-Tyne, 1993), p. 51.

49 *Financial Times Weekend Sport*, 8 August 1997.

50 *Guardian*, 2 March 1999. It is hard to imagine any Prime Minister before this moment doing such a thing.

51 Kate Hoey was interviewed in *Independent on Sunday*, 3 October 1999.

Conclusion

1 *Sunday Times*, 26 March 2000, p. 21.

2 Martin Jacques, 'Worshipping at the altar of sport', *The Observer*, 13 July 1997; a long and thoughtful piece on the new meanings of sport.

Select Bibliography

Note. Items marked with an asterisk (*) have been particularly useful. A full list of all references is contained in the chapter notes. Place of publication is London unless otherwise indicated.

Adams, A. (ed.), *50 Years of Sports Report* (Collins, 1999).
Allen, D. A., *Cricket on the Air; a selection of fifty years of radio broadcasts* (BBC, 1985).
Allison, L. (ed.), *The Politics of Sport* (Manchester University Press, Manchester, 1986).
*Aris, S., *Sportsbiz: inside the sports business* (Hutchinson, 1990).
Armstrong, G., *Football Hooligans: knowing the score* (Berg, Oxford, 1988).
*Baker, N., 'The amateur ideal in a society of equality: change and continuity in post-Second World War British sport, 1945–48', *International Journal of the History of Sport* 12 (1), 1995.
*Barnett, S., *Games and Sets: the changing face of sport on television* (BFI publications, 1990).
Bear, C. (ed.), *Official Report of the London Olympic Games* (British Olympic Association, 1948).
Birley, D., *Playing the Game: sport and British society, 1910–45* (Manchester University Press, Manchester, 1995).
Blain, N., Boyle, R., and O'Donnell, H., *Sport and National Identity in the European Media* (Leicester University Press, Leicester, 1993).
Blake. A., *The Body Language: the meaning of modern sport* (Lawrence and Wishart, 1996).
Booth, D., *The Impossible Hero. A Life of Gordon Pirie* (Corsica Press, 1999).
Bowler, D., *Danny Blanchflower: a biography of a visionary* (Gollancz, 1997).
Briggs, A., *The History of Broadcasting in the United Kingdom, vol. iv: Sound and Vision* (Oxford University Press, Oxford 1979).
Cashmore, E., *Black Sportsmen* (Routledge, 1982).
Cashmore, E., *Making Sense of Sports* (Routledge, 1996).

Chalke, S. R., *Runs in the Memory: county cricket in the 1950s* (Fairfield, Bath, 1997).

Chandler, J., *Television and National Sport: the United States and Britain* (Illinois University Press, Urbana, IL, 1988).

Chester, Sir N., *Department of Education and Science Report of the Committee on Football* (HMSO, 1968, 'The Chester Report').

Coe, S., Teasdale, D. and Whickham, D., *More than a Game* (BBC Books, 1992).

*Coghlan, J. with Webb, I., *Sport and British Politics since 1960* (Falmer, Basingstoke, 1990).

Compton, D., *End of an Innings* (Pavilion edn, 1988).

*Cosgrove, S., *Hampden Babylon: sex and scandal in Scottish football* (Canongate, Edinburgh, 1991).

Critcher, C., 'Football since the war', in J. Clarke, C. Critcher and R. Johnson (eds), *Working Class Culture: studies in history and theory* (Hutchinson, 1979).

*Cronin, M., *Sport and Nationalism in Ireland: Gaelic games, soccer and identity since 1884* (Four Courts Press, Dublin, 1999).

Cronin, M., 'Which nation, Which flag? Boxing and national identities in Ireland', *International Review for the Sociology of Sport* 32 (2), 1997.

Digest of Sports Statistics for the UK (UK Sports Council, 3rd edn, 1991).

Duncanson, N. and Collins, P., *Tales of Gold* (Queen Anne/Macdonald, 1992).

Dunning, E., Murphy, P. and Williams, J., *The Roots of Football Hooliganism* (Routledge, 1988).

Dunphy, E., *Only a Game?* (Penguin, Harmondsworth, 1977).

Evans, H. J., *The Story of the CCPR 1935–72* (The Sports Council, 1974).

Foot, D., *Wally Hammond: the reasons why* (Robson, 1998).

*General Household Survey, *Trends in Adult Participation in Sport in Great Britain, 1987–1996* (Sport England/UK Sport, 1999).

General Household Survey, *Participation in Sport in Great Britain 1996* (Sport England/UK Sport, 1999).

Gratton, C. and Tice, A., 'Trends in sports participation in Britain, 1977–1987', *Leisure Studies* 13, 1994.

Hamilton, I., 'Gazza Agonistes', *Granta* 45 (Penguin, Harmondsworth, 1993).

Harding, J., *For the Good of the Game: the official history of the Professional Footballers' Association* (Robson Books, 1991).

Hargreaves, Jennifer, *Sporting Females: critical issues in the history and sociology of women's sports* (Routledge, 1994).

Hargreaves, John, *Sport, Power and Culture: a social and historical analysis of popular sports in Britain* (Polity, Cambridge, 1986).

Harris, Reg, *Two Wheels to the Top: an autobiography* (Allen and Unwin, 1976).

Hawes, S., 'Making faces: when "Socu-soap" was young', *Soundings: a Journal of Politics and Culture* 13, 1999.

Hill, D., *Out of His Skin: the John Barnes phenomenon* (Faber, 1989).

Hill, J., 'The legend of Denis Compton', *The Sports Historian* 18 (2), November 1998.

Hill, J. and Williams, J. (eds), *Sport and Identity in the North of England* (Keele University Press, Keele, 1996).

Holt, R., *Sport and the British: a modern history* (Oxford University Press, Oxford, 1989).

Hughes, S., *A Lot of Hard Yakka. Triumph and Torment: a county cricketer's life* (Headline, 1997).

Hyman, D., *Sprint to Fame* (Stanley Paul, 1964).

Inglis, S., *Soccer in the Dock* (Willow Books, 1985).

Inglis, S., *League Football and the Men Who Made It* (Collins, 1988).

*Jarvie, G. and Walker, G. (eds), *Scottish Sport in the Making of the Nation: ninety minute patriots?* (Leicester University Press, Leicester, 1994).

Kew, F., *Sport: social problems and issues* (Butterworth/Heinemann, 1997).

*Marqusee, M., *Anyone but England: cricket, race and class* (Two Heads Publishing, 1998 edn).

Marshall, M., *Gentlemen and Players: conversations with cricketers* (Grafton, 1987).

Martin-Jenkins, C., *Ball by Ball: the story of cricket broadcasting* (Grafton, 1990).

Mason. T. (ed.), *Sport in Britain: a social history* (Cambridge University Press, Cambridge, 1989).

McIntosh, P. and Charlton, V., *The Impact of the 'Sport for All' Policy, 1966–1984* (Sports Council, 1984).

Moorhouse, G., *At the George and other Essays on Rugby League* (Sceptre, 1989).

Moorhouse, H. F., 'Shooting stars: football and working class culture in twentieth-century Scotland', in R. Holt (ed.), *Sport and the Working Class in Modern Britain* (Manchester University Press, Manchester, 1990).

Mosey, D., *Laker: portrait of a legend* (Queen Anne/Macdonald, 1989).

Motson, J., *Match of the Day: the complete record since 1964* (BBC Books, 1992).

Nicholson, G., *The Professionals* (André Deutsch, 1964).

Pilley, P. (ed.), *The Story of Bowls* (Stanley Paul, 1987).

Pirie, G., *Running Wild* (W. H. Allen, 1961).

Polley, M., *Moving the Goalposts: a history of sport and society since 1945* (Routledge, 1998).

Porter, D. and Smith, A. (eds), *Amateurs and Professionals in Post-War British Sport* (Frank Cass, 2000).

Richards, H., Stead, P. and Williams, G., *More Heart and Soul: the character of Welsh rugby* (University of Wales Press, Cardiff, 1999).

*Russell, D., *Football and the English: a social history of Association Football in England, 1963–1995* (Carnegie, Preston, 1997).

*Smith, D. and Williams, G., *Fields of Praise: the official history of the Welsh Rugby Union* (University of Wales Press, Cardiff, 1981).

Stewart, G. T., 'Tenzing's two wrist watches: the conquest of Everest and late imperial culture in Britain 1921–1953', *Past and Present* 154, 1995.

Sugden, J. and Bairner, A., *Sport, Sectarianism and Society in a Divided Ireland* (Leicester University Press, Leicester, 1993).

Tomlinson, A. and Whannel, G. (eds), *Off the Ball: the football World Cup* (Pluto, 1986).

Vamplew, W., *The Turf: a social and economic history of horse racing* (Allen Lane, 1976).

Wagg, S., *The Football World: a contemporary social history* (Harvester, Brighton, 1984).

Webb, S., *Footballers' Wives Tell their Tales* (Yellow Jersey, 1998).

Wenner, L. A. (ed.), *Media Sport* (Routledge, 1998).

*Whannel, G., *Fields in Vision: television sport and cultural transformation* (Routledge, 1992).

Williams, J. and Wagg, S., *British Football and Social Change: getting into Europe* (Leicester University Press, Leicester, 1991).

Winterbottom, W., 'The pattern of sport in the United Kingdom', Proceedings of the Conference 'Sport in Education and Recreation', July 1966 (UK Sports Council Library).

Wolfenden Committee on Sport, *Sport in the Community* (Central Council of Physical Recreation, 1960).

Index